MODERNITY, CIVILIZATIONS AND THE TRUTH

MODERNITY, CIVILIZATIONS AND THE TRUTH

KANNAN SOLAYAPPAN

Publisher:
SAI PUBLISHERS L.L.C.
Eagan, Minnesota

Copyright © 2015 by Kannan Solayappan

Modernity, Civilizations and the Truth
Kannan Solayappan

All rights reserved. No part of this book may be reproduced or transmitted in any form or by any means without written permission from the publisher.

Published by: SAI PUBLISHERS L.L.C.
Eagan, Minnesota

Printed in the United States of America.

ISBN 978-0-692-02804-9

Dedicated to my Guru
Shirdi Sai Baba

True words are not beautiful,
beautiful words are not true.

- Lao Tzu

யாதும் ஊரே, யாவரும் கேளிர்,
தீதும் நன்றும் பிறர்தர வாரா,
நோதலும் தணிதலும் அவற்றோ ரன்ன
சாதலும் புதுவது அன்றே, வாழ்தல்
இனிதுஎன மகிழ்ந்தன்றும் இலமே, முனிவின்
இன்னாது என்றலும் இலமே, பின்னொடு
வானம் தண் துளி தலைஇ ஆனாது
கல் பொருது இரங்கும் மல்லல் பேர்யாற்று
நீர்வழிப் படூஉம் புணைபோல் ஆருயிர்
முறைவழிப் படூஉம் என்பது திறவோர்
காட்சியின் தெளிந்தனம் ஆதலின் மாட்சியின்
பெரியோரை வியத்தலும் இலமே,
சிறியோரை இகழ்தல் அதனினும் இலமே.
(கணியன் பூங்குன்றன், புற நானூறு, 192).

To us all towns are one, all men our kin,
Life's good comes not from others' gifts, nor ill,
Man's pains and pain's relief are from within,
Death's no new thing, nor do our blossoms thrill
When joyous life seems like a luscious draught.
When grieved, we patient suffer; for, we deem
This much-praised life of ours a fragile raft
Borne down the waters of some mountain stream
That o'er huge boulders roaring seeks the plain
Tho' storms with lightning's flash from darkened skies.
Descend, the raft goes on as fates ordain.
Thus have we seen in visions of the wise !
We marvel not at the greatness of the great;
Still less despise we men of low estate.

Kaniyan Pungundranar, *Purananuru* - 192
(Translated by G.U.Pope, 1906)

Table of Contents

Acknowledgements xiii
Preface xv

History
1. An Ethical Interrogation into the Pre-Modern World.. 3

Falsehood
2. Western Modernity................................. 27
3. Post-Modernity...................................... 37
4. Civilizational Narratives......................... 44

Truth
5. Gandhi, India and the Quest for an Ethical Response to Modernity............................. 61
6. Expositions of the Truth......................... 83
7. Ethical Resolutions in the Light of the Truth... 106

Civilizations
8. An outline for a discourse on Civilizations....... 167
9. India: A World within the World.................... 177
10. The Chinese Mind..................................... 187
11. The Ethical and Historical Dimensions of Islam's Interaction with Modernity................ 201
12. Secular Historical Reflections on the Second Coming... 212

Destiny
13. The Way Forward.................................... 225

Appendix.. 251
Notes.. 265
References... 311
Index.. 329

Acknowledgements

Firstly, I need to profoundly thank my Guru Shirdi Sai Baba for initiating me on the path of love and showing me through everyday life experiences that love was both potent and auspicious. Secondly, I must be thankful to my late mother for getting me started on what has now become a lifelong interest in ideas that affect the world. Then, I must thank both of my parents for exposing me to faith and devotion while I was growing up. This book would not have been possible without the steadfast support and constant encouragement I received from my wife Vallikannu and daughter Yazhini Solachi. They are one with me in spirit. Finally the writing of this book coincides with a period of great economic gloom in America. We as a family managed to stay afloat during this period with timely assistance from my father, my in-laws (that is my wife's parents) and my brother-in-law Veerappan Nachiappan. I thank them for their timely assistance.

I would like to thank the Periyar Rationalist Library and Research Centre for the photographs of Periyar and the permission to use them on the cover of this book. I also would like to thank the Gandhi Ashram at Sabarmati for the photographs of Gandhi and the permission to use them on the cover of this book.

Preface

I am not a scholar. I am not trained either formally or informally in the ways of modern scholarship. I however do not regard it as a particular disadvantage. Any work of scholarship is delimited by its presuppositions. Modern scholarship to be credible has to conform to the bedrock of objectivity. In the Islamic middle ages there were Islamic scholars but their presuppositions were rooted in what they perceived to be the message of Islam. Likewise in medieval Europe, Christian scholastics pursued rigorous critical scholarship and reconciled their thought with works from other traditions but would not deviate from their orthodoxy.

This is a book about the Truth. Truth, by any definition, constitutes the very presuppositions on which all subsequent scholarship is built. In referring to this book as a book of truth, I am not in any way suggesting that I have a new truth to offer to the world. I don't. I am merely reiterating an age old truth that is now practically lost upon humanity. I have to do five things to reiterate this truth. First I need to set the context for our discussion. Next, I need to expose the various faces of falsehood that are prominent in our midst. Then, I must present this timeless truth in the context of our times - which is to say that I must be cognizant of the historical circumstances in which we find ourselves, where our major civilizational traditions are substantially disrupted by the cascade of modernity and are seemingly edging towards a confrontation with each other. Finally I must be positive and show a way forward for humanity.

This book brings together two distinct strands of my life. One is my faith and the other is a general interest in ideas. Ever since my late adolescence, I have been mostly sincere in what I took to be my faith. The subject and content of my faith might have changed but my disposition to faith itself remained essentially intact. Likewise my general interest in ideas began in my late adolescence. Ever since, I have been fascinated by politics, philosophy, religion and history. By themselves, these personal inclinations of mine wouldn't have accounted for much. Fortunately for me I was drawn to my Guru, Shirdi Sai Baba, a perfect master who lived in Western India. As a result of my Guru's grace I was initiated into the path of love. I was shown through events in everyday life that love was auspicious and potent. Further reflection on my Guru's abode clarified for me the fundamental relationship between love and truth. I then believed that I should take this notion of truth to my politics. Writing this book seemed like the natural next step to me. In addition writing this book helped to clarify my worldview.

Truth, especially when one becomes aware of it from religious sources is likely to be associated with perfection. But I am no paragon of perfection. My understanding of the potency of love came from co-relating arbitrary acts of love with successful outcomes. My further understanding of the truth was purely intellectual. To be sure I got streamlined a short while after I had passed the carelessness of my adolescence. Ever since, I have led an essentially streamlined life making streamlined choices. But that certainly doesn't make me perfect by any stretch of imagination. Indeed I have not even made an effort to be perfect. It is not that I do not value perfection. I sure do. To me perfection must come when I am ready for it. It must come as a result of my Guru's grace.

My religiosity is strictly personal to me. I have merely recounted it here as part of my motivation for writing this book. The reader ought to encounter the contents of this book for its own sake.

Kannan Solayappan
Eagan, Minnesota, U.S.A.
18th November, 2015

History

1. An Ethical Interrogation into the Pre-Modern World

The technological, scientific, industrial and material changes that have been brought about as a consequence of modernity is so large that one could say that modernity constitutes a transcendental[1] moment in human history. Respected scholars like Paul Kennedy, Jacques Barzun and Cornel West are in agreement that this historical process that would come to be recognized as modernity began in Western civilization around the year 1500 of the Common Era[2]. Paul Kennedy believes that up until the year 1500 C.E. all the major civilizational traditions of the world viz. Islam, Confucian East Asian, India and the West were roughly at the same level of development. Only then did the West take off. These civilizational traditions believed in vastly different narratives and were products of different experiences but there were a common set of historical categories that characterized most of them and common historical themes ran through all of them. We will use the term pre-modern to refer to this world at large that existed prior to the advent of modernity. It is not necessary to historically classify the world based on stages of development as primitive communism, slave society, feudalism, capitalism, socialism and communism[3] as Marxists do because it is not self-evident that history moves in a neat linear fashion. For instance, chronologically, European feudalism preceded slavery practiced in the new world in variance with the prognosis of Marxist theory. Similarly, according to Marxist theory, feudal society cannot evolve to into a communist society without large scale

3

industrialization but in China under Chairman Mao, communism preceded large scale industrialization[4]. We however recognize that considerable variation existed in the pre-modern world. For instance in remote antiquity, humans organized themselves into tribes. Later, in the few centuries before the Common Era, we see the emergence of large unifying empires in all the major civilizations. We however are not attempting to understand the pre-modern world in a historically comprehensive manner. We seek to understand the pre-modern as a predecessor to the modern and for that purpose it is sufficient if we realize that modernity constitutes a transcendental moment in world history and that the essential historical distinction which ought to be considered is the one between the pre-modern and the modern.

To more clearly understand the significance of modernity as a historically transcendental moment, it will be helpful to look at other transcendental possibilities so that through analogy we can better appreciate the significance of our times.

If miraculously the cognitive capabilities of all animals transformed in an instant so as to enable them to learn the languages we speak and through some innovative method we are able to teach all the animals to learn and speak the respective languages we speak then one could say that it would result in a historically transcendental moment. Animals will then be able to talk like us and respond to us. They will be able to express their desires and preferences. Animals will also be listening to all our conversations, including our political conversations. They will see us fight for our respective rights. They will then compare our circumstance to theirs. They may begin to see how much better our lives are with respect to theirs. We can try to envision their reasoning. They may begin to see their life in the forest as abandonment to barbarianism and the domestication of animals would be seen as slavery. All acts of meat eating, hunting, fishing, horse racing and use of animals for transportation would be considered crimes committed by humans. The circus that we delight in watching would be viewed very ungenerously and the zoo would be regarded as life imprisonment for no crime on the animal's part. Animals would justly take issue with every derogatory depiction and condescension of them in human history and culture. If animals in addition to speaking were able to learn, be educated and equally function in professions occupied by contemporary humans then they would justly want equal opportunities like humans.

Another transcendental moment could be imagined if humans conquered death through medical and technological advances. American inventor and futurist Ray Kurzweil actually anticipates it in the not too distant future[5]. If humans never died, then that surely would have social, cultural and historical ramifications. If humans were immortal then all humans who were born in this world would continue to live forever. If all humans lived forever then there would be a population explosion. The sheer lack of space and other resources in our planet would force humans to migrate to other worlds or alternately humans would have to forever stop procreation. If humans stopped procreating they would forever be deprived of the opportunity to cherish the joy of bringing a child into this world and raising it. Then there would be no social need for the family as an institution. Likewise prophets, messiahs, buddhas and avatars after having been born into this world would have no way to leave it. All these great souls, each with a highly evolved consciousness will have to live alongside humans. The realization of divine prophecy can be objectively verified as the prophet will be present both to confirm the realization of prophecy and to explain the delay in its fulfillment. Misinterpretation of religion and the degeneration of ethical ideals can be checked and corrected at its source as those who were present at the founding of religious and ethical orders will be present to ensure right interpretation. The Hindu notion of full avatar is nothing but the omnipotent, omnipresent and omniscient God being born as a human being in this world of ours to protect the good and destroy the wicked. When such an avatar comes to this world it will not have a natural way to leave this world as death will not be an option. Many of the religions of the world state that heaven is where God resides. If God came to this world as an avatar and is not able to leave it because humans have transcended death then this world will become the home of God. That is to say that heaven and earth would have reversed roles. With such a reversal of roles, in addition to being aided with the spiritual powers that messiahs, avatars, prophets and buddhas bring to this world, immortal humans and their spiritually gifted co-planetary inhabitants may evaluate the way other worlds had operated until then. Throughout the eons were the Gods harsh with humans? Did humans endure more than that which was necessary? These may be issues that would dominate global discourse on that day.

Yet another transcendental moment that could be imagined, though it may not be intuitively apparent, is if all children at the moment of their birth were able to walk, talk and function in this world as adults. If that were to happen then with time the very institution of family would seem to be oppressive. Parents would be regarded as needless bullies who have unnecessarily dominated the life of their children ever since the dawn of human history.

So also is modernity, a historically transcendental force. It may not seem to us as we have imbibed it and live in it. If we were living in the pre-modern world then the idea of a modern aircraft can only be comprehensible as a piece of metal flying, taking people from one corner of the world to another. Surely a piece of metal flying people from one corner of the world to another must seem like a miracle for one who lives his or her life in the pre-modern world. Illuminating a room with the turn of a knob, as electricity makes possible, would be reason for great astonishment. The telephone, television, anesthesia, computers, temperature control with heaters and air conditioners must fill one with awe and wonder.

Modernity comes as a cascade to nations and civilizations. Overwhelmed by the cascade of modernity we are caught between our inability to change and the necessities of our times. In such moments we either tend to be romantic about the past or deride it. Our derision of the past often has a moral tone to it. When viewed from this perspective the past seems to be very oppressive. The pre-modern world certainly restricted possibilities for many and was definitely oppressive to some. To what extent can modern resentments with the pre-modern world be traced to originate in human malice and to what extent were they necessities of pre-modern times. Could there have been a structural remedy to some of the institutional hardships? What were the ethical possibilities of the pre-modern world? How could ethics have been practiced in the pre-modern world? Could the pre-modern world have been any better than it actually was?

Answering these questions may not be easy. We evidently cannot go back in time and recreate the old world in its entirety. We can use our intuition to look at a broad set of categories that characterized the pre-modern world to form judgments of an age increasingly fading way. Also by ethical interrogation we do not mean enquiring into an individual 's personal ethics as in being honest, speaking the truth, keeping one's word, not stealing, not killing, being committed to one spouse, not harboring malicious intent and the like. As we understand the pre-modern past from history, it is quite possible that these personal ethical traits were widely practiced. Indeed if humans had been constantly lying to one another, stealing from one another, killing one another and indiscriminately sleeping with one another there would have been total anarchy devoid of any semblance of order. On the other hand we seek to understand whether a better social, political and economic order was possible in the pre-modern world and if possible how could it have been brought about. Alternately if a better socio-political and economic order was not possible then why was it not possible? In an effort to answer some of our questions let us ponder over some historical and ethical categories that characterized different civilizations in pre-modern times.

Aristocracy: Aristocracy, as is generally understood, is referred to as the presence of a dominant class usually made up of a hereditary nobility. The very existence of the aristocracy would have implicitly foreclosed the prospects for equal opportunity in the pre-modern world. We need to ponder over whether the existence of the aristocracy was inevitable in the pre-modern world. The pre-modern world was a period when life expectancy was very low and infant mortality rates were very high. Scholars tell us that life expectancy in the Roman Empire was no more than twenty five years[6]. As late as the first decade of the twentieth century, even when it was beginning to be characterized as the American century, in America a fourth of all children below the age of five used to die[7]. Also the pre-modern world was a world without electricity, modern transportation and modern machinery. In such a world much of the necessities of life like food, clothing, provision for shelter and transportation had to be made possible only by intense physical labor. Since the majority of the people had to labor, only the remaining few could pursue a literary education. Division of labor was inevitable in the pre-modern world. Since life expectancy was low, people tended to pass on their learning, trades, occupations and skills to their children. In reality many of the fruits of civilization like writing, literature, arts, philosophy and religion that humanity claims as its own are a result of broad division of labor that existed in the pre-modern world. In all of the four major cultural traditions that have come down to us Indian, East Asian, Islam and Christendom there is little or no evidence of equal opportunity for all citizens in pre-modern times. China through the ages had a two tier society made up of the gentry-scholar[8] and the laboring class. Japan and Christian Europe had feudal orders. A closed aristocracy was at the helm in pre-Islamic Iran. The Greco-Roman world had its classical aristocracy and even in Islam with its emphasis on equality and inclusiveness the two classes were unavoidable[9]. The Hindu Indian caste system was also division of labor though it did not merely evolve out of necessity as other aristocracies had but was superimposed by a harsh and humiliating alien occupation[10]. During pre-modern times across cultures all over the world, for overwhelming majority of laboring people either sustained poverty or mere subsistence living over many generations was a fact of life. However, if aristocrats, royals and other rich people had been thrifty in their personal expenses, generous in charity and if capable citizens had been forthcoming in undertaking responsibility for the well-being of all the people then the burden of the working poor would have been lightened. Likewise, if these privileged people had nurtured the presence of conspicuous human talent among the laboring classes and made provision for the self-expression and elevation of such talent, it might have been a source of hope for the toiling multitude. There however could not have been a structural alternative to the condition of the toiling poor in the pre-modern world. While it is true that some members of the working orders went onto to be founders of imperial dynasties and occasionally in some cultures it was possible for individuals from the laboring classes to attain to power, wealth and dignity [11], equal opportunity for all was a near impossibility. It is instructive to look at the perspectives of two different thinkers Aristotle and Machiavelli drawn from different regions, affiliated to different cultural traditions and separated by almost two thousand years for their views on the aristocracy. According to Aristotle's definition, aristocracy was practice of ethics in the public sphere by society's privileged citizens. Aristotle extols the aristocracy. Machiavelli on the other hand warns the Prince not to derive authority for his rule through the support of the nobles as their desires had no limits. This radical difference between the perceptions of Aristotle and Machiavelli about the aristocracy[12] is far more a reflection of the times in which they lived rather than a commentary on the aristocracy itself. In Classical Greece, with the advent of the Athenian Academy and its rational realization in the value of ethics, the aristocracy was hailed as the vehicle for the creation and preservation of an ethical order. Florentine Italy where Machiavelli lived during the Renaissance was not only a period of great artistic ferment but also one in which avarice and materialism was rampant[13]. Not surprisingly, Machiavelli does not have a charitable view of the aristocracy. The ethical character of the aristocracy was largely dependent on historical circumstances. On the whole, one could say that in the pre-modern world, aristocrats were sometimes virtuous, sometimes rapacious and often somewhere in between.

Economy: The vast majority of the people in the pre-modern world were the working poor. There could not have been a structural remedy to the vast economic inequities that existed in society. Communism was attempted only in small city states. Even Marxist theory insists that primitive communism was practiced only at the dawn of history and that in all other previous ages communism was inherently not possible. Under these circumstances the most ethical course that a society could have embarked on in pre-modern times was to have reduced the hardships on the poor by avoiding extravagant expenses, avoiding consumption and trade in non-essential commodities like gold, silver, silk, spices etc., banning usury, avoiding long distance trade and directing all such resources towards ameliorating the conditions of the poor. In practice, however intercontinental trade flourished and the rich and affluent continued to live ostentatious lives. Usury was practiced across generations by specific communities. Jews in Europe took to money lending because that was really the only occupation left to them as Christians regarded usury as sinful and Jews were stigmatized in Christendom to be able to freely practice other occupations[14]. Likewise in Hindu India, the Brahmins created a social order based on caste. Each caste had an occupation associated with it. There was a caste of thieves, a caste of prostitutes and so also a caste of money lenders. In pre-modern times the only way the hardships of the poor could have been reduced was through charity and benevolence. Islam advocates charity and wealthy members of the community gave away money in alms to the poor, though money so given may not have always been as much as was prescribed by the religion. In India, in the Tamil tradition, there is great emphasis on charity. In China, mercantilism was derided and a certain Confucian public spiritedness of the gentry often provided leadership to ensure at least subsistence for the poor. In 18th century England, social work undertaken by the Methodists would come to be regarded as an expression of the moral sentimentality of the English

Enlightenment[15]. Just as equal opportunity was almost impossible in the pre-modern world so also it was inherently not possible have communism. While across cultures charity was generally cherished, affluent people almost always consumed far more than what they needed. **Ethnicity.** Humans through the ages have inflicted great suffering on peoples who have been ethnically, linguistically and culturally different from them. Most of the institutionalized forms of oppression through the ages have been inflicted by people on people who have been very different from themselves. The arrival of modernity has not ended such oppression. Hitler persecuted and exterminated hundreds and thousands of Jews who differed from Germans in ethnicity, language and civilizational affiliation. Hitler did not treat the French and the Poles anywhere as cruelly as he had treated the Jews. People of European descent imported, bought, whipped and sold hundreds and thousands of Africans who were ethnically, linguistically and culturally different from them as chattel slaves in the new world, they didn't inflict such hardships on other Europeans. The alien origins of the Aryans made the Hindu caste system easily more rigid and shamefully more insulting than any other feudal order anywhere else. Human history is however not entirely hopeless. The prevailing contemporary ideology has significantly influenced inter-ethnic relationship. When the prevailing ideology explicitly insisted on being multiethnic then the relationship between communities has had a greater likelihood of being amiable. On the other hand when the ideological narrative of a people was based on its sense of being superior to others then condescension was inevitable and it resulted in humiliation and great suffering for those who happened to be depicted as inferior. Islam has been a relatively inclusive multiethnic civilization because the narrative insists on it. All

Muslims were one before Allah without distinction or hierarchy. The Hindu caste order on the other hand came after early conflict between two peoples and the narrative that evolved was based on the superiority of the one that emerged triumphant in the struggle over the other. Not surprisingly, the Hindu Indian caste order would be far more rigid, insulting and humiliating than any other feudal order in the world for most of its adherents over the millennia. The moral sentimentality of the English Enlightenment gave way to the anti-slavery movement[16] which successfully resulted in abolishing slavery in the British Empire and contributed to abolishing slavery worldwide. Here again, ideological consideration, resulted in successfully ending one of the worst forms of slavery that was practiced in the western hemisphere. After the civil rights movement in the 1960s multiculturalism and celebration of diversity have become central tenets of American life. Not surprisingly America continues to be a very attractive destination for immigrants from all parts of the world. So we see not just in the pre-modern world but even afterwards ethnic difference has been the cause of some of the worst forms of oppression and the willful acceptance of an ideology of ethnic inclusiveness has been an effective remedy against such oppression.

Religion: We must recognize that we will not be able to entirely grasp the social conditions in which the major religions of the world came into existence. In addition if we make some allowance for the dissipation of the truth over time, then we could persuasively make a case that all the major religions of the world, in their inception, will withstand ethical scrutiny. Islam during the time of Prophet Mohammed, Christianity during the times of Jesus, Judaism during the time of Moses, the Hinduism of perfect masters called Siddhars and the ideas of Buddha, Confucius and

Lao Tzu would be able to withstand such an ethical interrogation[17]. All of these great spiritual teachers advocated love for all of humanity[18] and many of them advocated nonviolence. All of them were well disposed to charity and discouraged selfishness. They even offered heaven and release from the cycles of birth and death as rewards for selflessness. Charity and selflessness were not arbitrary values that were espoused. They were pertinent to the necessities of life in the pre-modern world. Only through the benevolence and selflessness of the able and the privileged could human misery have been reduced, if not eliminated, in that world. Some of these great spiritual teachers like Jesus and Confucius relied essentially on individual transformation. Others like Prophet Mohammed enunciated laws both for the individual and the community. If the wisdom of these great religious teachers were adhered to, human suffering and inequities in our world could have been considerably reduced and many of the wars could have been avoided. Unfortunately the message of these great teachers degenerated after them[19]. An oppressive and humiliating caste order persisted in India through the millennia. Bloody wars were fought in the name of Christianity and Islam. Confucianism gave way to the Chinese empire and the Christian faith was sustained with total disregard for Christian ethics. In addition religion which in its origin was meant to be a source of peace and amity became the object of contention. The conflict between Protestants and Catholics in Europe was bloody and the millennial conflict between Hindus and Muslims tragically continues to the present day in the Indian subcontinent. In recent times resentments against religion in general have come from those who adhere to a secular liberal world view. They find religion to be the very antithesis of liberal permissiveness especially in realm of human sexuality. Should we regard sexual taboos of the pre-modern world as being oppressive? This is a question that is inherently not possible to answer. Even today we do not have universal agreement that sexual permissiveness is good in the same way that we have universal agreement that truth, love, benevolence, equality, justice, freedom and non-killing are good. Outside of some sophisticated urban elites there is little resonance for permissive sexual mores in the continent of Asia and in the wider Islamic world[20]. If we are not able to find broad agreement for permissive sexuality even in our age then how are we to use it as a criterion to evaluate the ethics of a previous era? We must first be sure of the value of something before we can examine whether it could have been practiced in a previous age.

State: The State in the pre-modern world was anything from a small city state to a vast polyglot, multiethnic empire. The function of the State was to ensure political stability and provide security for the citizens. The state was a bulwark against invaders, marauders and encroachments by bandits. The State could have taken responsibility to ensure that roads and sea-routes were made safe for travel and commerce from robbers and pirates. In some cases the State might have undertaken large scale projects as in the construction of the Great Wall of China. The State encouraged learning and often patronized the arts and culture. To a limited extent it could have protected private property and provided conflict resolution among citizens in the name of justice. But in the pre-modern world, did the State contribute to the creation of a more meaningful socio-economic order? Aristotle says the end of politics is ethics. That may be true for a small city state in classical Greece when the aristocracy practiced ethics. Outside of certain ideal states in classical Greece which contributed to the Aristotelian world view, in the pre-modern world the role of the State in creating an ethical order has been limited. The most enduring political structure in the pre-modern world has been the empire. Emperors have from time to time embraced specific ideologies; almost always these ideologies have been religious. These emperors then promoted these ideals and religions within their empires. The citizen's acceptance and conformance to religious ideals was supposed to transform the individual and ultimately be beneficial to society as a whole. Social transformation could only have been brought about in the pre-modern world through individual transformation. In practice however the religious ideals had been distorted to varying degrees. Often distortion of religion took place fairly early in a religion's history. More often than not the State and its citizenry became united in a common enterprise through religion. Empires propagated religion and religion sustained empires. Those outside the gambit of the chosen religion were viewed either as targets for conversion or as enemies to be defeated. In the pre-modern world, specifically in large empires, it was inherently not possible for the State to create an ethical order in the same way that newly independent modern nations in the twentieth century embraced secular ideologies like democracy and socialism based on ethical considerations. What then was the value of the state in the pre-modern world? Was the state at all necessary? The patronization of arts and culture might have provided entertainment for the peasantry but patronizing of learning was inherently elitist. The main benefit in promoting learning, arts and culture was having preserved the achievements of civilization for posterity. As a result today these achievements can be claimed by many nations and peoples as their cultural inheritance. Protecting long distance trade provided for the consumption of the elites, it did nothing for those who lived at subsistence levels. The security provided by the state against invaders, pirates and robbers could have been useful. The state often generally identified with a religion and actively promoted it. Religion while extraordinary in its inception had almost always become corrupt before the state embraced it. Since the ethical substance of religion was already distorted, the state's promotion of religion did not result in the creation of an ideal pre-modern society. In addition the state in the pre-modern world spent enormous resources in pomp, pageantry and ostentation besides squandering national treasure in unnecessary wars. In a world where most of the people were living at subsistence levels such ostentation and pomp were unnecessary and these resources could have been better used for the wellbeing of the teeming poor. Overall the state merely provided some physical protection for the people and helped in preserving the literary, artistic and cultural achievements of civilization. The state in the pre-modern world was more a burden for society as a whole. The larger the state the more burdensome it was. In the biblical narrative, the inherent inability of the state to establish ethics through politics is possibly implied in God's hesitation in giving into ancient Israel's desire for a king.

Women. The pre-modern world was one in which infant mortality rates were high, life expectancy low and modern birth control methods were not available. As a consequence of all this the size of family was large. Most women must have married very early and spent much of their adult life being pregnant or raising children. In the case of poorer women, they had in addition to do manual work outside the home. As with the working poor, women too were restricted in the opportunities that were available to them in the pre-modern world. However some of the most gruesome hardships that women endured through the ages were not a consequence of inherent structural limitations of the pre-modern world but a result of the institutionalized exploitation of the physical weakness of women by oppressive men. All the major cultural traditions in their own respective ways stigmatized or oppressed women. In Hindu India, the pursuit of chastity was taken to atrocious heights where a widow self-immolated herself in her husband's funeral pyre. Islamic societies imposed the veil on women. Foot binding of women was practiced in China well into the 20th century and might have been completely removed only after the communist takeover. In Christendom, women were depicted as the source of sin. Over and beyond specific ways by which each of the cultural traditions oppressed women there were universal modes of oppression that some women everywhere had to endure like prostitution, rape - especially rape of alien women during military conflict and wife battering.

Outcastes. No attempt to discern the ethical dimensions of the pre-modern world can be meaningful without reference to Outcastes. Outcastes are a category all unto themselves and as people they have been associated with occupations which were considered impure or polluting. The Dalits or untouchables in India, the Dowa in Japan and the Osu in West Africa are all outcastes from different regions of the world. These outcastes are different from victims of racism in that they are ethnically the same people as the general population which ostracizes them. Also these outcastes have been ostracized for centuries in their respective societies. In all these cases the impurity associated with these outcastes has had a spiritual origin. Modern scholars[21] say that untouchables in India were regarded as untouchable because they were associated with inauspicious powers. India's untouchables were avidly sought by kings and chieftains for their skills in controlling these inauspicious powers and for the assistance they provided to the King in transforming inauspicious powers to auspicious powers. When the Brahmins of India came in contact with these indigenous kings they were able to provide a religious alternative to them that was wholly auspicious. The untouchables became the "polar opposites" of the Brahmins and their services were no longer sought after by the kings. The stigma associated with the untouchable however remained and their condition in society greatly worsened. So much so today the untouchables continue to be victims of crimes listed in the Government of India's Indian Prevention of Atrocities Act like forced consumption of noxious substances, forced labor, denial of access to water and other public amenities and sexual abuse of untouchable women. Though we may not have as detailed a narrative for the Osu in West Africa and the Dowa in Japan, their history is characterized by the same broad themes that affected the untouchable in India. In the case of the Osu their condition could have worsened after colonial intervention[22] whereas among the Dowa of Japan their condition seems to have worsened without foreign intervention. Could there have been a structural alternative to the creation of the outcaste? Was it human malice that was responsible for creating the untouchable in the first place? At the outset, it was and is certainly wrong to regard one's fellow human as an outcaste. If on principle untouchability is wrong then we need to look at the context once again to understand the nature of the crime. Again we will turn to the practice of untouchability in India for further elucidations. Modern scholarship has traced the origin of untouchability to early indigenous Dravidian society. Early Dravidian society was one in which people lived in constant fear of malevolent spirits and the primary preoccupation of their society was to protect themselves from the harmful effects of these spirits. In this society untouchables were associated with the inauspicious. However they were sought after by Kings and to a lesser extent by rich people as they believed the inauspicious was the raw material for the auspicious. Therefore, though the untouchables were regarded as lowly[23], socially they enjoyed considerable mobility. This was the world of the ancient Dravidians and it stemmed from their understanding of reality. Dravidian civilization at this time was in an archaic period of its classical antiquity. The archaic period typically precedes some of the more profound ethical and metaphysical developments of a civilization's axial age. Such ethical development did indeed take place in Tamil Dravidian society. One of the world's greatest ethical texts, which to this date remains relatively unknown to the world, the Thirukural, is a product of such a period. Tragically for Tamil Dravidian society such a period was also one in which alien Aryan penetration deepened in their midst. Therefore the early Dravidians did not have the historical opportunity to morally grapple with the world around them and order life in accordance with their preferences. At any rate untouchables did enjoy considerable mobility in their world. Therefore, in a technical sense, we certainly can take note of the fact that untouchability had a nascent presence in early Dravidian civilization but it would be too harsh to hold them responsible for the subsequent fate of untouchables in Indian history. However the contrast becomes stark when we begin considering the fate of untouchables after Brahminical penetration of indigenous Dravidian society. The Brahmins could have initially positioned themselves as polar opposites of untouchables so as to market their religion as one which was wholly auspicious. Once they succeeded in converting all of indigenous India into their religious order then what was the need to further ostracize the untouchable and heap untold cruelties on them? After all Hindu philosophy emphasized truth, non-killing and universalism. The supreme Hindu god Sivan was synonymous with love and was a source of auspiciousness, implying that love was auspicious. The Hindu high god Vishnu was recognized as Sathyanarayana, meaning god who embodied the truth and therefore encompassing love. Why then did the Brahmins not spearhead the effort to remove the stigma associated with the untouchable through the millennia? For one thing this would have meant dethroning themselves. The more the Brahmin relaxed the grip on the untouchable the more rest of the population would want to be proximate to the Brahmin. The early history of Aryans in India and the social philosophy of Hinduism are unapologetically racist and so it is hardly surprising that the Brahmins would want to keep the distance between them and others as far as it was possible. Untouchability, at least in India, is then a case of classical racism in which outcastes of a subjugated civilization were most victimized.

Vegetarianism. Could vegetarianism have been practiced in the pre-modern world? Vegetarianism could only have been practiced if there was adequate vegetarian food for all in the pre-modern world. The essential nutrients that a human body needs are carbohydrates, proteins, fats, vitamins, minerals and water. With the exception of proteins and possibly fats the other essential nutrients that a body needs may have been obtained by observing vegetarianism. It may not have been possible to obtain the needed proteins from cultivated plants alone. Dietary sources that are rich in proteins are pulses, nuts, soya, eggs, chicken, meat, fish and milk. Among these only chicken, fish and meat also have a high calorific value. In pre-modern times among working people who expended more calories in hard physical labor, eating meat, chicken and fish may have been the only way in which they could have obtained both needed calories and proteins. The only civilization that embraced vegetarianism in any substantial way was India. We do not have any reliable way of knowing the degree to which vegetarianism would have been practiced in India in the pre-modern world. Today India has a substantial population of the world's vegetarians. So it helps to look at the dietary sources in India today before making ethical judgments on the possibilities for vegetarianism in the pre-modern world. The largest producer and consumer of pulses in the world today is India. In addition, India also imports pulses. Also India is the largest milk producer and of late even an exporter of milk to the world. One may assume the legacy of growing more pulses and producing large amounts of milk were consequences of an effort to make vegetarianism possible. Religious and ethical perspectives that have had their origins in India have almost always advocated non-killing which in time extended to vegetarianism. As a result, according to a certain study[24], 40% of today's Indian population could be classified as vegetarian. That still leaves more than half the population in the meat eating camp. Also greater percentages of people from India's forward castes who traditionally did white collar jobs refrain from eating meat than people from backward castes who traditionally did blue collar jobs. Despite being the largest producer of milk and pulses in the world and despite religious and ethical ideologies proscribing meat eating through the millennia, India still has more than half its population eat meat. We must then conclude that it is the unavailability of adequate of protein sources that keeps Indians away from a vegetarian diet today. If that is the situation today when modern methods are increasingly being applied to agriculture, dairy farming and distribution then we may say that it must have been at least equally difficult in pre-modern times to observe vegetarianism. There can be little doubt in the value of an animal's life or a bird's life or for that matter any life. Animals certainly are vested with consciousness like humans. When they are hurt, animals experience pain like humans; though animals are not as dramatic as humans in exhibiting pain, they certainly display conspicuous signs of enduring pain. It is certainly wrong to hurt or kill animals. But when we look at the availability of nutrients in the pre-modern world, we must say that it must have been nearly impossible for any society to observe vegetarianism in any comprehensive way. In the case of India, religious and ethical ideologies motivated sizable sections of the people to refrain from meat eating and that is remarkable. We however cannot blame other civilizations for not doing so as it was very difficult in the pre-modern world to show equal consideration for all humans in the first place and therefore it would be unreasonable to hold them responsible for not extending such consideration to animals.

Ethical possibilities of the pre-modern world

Many of the inequities that humans faced in the pre-modern world lay inherent in its structure. There could not have been a structural remedy to these inequities. All the major religious and cultural traditions, in their inception, at once, both advocated the path of ethics and love to their adherents and simultaneously established transcendental incentives for following such a path. With love and ethics, individuals and dominant groups could have lightened the miseries of others. The pre-modern world was an opportunity for individuals and historically dominant groups to love and practice ethics. Humans, both as individuals and groups, sometimes were well disposed to the well-being of others but more often out of greed, ambition, lust, pride, arrogance, ignorance, frivolousness and mediocrity have inflicted enormous unnecessary suffering on those who were weak and helpless. Women, outcastes and aliens were victims of some of the most horrendous institutionalized crimes that seemingly spanned all of history.

Falsehood

2. Western Modernity

Historically, the sheer magnitude of scientific, technological and industrial advancement that has been achieved in Western civilization in the last 500 years has been unprecedented. In terms of the scale of advancement, it is only comparable to the establishment of river valley civilizations at the dawn of history[1]. The philosophical basis for this advancement is the method of science, whose central tenets are founded in empiricism, logic and mathematics. The essence of empiricism is demonstrable evidence. Empiricism is useful in validating a thesis and could provide data for formulating a hypothesis. Science has been extremely successful in understanding and manipulating the physical world. The role of science has been far less effective in understanding the social realm of humanity. The role of science has been even more limited in creating socio-political institutions. At best empirical data could shed light on certain policy choices but has not resulted in the creation of fundamental social or political institutions. The family, bureaucracy, democracy, constitutional government, the rule of law and even communism, preceded[2] the advent of modern science.

Historically, in the modern West, two sources have provided the philosophical underpinnings for organizing the sociopolitical sphere - one being the ideals of the Enlightenment and the other from Germany using history as source material[3].

The European Enlightenment was an 18th century historical movement. Europe in the 18th century was essentially an agrarian pre-modern society. Though the Industrial Revolution took place in England in the 18th century, the way of life of most of the people was still pre-modern. The European Enlightenment as a historical movement sought to secure and preserve individual freedom through the use of reason. The church, absolute monarchy and aristocracy were regarded as obstacles to individual freedom that had to be removed. The acceptance of this Enlightenment world view was completely arbitrary and not a consequence of enquiry. More importantly, proponents of the Enlightenment never demonstrated with reason the relevance of their worldview to the circumstances they inhabited. To be sure there was vast discrepancy between Christian ideals and Christian practice. Indeed, Christian practice quite often has been diametrically opposed to Christian ideals. However, the intensity of the message of love that had been central to the religious doctrine found little resonance among Enlightenment thinkers. No serious attempt was made to seek a meaningful resolution between reason and love[4]. Likewise the European Enlightenment sought to overthrow absolute monarchy. In the pre-modern world, birth right provided the legitimacy for succession. Whether a nation had a representative form of government or monarchy, the existence of the authority of the state has been for the most part and in most places an inescapable fact of civilized life. If anything in the twentieth century as a consequence of advances in communication and information technology, progressively central control over citizen's life has been increased either through state control or corporate control. In the newer suburbs of developed nations all homes fall into certain patterns chosen by the builder. It is not cost effective to build custom homes for everyone. In a Marxist society the size and patterns of homes would change based on the needs of the family. In the modern era, cost consideration and historical ideology has restricted the very freedoms that the Enlightenment espoused to a far greater degree than what any absolute monarch would ever have restricted in pre-modern times. In some countries like Japan and Britain, one may argue that the monarchy has been an invaluable source of national unity and continuity. If a nation does not have an inherent capacity to democratically create and uphold the rule of the law in a spirit of fairness and equality for all citizens, then absolute monarchy is no more depraved, as a form of government, than representative democracy. In such cases representative democracy may become the tyranny of the majority. Aristocrats, to our very times, still have a role to play. In the almost 300 years since the dawn of the European Enlightenment, there is hardly an occasion when any sort of idealistic socio-political order was created without active aristocratic participation. The American Revolution was an aristocratic enterprise. Lenin was a Russian nobleman. The Indian independence movement and every other cadre based idealistic political movement, both before and after India's independence, that has remained essentially idealistic when it was entrusted with political power, did so only when it had the enthusiastic participation of castes that had historically been better placed in the Hindu caste order[5]. The Enlightenment however regarded the aristocracy only as needless authority that needed to be overthrown. The aristocracy did not have an obligation to serve. The Enlightenment dismissed all pre-modern institutions and structures as superstition.

A host of values were entirely arbitrarily espoused during the Enlightenment; the most prominent among them, of course, was reason[6]. No attempt was made to resolve between conflicting values. Ethics was noticeably absent in the Enlightenment discourse[7]. Even at the level of terminology the only occasion when one comes across terms like "virtue" or "ethics" or 'righteousness" or "morality" acquiring a centrality in the

Enlightenment discourse pertains to the moral sentimentality of the English Enlightenment[8]. During this period, for morality, mere sentimentality was all that was advocated. This is in sharp contrast to an earlier occasion in Western history when Socrates used his method. The Socratic Method involved the rigorous application of reason. The Socratic Method was still only a method. It was the conclusions of the Socratic Method that was truly profound. Using his method, Socrates demonstrated that it was advantageous to be good[9].

The Enlightenment was immediately followed by one of the most horrific political spectacles in Western history – the French Revolution. While majority of the stalwarts of the Enlightenment had passed away, the French Revolution was certainly inspired by the Enlightenment[10]. The French Revolution in many ways constitutes a crystallizing moment in Western history. Posterity would commemorate the ideals of the French Revolution through the motto 'Liberty, Equality and Fraternity'. When viewed superficially 'Liberty, Equality and Fraternity' resonates with our sense of decency but can it withstand ethical scrutiny? Liberty is not accompanied by an ethical directive as in 'Love thy neighbor as thy self'. One is at liberty for what purposes? The motto is silent about it. The inherent equality of all living beings is an irrefutable truth. In the Enlightenment world view, equality is tacitly presumed to be the equal capacity to perform. In part, equality is confused with difference and in part there is a great dishonesty in comprehending the existential circumstances of the world in which we live. Adults differ from new born children and new born children cannot survive in this world without the loving care of adults. Similarly teachers must impart knowledge to students and are different from their students in the knowledge they possess about the subject matter they would teach. Likewise we can identify other differences like cultural differences and historical differences, all of which may provide opportunities for honorable co-operation. Fraternity means brotherhood of all. As the difference among people is large there is an existential need to co-operate. Therefore all relationships cannot be fraternal relationships alone; some relationships must be parental relationships as well.

The intellectual origins of political discourse in Western civilization for the last 200 years can be traced back to the pamphlet war that was started by Edmund Burke during the French Revolution with his "Reflections on the Revolution in France". Burke evidently defended the ancient regimes, but in time his perspective would evolve into modern conservatism[11], whose central tenets would be national self-preservation and resistance to change advocated by the European Enlightenment. A number of illustrious writers responded to Burke, most notable among them being Thomas Paine with his Rights of Man and Mary Wollstonecraft with her feminist response. The response to Burke marks the beginning of liberal advocacy in Western civilization and the world at large. Liberals from then on would become advocates for the ideals espoused by the European Enlightenment. Liberal advocacy would become a never ending quest to reduce the scope of all forms of authority – religious, political, social, cultural and even parental. As a consequence of liberal advocacy slavery was ended worldwide, natives in European colonies were inspired to seek independence from their colonial masters, racial segregation was ended and women began obtaining their rights and all of it was good and welcome. If the European Enlightenment was devoid of ethical consideration then how could it have helped free women, free slaves and inspire anti-colonialism? In reality all the constructive socio-political change that occurred after the

European Enlightenment coincided with the inevitable societal transformation which was a consequence of progressive technological and industrial development that was unleashed by modernity. Industrialization made mass manufacture possible on scales hitherto inconceivable providing people with much greater material goods. Also with advances in medicine people started living longer. Transportation and communication became revolutionized and distances became shorter. People could move easily from place to place. Populations moved from rural areas to urban areas. The call for freedom resonated with social dislocations that were a consequence of modernity. After all why would it be necessary to possess slaves if machines did the task, or why should parents have more than one or two children if infant mortality rates were dismally low. If parents had fewer children then the woman, who traditionally raised children at home, would have more spare time which she could use for pursuing a career. Likewise, as the benefits of modernity percolated to the colonies, decolonization was inevitable. The European Enlightenment could have inspired the leaders of colonies through the content of liberal education, but the colonizer simply did not have the resources to hold colonies against their will. Gandhi pertinently observed "100,000 Englishmen simply cannot control 350 million Indians, if those Indians refuse to co-operate"[12]. The same was true in South Africa at the beginning of the last decade of the twentieth century. The apartheid system simply could not be sustained any longer. The necessities of modern life made apartheid impractical[13]. The post Enlightenment liberal advocacy has always clothed its argument in moral terms - freeing slaves, freeing women, freeing colonies and the like but it was the increasing irrelevance of these institutions in the face of modernity that has undermined and even eradicated them.

In the modern era, democracy in Western civilization was instituted initially for pragmatic not ethical reasons. Only propertied white men could participate in democracy initially. With time democracy was expanded with the ideals of the European Enlightenment to include women and racial minorities. Democracy when it is accompanied by universal suffrage is certainly ethical. It is better to elect one's rulers than to have rulers imposed on oneself. However, democracy in Western civilization has not been used for conducting ethical deliberations. Modernity is a new phenomenon which continuously has been transforming life in the Western world for at least 200 years. One would have expected that the ideal way to live in this emerging new world would have been the central national preoccupation of the polity in the West. Then such issues as the social misery of ethnic minorities, immigration, poverty in third world nations and health care for those who are unable to afford it would have acquired due attention. Unfortunately that has not been the case.

The English speaking countries where the democratic tradition continued relatively uninterrupted managed the transition to modernity rather smoothly without major upheavals like the Russian Revolution, Chinese Revolution or the Iranian Revolution. The civil war in the United States may have been the notable exception to the relatively smooth transition to modernity in the English speaking world. If modernity constituted a transcendental moment in world history then liberal democracy in the English speaking world has succeeded in maintaining order during a period of massive transformation. Even in America where the founding fathers of the United States engaged in a collective discourse on the contours of the independent nation they were creating, their political creation was based on a happy mixture of human experience, Enlightenment ideals, classical learning and Hobbesian ideas. Indeed it would have been inherently impossible for them to create a structural arrangement that would have been an ethical response to modernity as America at the time of its founding was largely an agrarian nation in which people were living in pre-modern conditions. This same theme is repeated in international affairs as well. English speaking countries have succeeded in preserving order in the world during the last 200 years when modernity was transmitted to cultural spheres outside Western civilization. The 19th century increasingly came to be dominated by Anglo-Russian rivalry, the object of which was to check Russian expansionism[14]. America sided with Britain and Russia and successfully thwarted German and Japanese aggression in the first half of the 20th century and alongside exerted pressure on Britain to decolonize. American policy of containment succeeded in preserving the international order during the cold war. Likewise during the last four decades, America succeeded in co-opting China into the international system. The great legacy of the long standing democracies – Britain and America - both domestically and internationally was the preservation of order. Neither of these two prominent countries nor Western civilization as a whole strove for an ethical response to modernity.

The alternative way in Western civilization to order the socio-political and economic sphere is based on ideas largely from Germany which uses history as source material to discover innate social laws. Herder, Hegel, Spengler, Marx and possibly Nietzsche and Weber were some of the more influential thinkers who expounded this line of reasoning. The most prominent political system that emerged from this perspective was Marxism. Though Marxism never politically took root in the West, the intellectual origins of this line of reasoning are unmistakably Western. Marxism like democracy has a basis in ethics, but Marxism is not a consequence of ethical enquiry. Marx develops Hegel's dialectical method along economic lines. While Hegel develops the political strand dialectally through history and arrives at the nation as its final expression, Marx develops the economic strand through history as dialectical class struggle and predicts that communism constitutes the final stage of development[15]. Marxism is an existential ideology and not an ethical ideology. It is existential because it is time based – time, matter, energy and space are, among others, facets of existence. Several thinkers in the past have advocated communism like Socrates, Plato and Thomas More. One may even argue that Jesus himself was a libertarian communist in that Jesus sought individual transformation through love. If all people sold everything they had and gave it to the poor, as Jesus advocated, it would have had the consequence of creating a communist society. Marx himself differs from other prominent pre-modern communists in that he predicts that history will evolve and culminate in the establishment of communism worldwide. To Marx, communism was inevitable with the advent of modernity. Since it is deterministic one has to wait for the various stages to be exhausted before the classless society can be created. In Marxism, there is little incentive to act in certain way and as a consequence realize the benefits of one's actions. In this sense Marxism is almost fatalistic.

Marxism is supposed to have been the final system in the class struggle. If this was so, then how does one explain its collapse in the former Soviet Union and its enormous dilution in China during the last 30 years? A final system ought not to have regressed even temporarily or tactically. Indeed the idea of tactics ought to be irrelevant to a historical ideology. There is no need to be tactical when the end is inevitable and the path is pre-defined. Why did Marxism not resonate among large population centers elsewhere?

Part of the reason may be Marxism's view of religion and even nationalism. To Marx, religion was the opiate of the masses. Outside of China and Russia, in other cultural traditions the state's authority was delimited by the religious tradition the state identified with. For instance, in self-governing Islamic societies Marxism could not supersede Islam. On the other hand in Russia, God was the Czar's junior partner[16] and in China the Emperor was regarded as God. So in China and Russia the State could supersede religion by tradition. In societies in which the State could not override religion by tradition it was far harder to impose communism. Just as Marxism rejects religion, it also rejects concepts of nation and language. The reality however is that people cherish and willingly identify with their respective nations and languages and to that extent Marxism is unable to penetrate the political consciousness of such people.

In the twentieth century, Classical Marxism has been modified to correct some its inadequacies and this modified Marxism is referred to as neo-Marxism. However the cumulative impact of all the strands of neo-Marxism in affecting the social, political or economic landscape of the world is negligible.

So we see that both historical movements, the European Enlightenment and Marxism, which have actually been used to order the socio-political and economic sphere, were not a consequence of ethical enquiry.

3. Post-Modernity

Post-modernity[1,2] is a term that we choose to use to distinguish ideas that were at the heart modernity from more recent ideas that that are passionately advocated in the liberal academy. Post-modernists insist that there are no absolute truths and that all truth is relative and local. Post-modernists believe that humans have a great desire to create order and such orders need grand narratives. A grand narrative or a meta-narrative has a story that self justifies itself and is used to create orders. Such narratives, postmodernists say, overlook inherent contradictions laden within them. Such narratives may be secular like modern Science or Marxism or religious like Christianity or Islam. In addition, language as it has evolved over the centuries is full of binary oppositions like order and disorder, tall and short, man and woman and language always picks one over the other. They say, such terms are not value free. Order is preferred to disorder, tall is preferred over the short and man is preferred over woman. Hence post-modernists insist that disorder is not bad. An influential strand of thought associated with post-modernity is called Deconstruction[3]. Deconstructionists take issue with the process of writing. They say that when one writes, one not only says something but one also simultaneously leaves many more things out. Writing they say is a process of choosing. Just as one leaves something out when one writes so also narratives tend to leave out specific groups. The post-modernist strives not to leave out specific groups, minorities and those in the margins of society. Some post-modernists even insist that all meta-narratives and by extension all truths are inherently elitist. Post-modernists are particularly critical of white males in Western civilization. They are also critical of the concept of modernity and Christianity. Post-modernists attempt to take the side of the "other", i.e. women, third world nations, African Americans and the like. Regardless of the truth one espouses, any advocacy for truth must give due consideration to the post-modernist viewpoint and must try to convincingly respond to them.

Post-modernity and the European Enlightenment. Post-modernists often contrast themselves with the European Enlightenment and see themselves as being different from it. Post-modernists regard the Enlightenment's case for reason as just another narrative that ought to be undermined. However there are very important similarities between the European Enlightenment and post-modernity. The European Enlightenment didn't concern itself with ethics. Reason happens only to be a method. In the case of the European Enlightenment, no serious attempt was made to use reason to arrive at ethics. If the idea of Post-modernity is taken to its logical end then it will affirm anything as ethical as long as it is subjective. Any system of thought that affirms anything as ethical affirms nothing as ethical. Both the European Enlightenment and post-modernity are non-ethical ideological systems. The European Enlightenment used reason to overthrow contemporary institutions like church, monarch and aristocracy. The narrative of the church was the only narrative known to Europeans at the time. Post-modernists today are aware of other narratives from other cultures, so the fact that they are against all narratives is only an ideological extension of the European Enlightenment. There however is also one very important difference between the European Enlightenment and post-modernity. The European Enlightenment had reason by which it sought to create a new order. Post-modernity on the other hand does not have any alternative to the existing status quo. At best it simply could claim to undermine it.

Post-modernity, meta-narratives and the yearning for the local and the subjective. Post-modernity does not seek to create any new order; it simply seeks to undermine universal claims made on behalf of existing orders. Existing orders may be based on truth which have degenerated over time or on outright falsehood which continue exercising their sway over human life. If orders were originally based on the truth and in time have degenerated then they must be returned to their original ideals. If orders were based on falsehood, then the falsehood must be countered with the truth, so that new ethical orders could be constructed on these truths. Post-modernity does neither of these. Post-modernity simply undermines the universal claims on which these orders are based. The integrity and relevance of the ideals espoused by the different narratives are never examined. In the meanwhile orders that tend to have the most profound impact on human life continue to be based on grand narratives. Indeed the Post-modernist insistence on acting locally is irrelevant to decrees set nationally, internationally or religiously. There is nothing local when a Muslim bows towards Mecca to pray to Allah or when the when the faithful worldwide read the Quran which was revealed 1400 years ago in Arabia. Easily the most important thing in the life of a Muslim is turning towards Mecca to pray. There is only one Mecca for all Muslims. So also in the United States, if people do not file their tax papers by April 15th each year, the IRS will be behind their back and offenders could very well end up in jail for tax evasion. There is nothing subjective in paying taxes on time in the United States. National, International and Religious structures have a profound impact on human life and such structures are founded on an ideological core. Such ideologies are rooted in the historical and cultural experiences of different peoples. In practical terms post-modernity does not offer an alternate vision for society. In rare moments of intensity post-modernity creates a few blasphemous ripples in society and quietly disappears. One must conclude then that post-modernity is the happy underside of a decadent status quo. Post-modernity helps educated members of marginalized groups sustain themselves in an age of decadence. It is provides psychological recompense in place of constructive change.

Post-modernity and binary opposition. Another theme that resonates very loudly in the post-modernist view is that language chooses one in a pair of the binary opposites. Order is preferred over disorder, light over darkness, man over woman and the like. So the argument goes that language is inherently hierarchical and elitist and post-modernity seeks to ensure that those who are left out are represented. The metaphysical dimensions of binary opposites can be better understood with eastern thought than through linguistic theory. According to eastern thought, opposites came into existence when the universe came into existence. Opposites are an existential phenomenon. Opposites will find expression in existence at different times and in different existential contexts. At any given time one of the opposites may either be valued or relevant and therefore is preferred over the other. Preference is determined by the existential circumstance. But inherently neither of the opposites is superior to the other and both find equal opportunity for expression and are valued at different moments in existence. This is true but one cannot prove by empirical methods. However adequate evidence is available in nature to sustain a belief in the inherent equality of opposites provided we are open to seeing it. It is advantageous to be tall on the basket court, while it is advantageous for a jockey in a horse race to be short. In existence, light and order are preferred. According to eastern metaphysics[4], prior to existence and non-existence, nothing can be said about being except that its images were dark and chaotic. That is the primordial representation of being is dark and chaotic. Which is more valuable? If we cherish what is fundamental to being then we would say its primordial representation is valuable. If we isolate existence, then in it light and order will be invaluable because light gives potency to our ocular faculty and order provides us with predictability to operate in. Despite the post-modernist depiction of chaos and order in concrete terms rarely do we see them in isolation. Despite the Postmodernists disdain for order, and romance with chaos, life would be impossible to live amidst absolute undifferentiated chaos. One only needs to imagine how life would be if there is total chaos. To begin with, in the socio-political realm there would be no family, no government, no bureaucracy, no education, no law and no regulation. If there was no family after kids are born who will raise them? Left alone with no one to nurture babies, the entire human species will be extinct in one generation. Without laws or regulation or government there would be total anarchy and without education the knowledge accumulated by humans over the millennia cannot be passed on to posterity. Other expressions of opposites can be found in the fullness of history. Jews who were once persecuted and ostracized in Christian Europe as Jesus killers today are acknowledged as being high achievers with intellectual predispositions in Western civilization. Regions occupied by dark skinned Dravidians of Southern India, who are depicted as demons[5] in Hindu mythology, outperform regions inhabited by North Indians from the Hindi heartland, where the so called 'noble' Aryans lived, in every objective measure of modern development. In addition to opposites finding expression in history

41

we see ample evidence for change. Things are never static. In the medieval period the most ascendant civilization was Islam, in the last 400 years, it has been Western civilization that has been growing. Russia attained historical parity with the West immediately after the Napoleonic wars and it continued right through the cold war years. The imminent possibility of change inculcates a belief that change is inevitable and when the process of change is extended it culminates in opposites finding expression.

Post-modernity and elites. Post-modernity shares the Enlightenment's obsession with dethroning elites. While the French Revolution which followed the Enlightenment thirsted for aristocratic blood, post-modernity is far more benign in that it only seeks to ensure that those in the margins of society are heard. Since any narrative is inclusive of a large section of the general population, post-modernity in attempting to bring those in the margins of society to the forefront of the discourse leaves the majority out or worse still sets those in the margins on a confrontation course with the majority. There is a certain dishonesty about human differences that post-modernity inherits from the European Enlightenment. Different peoples are products of different historical experiences. So some peoples have accumulated greater cultural capital to operate and function in the modern world. Such cultural capital cannot be transferred; it can only be expended in the collective well-being of everybody.

Post-modernity and our times. In fairness, the aims of post-modernity are not conspicuously dishonorable. After all, it wants those in the margins of society be heard. But then modernity is a transcendental moment in world history and humanity has yet to arrive at a relevant structural arrangement to order human life. Several cultural traditions and political philosophies are claiming to be relevant responses to modernity and are generally successful in subscripting people. Post-modernity has not been able to penetrate the consciousness of vast numbers of these people because it is unable to relate to their historical and cultural experiences. To side with marginalized people and spend a lifetime celebrating them may be very therapeutic to privileged citizens who are guilty but it does not bring about substantial change in the lives of the marginalized. There is nothing wrong with a local, disordered, subjective worldview. Only the current of history is against it. Technology, modern methods of communication and transportation are all reducing distance and increasing contact between people from different continents. Such a world makes centralized control and planning very viable and often advantageous. One only has to witness the mergers between large private corporations or the almost complete absence of mom and pop stores in America to understand the rationale for greater centralization.

4. Civilizational Narratives

Almost all the people in the world can trace their cultural origins to one of the four major cultural traditions of the world namely Confucian, Indian, Islam and Christendom. These traditions can be regarded as having been ideal and perfect in their inception. All these traditions were truth in their inception and only became narratives when these traditions strayed away from their ideals. All four of these cultural traditions have their origins in the continent of Asia.

The civilizational narratives that are with us today differ from the ideals of the European Enlightenment and ideas of post-modernity in one important respect. While the ideals of the European Enlightenment are founded in untruth and Post-modernity in effect denies the very existence of universal truth, these civilizational traditions were founded on the truth but fairly early on in their history became tainted by untruth. The untruth associated with these civilizational narratives persists with us to this very day. Even though these narratives have conspicuously deviated from their ideals, one cannot deny that they have sustained human life for thousands of years. People have lived by these civilizational narratives through the millennia. The fact that people have lived by these narratives does not enhance the moral content of these narratives. On the other hand it points to some degree the inherent difficulty in creating an ethical order in the pre-modern world and to a much larger degree to the concessions made to human weakness.

It is not difficult to see that the different civilizational traditions are founded on the truth and would stand the test of ethical scrutiny provided we make adequate allowance for the different historical circumstances in which these truths were expressed and conspicuous loss that has occurred in perception, interpretation and transmission. There is a recognizable early moment in the historical evolution of all these major cultural traditions, except China, when truth dissipates and narratives are created. In the case of China the recognizable moment occurred a little later. Once the narrative is created from that point onwards the narrative is adapted to meet challenges that arise and to cope with different circumstances. However despite all the adaptations and changes through the ages, these narratives have preserved a certain core. Indeed it couldn't have been otherwise. Without a certain ideological core as a reference neither order nor continuity would have been possible. Also civilizational narratives have been accommodative of conspicuous acts of evil, tolerant of oppression and have facilitated the humiliation and dishonoring of others. Occasionally a visionary leader may seek to interpret the narrative in the light of the truth, as Gandhi did in India to the Hindu narrative[1], but fairly soon human failings catch up. As these cultural traditions have successfully adapted their narratives and are currently being confronted by modernity it is useful to examine the ethical integrity of the origins of our major cultural traditions and the reality of their respective practice as is evident in their subsequent histories[2].

Indian Truth. Indian metaphysical ideas are spiritual insights and inspired proclamations of highly evolved individuals. These individuals have been differently referred to as Siddhar, Buddha, Bodhisattva, Qutub, Sarguru, Rishi and Muni by different traditions in India and outside India they may be understood to be

Sages. Indian metaphysical ideas seek to transform the consciousness of an individual so that a person ceases to identify with his body and leads an egoless life. This is to be aspired for as it is a blissful state. Those who attained this state may be able to free themselves from the cycles of birth and death. Only a few spiritually gifted students could attain this through meditation. Other less spiritually gifted individuals ought to prepare themselves for liberation through good actions, service to others, ethical pursuit, sacrifice, devotion, respect for parents, good conduct, humility, charity, love, meditation and other such noble deeds. Mythology was created to cater to the needs of these less spiritually gifted individuals. Those who falter in this pursuit would slip in their evolutionary trajectory taking them longer to free themselves from the cycles of birth and death. The Hindu variation of Indian metaphysical thought philosophizes that the same universal consciousness pervades all of existence. If universal consciousness pervades all living beings then one's identity is inseparable from everything else in the universe. It follows that one should be able to feel others pain, know others desires and experience others longings and every individual must prioritize their actions based on the collective need of everybody, just as we treat the more lethal wound in the body first. These are the truths associated with the Indian tradition. Indian metaphysical ideas are addressed to the individual. In the pre-modern world where it was inherently not possible to bring about an order that would provide a comprehensive socio-economic and political solution to human problems the only way to lessen the hardships on the vast majority of people was through individual transformation. Indian metaphysical ideas, if seriously undertaken and followed by all individuals, would have precisely done that.

Indian Reality. About a thousand years after the beginning of civilized life in the Indian subcontinent a group of light skinned Indo-European Aryans migrated to India in horse drawn chariots. Their national narrative was the Rig Veda. On arrival in India they confronted a largely dark skinned Dravidian people. Contact with the Dravidian people of civilized India could possibly have exposed the Aryans to the metaphysical ideas espoused by the Siddhars[3]. These metaphysical ideas were so persuasive that they were co-opted into the Vedic canon. Likewise indigenous Gods and local magic incantations were also co-opted[4]. A stratified social order - the Hindu caste system - was propounded. A group of Aryans called the Brahmins, who created the order, self-appointed themselves at the apex of this social order. Overwhelming majority of indigenous Dravidian people were stigmatized as "Sudra" and absorbed into the Hindu caste order to do menial work, while the Aryans wore a sacred thread to indicate divine status. The same process would be repeated with Brahmin migration to Southern India with only one difference. In Northern India from time to time powerful groups were given Aryan status out of necessity, in the South all the Dravidian peoples, whether rich or poor, educated or illiterate, good or evil, white collar worker or blue collar, were without discrimination dubbed "Sudra". The representation of the Dravidian in Hindu writing through the millennia must make any conscientious human being sick to the stomach. The ethnically Dravidian Sudra were considered to be sons of prostitutes[5]. In addition the Dravidian is represented as a demon in Hindu mythology[6]. To this day scores of untouchables all over India are denied access to drinking water, cannot walk the streets of their villages and are subjected to random acts of violence and sexual abuse just on the basis of their birth. Even today all over the world, including in America where equality before the law is a much cherished ideal, only people belonging to the Brahmin caste are priests in Hindu temples. The only things that were upheld through the ages were reverence for the Vedas, the caste order, the hierarchical primacy of the Brahmin community and the Sanskrit Language. While it is true in pre-modern times all the major civilizational traditions had a two tier social order in which the vast majority of people were doomed to hard physical labor - the cruelty, the inhumanity, the demonic representation, the rigid segregation and shameful humiliation that characterized the Hindu caste system has had no parallel in world history. It would be wrong to regard the Hindu caste system as a variation of feudalism or an aristocracy that had become perpetually corrupt. The Hindu caste system was an enslavement of a people by another people cherishing a different language, identifying with a different race and adhering to a different civilization. One could use the terms slavery, oligarchy, racism, imperialism and feudalism and yet even when all these terms are taken together they will not capture all the oppression that took place in Hindu India. However one must not suppose the vast majority of the people of India were abandoned with despair. Right in the vicinity of Hindu India, all through the ages there were casteless alternatives to Hinduism in Buddhism, Jainism and Islam engaged in passionate millennial struggles only to be out done by Hindu India. Likewise the oppression of women in Hindu India has no parallel in world history. Fidelity in sexual relations was a universally cherished ideal in pre-modern times, but the extreme degree to which it was taken to in Hindu India has no parallel. Widows were forbidden to remarry. Women in certain communities of Hindu India had to burn themselves on the funeral pyre of their respective husbands as part of the practice of Sati. On the positive side however, India hardly ever conquered or occupied any other country. Likewise, Vegetarianism was practiced by the elites in Hindu India. India, among the civilizations of the world, has been more inclined to cherish non-killing as a value.

Christian Truth[7]. The message of Jesus was a message of love. It was as simple as it was profound. Like Indian metaphysical ideas, the message of Jesus was addressed to the individual. Jesus spoke to the ancient Jews and reinforced their faith in the worship of the formless God. Jesus asked people to love their neighbors as they would love themselves. As a reward for a life of love they would be admitted to heaven. The intensity of love that Jesus expects becomes apparent when he asks everyone to sell everything they had and give it to the poor and when he admonishes that a camel can enter the eye of a needle but a rich man cannot enter the Kingdom of Heaven. Rich and poor are relative terms. Even among the poor there is difference. All people are not uniformly poor. One who has slightly greater possessions than his or her neighbor is rich relative to his or her neighbor. If the message of love that was espoused by Jesus was embraced by all human beings, then nobody would have possessed anything and all the resources of society would have been directed to the neediest citizens. Again if everybody had adhered to one of the two commandments favored by Jesus namely - Love thy neighbor as thyself - then that alone would have created and maintained a harmonious social order. There would have been no need for either government or laws. No outside nation would have attempted to capture such a country because there would be nothing ostentatious in it. If there happened to be another conquering nation that actually was poorer than a nation that lived by the message of love then citizens of the nation which lived by love would not only have given up without bloodshed all their wealth but would have voluntarily made it their first order of business to alleviate poverty in the conquering country. So much so the conquering country would have been transformed by the message of love that characterized the conquered country. In this way the territorial orbit of love would have unceasingly expanded. It is hard to imagine a better way to live in the pre-modern world. But wouldn't such a people be gullible targets for exploitation? After all wasn't there slavery? Weren't the working poor doomed to a life of hard labor in pre-modern times? Not likely. A nation is made of both the intelligentsia and the teeming poor. In a nation of love, the intelligentsia would have lived by love out of conviction. They would have articulated their conviction to their oppressors when they came in contact with them. The message of love would have initially subverted the unity of their oppressors and later conquered them.

Christian Reality. After the mission of Jesus ended, historically the most significant event in Christianity was the advent of Paul. Paul effectively takes over the Jesus movement within a few decades after Jesus and defines it for the rest of history. Up until the time of Paul, one had to become a Jew before one became a Christian but Paul changed that. Paul threw membership into the church to Jew and Gentile alike. Many of the ancient Jewish practices like circumcision were abandoned. The single obsession for Christianity from then on would be the destruction of polytheism in the Mediterranean world and beyond. The images of the polytheists were replaced with new images of the crucifix, Jesus and others. The Church grew through aggressive proselytizing. The growth of the Church was achieved through extreme ruthlessness. We are only left with an architectural residue and literary remnants of the old world of the Greeks, Romans and all other Near Eastern cultures. At least after the triumph of Christianity, the message of love certainly must have had some impact on some people but the cumulative impact of such individual transformation was not substantial enough to make a significant difference to society as a whole. Indeed when the 2000 years of Western Christendom in its entirety is viewed from an ethical perspective nothing can be said about it in concrete terms. It is true that the advent of the Church ended slavery in the Roman Empire. Nevertheless, later on one of the worst forms of slavery - the whip on the back kind of plantation slavery - was practiced in the western hemisphere, only to be followed by an anti-slavery movement which originated in Britain and led to the emancipation of slaves worldwide. Classical forms of slavery have not been conspicuously noticeable after that, but that is a result of the proliferation of industrial technology and not the ethical rectitude of the beneficiaries of slavery. The same is also true of usury. The Church initially only banned the practice of usury by clerics[8]. Later probably with awareness of Islamic law and the influence of Aristotelian ideas, the church was more comprehensive in its opposition of usury. Even then the Church was only partially successful. However after the Reformation and the English Enlightenment money lending was practiced with little or no moral restraint. Indeed the Reformation and much more so the English Enlightenment provided the philosophical foundations of modern capitalism. When seen in its entirety, the ethical legacy of Christendom thus far must be regarded as the pursuit of sentimentality.

Islamic Truth[9]. Islam, unlike Indian metaphysical ideas and the message of Jesus, was addressed both to the individual and to society at large. Islam like Judaism contains a system of laws for society. All through history humans have slaughtered and humiliated others on the basis of ethnicity, language and culture. Islam with its explicit and emphatic insistence on equality among the community of believers seeks to avoid divisiveness within the community. Given the corruption of ideals among other religions, Islam tolerates limited violence to preserve the ethical integrity of the community. Islam is explicit about freedom for individuals to practice other religions, not just monotheistic religions. A chapter in the Quran is titled "Idolaters", in which God asks Muslims to tell the idolaters "you your way me my way". Islam bans usury. According to Islamic tradition usury is a far greater sin than infidelity. Great emphasis is placed in Islam on charity. Charity is one of the five pillars of Islam. In Islam, charity is next only to submission to Allah in importance. While the Quran does not stipulate the percentage to be given as charity, it asks Muslims to give charity immediately after income is earned. The wealthy have a special responsibility to ensure that the poor do not suffer. The rich ought to lift the poor up. In making polygamy preferable to the existence of prostitution, Islam forces men to be responsible for their actions. There is absolute intolerance for rape and theft in Islam. Islam allows for divorce and allows both divorcees and widows to remarry. Besides women have a right to inheritance in Islam - though not equal inheritance. Slavery was allowed only under certain conditions. The slave had a well-defined legal and moral status in Islam[10]. Manumission was a very meritorious act under Islam[11]. The institution of slavery under Islam must be seen in the backdrop of historical circumstances of the pre-modern world. The pre-modern world was one in which the possibilities of the free poor were very restricted. At least the slaves had somebody to take care of them. In short through law, ethical directive, God's grace and the promise of heaven, Islam sought to redeem a world in which all the religions had conspicuously fallen from their ideals.

Islamic Reality. Soon after the Prophet Mohammed's life, violence and a quest for power - far beyond the prescriptions of the Prophet - were utilized both to expand the territory of Islam and also to fulfill the ambitions of some members of the Muslim community. A degeneration of the faith has been self-evident to adhering Muslims all along. Shiite and Sunni Muslims attribute different recognizable moments when Islam deviated from its pristine form. To Shiite's the violent death of Hussein[12], the second son of the Prophet's cousin and son-in-law Ali on the day of Muharram would be that recognizable moment. To Sunni's the first four Caliphs were regarded as being rightly guided[13], the death of the fourth Caliph Ali and the transfer of the Caliphate to Syria would be that recognizable moment when Islam deviated from its pristine nature. Right from these very early moments onwards unnecessary violence and a quest for power have continued to be constant themes in Islamic history. Then did Islam grow by the sword? Respected scholars like Ira Lapidus persuasively argue that while forcible conversions were not unknown, overwhelming majority of the people converted to Islam voluntarily[14]. Initially at least Islamic rulers were more absorbed in conquest and securing political power than in conversion. One of the largest trafficking of slaves also took place in the Islamic world. Some scholars like Bernard Lewis have not incorrectly argued that a slave had a certain legal status in Islam and was treated a lot better[15] than the slaves of antiquity or the slaves in 19th century America. No matter how well slaves were treated, people can never compensate the pain associated with the capture of slaves and the violent separation of slaves from their environments and their loved ones. Islamic societies also imposed the veil on women. On the positive side, when viewed from the fullness of history, Islam has easily been the most inclusive of the major cultural traditions we have surveyed here. Likewise Islam has been the most progressive of all pre-modern cultural traditions, in part because it was the last of the major pre-modern cultures and partly because Muslims have for the most part followed the teachings of Islam in the social sphere.

Chinese Truth. In China, during the feudal period, the ruling dynasty directly ruled only the areas immediately around the capital. The Emperor who lived in the capital was the son of heaven and ruled with the mandate from heaven. The rest of China was divided into hundreds of fiefdoms and each was ruled by family members of the ruling dynasty relatively independently[16]. During this period ritual was used to cultivate self-discipline among the people. The feudal states period was followed by the warring states period. During the warring states period these small fiefdoms had given way to a few large principalities that were at war with each other. The warring states period lasted from 476 B.C to the unification of the Chinese Empire in 221B.C[17]. The warring states period was also a period of great intellectual ferment where many schools of thought sprang up and many ideas were debated. Two schools of thought, Confucianism and Taoism won out and have been used to guide Chinese thought ever since. Confucius[18] was the founder of Confucianism. While several new ideas were proposed for the emerging new times, Confucius saw wisdom in continuity. He espouses ritual, learning and humaneness. Through ritual, discipline was inculcated and continuity with the old China was maintained. Confucius advocated both learning and thinking. One learned about the past in order to apply to the present circumstances[19]. Humaneness is compassion for all. Humaneness was not doing to others what one wouldn't want to be done unto oneself. Confucianism had been the central tenet of the Chinese people for much of Chinese history since the feudal age period. If everybody didn't do unto others what they didn't want to be done unto them then that would certainly be a very reasonable place to live. The central text of Taoism was Lao Tzu's Tao Te Ching. It builds on another tradition from the feudal age period namely that of change. Understanding change in nature is understanding reality. Taoism however goes way beyond reality and well into truth. It advocates passivity, stillness and inaction. Taoism abhors war, decries possession and elevates 'unutterable simplicity' above all else. It explicitly advices the rulers of a country to protect and guard these last citizens to get the choicest blessings of heaven and earth. Taoism warns the rulers against the enslavement of those who were unutterably simple. In the pre-modern world when most of the laboring poor could only merely subsist one must regard Taoism as ethically profound.

Chinese Reality. All of China came under the direct control of imperial authority only after the Chinese empire was unified in the year 221B.C. After that China had been politically unified through much of its history under different dynasties. It was inherently not possible for any large state or empire to establish an ethical political order in the pre-modern period. Therefore in Imperial China, the pursuit of ethics was intertwined with realities that the empire confronted. The Chinese empire was created and sustained through the millennia with considerable violence and bloodshed. This is in sharp contrast with the feudal age period when the Chinese gentleman known as junzi showed great civility and restraint on the battlefield[20]. Like empires everywhere the Chinese empire too spent enormous resources on ostentatious expenses when this could have been used to lessen the burden of the working poor. The state in the pre-modern world patronized religion. In the pre-modern world, the state sought to transform the individual through religion. In China, Taoism became mystical and

Buddhism was transcendental. Though both Taoism and Buddhism could have had an effect in transforming the individual for society it was Confucianism that had the greatest prospect for socially pertinent individual transformation. The essence of Confucianism was self-cultivation. Self-cultivation through ritual was already well entrenched in the Chinese culture of the feudal age period, way before the Chinese empire was unified. Then certainly the self-cultivation that was advocated, the deviance that was corrected through peer pressure and the conformance that resulted due to the Confucian culture were not a consequence of empire. The Chinese were the first to institute the examination system to select bureaucrats. However, many of the candidates got in through nepotism[21]. Not all of China's inequities in the pre-modern period were a result of empire. The Chinese narrative all along had depicted the non-Chinese as *barbarian*. The lowering and inferior representation of the non-Chinese was a central facet of China's national narrative and was conceived well before the Chinese empire. Many nations and peoples consider themselves chosen or superior but in China this sense of superiority was both continuous and central to its narrative. Needless to say, the non-Chinese is no way inferior to the Chinese. But as a practical matter in the pre-modern world it was the so called barbarian, who dominated and ruled China more than China dominating the so called barbarian. China surely had other social problems unrelated to empire as in the foot binding of women. On the positive side, through the ages up until modern times, China did not seek to invade other nations. Indeed it is the inner Asian tribes that conquered China and ruled it for most of the last thousand years. Therefore most of China's military intervention in history must be seen as attempts at self-preservation. Likewise the public spiritedness of the Confucian elite was clearly better than their counterparts in other parts of the world like the Brahmins in India or the nobility in Europe. China avoided a formal caste system as in India and a formal feudal arrangement as in the serfdom of Europe. It is all the more remarkable because all through the ages China has been densely populated and essentially agrarian. It was far more difficult to preserve the self-respect and dignity of the working poor in an agrarian society of the pre-modern world than among nomadic peoples. The most prestigious occupation in China was that of the scholar-bureaucrat. Though nepotism continued in bureaucratic appointments, the examination system in China provided a path by which people from other sections of society, besides the gentry, could also become scholar-bureaucrats.

Conclusions. Three out of our four major cultural traditions are religious traditions. Only the East Asian Confucian civilization is mostly secular. An average human's life span is so small in relation to human history and infinitesimal in relation to the life of the universe. Therefore the center piece of our religious narratives was not secular but transcendental. Despite three of our cultural narratives having a transcendental basis, all our civilizational narratives were perfect and ethical in their inception. They however degenerated fairly soon. The Hindu and the Christian narratives relied on individual transformation whereas the Islamic and Confucian traditions sought to bring about transformation through laws and self-cultivation enforced via societal pressure, respectively. The Hindu and Christian ideals offered greater scope for ethical growth to privileged individuals and ended up being harsher on society as a whole. While Islamic and Confucian systems, in very different ways restricted moral choice, they secured for their respective societies a relatively more equitable social order in the pre-modern world. Recent research in social and cultural anthropology, primatology, evolutionary biology and evolutionary psychology[22] have attempted to uncover innate human nature. At the time of their inception our major cultural traditions recognized, that in the pre-modern world with all its inequities, if people simply lived by human nature it wouldn't suffice. So they sought to propel individuals to acts of service, sacrifice, love, charity, humility and selflessness with rewards and incentives in the afterlife.

Truth

5. Gandhi, India and the Quest for an Ethical Response to Modernity

With the advent of modernity it was only in India, during the first half of the 20th century, that a discourse on ethics was carried out in the public sphere. The ethical discourse was spearheaded by Gandhi, but it was a discourse nevertheless. This conversation took place in an ancient civilization that was simultaneously breaking free from the shackles of colonialism and attempting to chart its course in the face of modernity. Eminent individuals representing different ethnic, religious and ideological groups participated in this national conversation. To begin with there was Gandhi, whose quest for the absolute truth included his active participation in politics. There were the British who obviously had their reasons to resist Indian independence. Then there was the concept of modernity in all its dimensions that was part of the discourse. Nehru championed for the ideals of the European Enlightenment albeit with a socialist tilt. There was the Muslim leader Mohammed Ali Jinnah who wanted India partitioned into Pakistan and India. There was the very erudite Dalit leader B.R.Ambedkar who spoke for the rights of the untouchables. There was another idealist, E.V.Ramasamy Periyar, who located himself amongst the Dravidians of South India and espoused his ideal of self-respect. There were Marxists and Hindu Nationalists as well on the fringes. The sheer range of ideas that were grappled with in this conversation - truth and morality, Asia and Europe, capitalism and socialism, communism, modern and the pre-modern, to industrialize or not, science and religion, Islam, Hinduism and

Christianity, caste and equality and more is truly staggering. It was almost as if a microcosm of the world was talking to itself in the wake of modernity. This was not a conversation that took place in a structured artificial academic setting, but was historical and evolved naturally. The most significant aspect of this conversation was not the diversity of opinions that engaged in the national conversation. Diversity certainly enriched the conversation but the most significant aspect of this conversation was that truth and ethics were deliberated in the public sphere. Perhaps the only other time in world history when ethics was so deliberated was in classical Greece. There were again important differences between classical Greece and India in the first half of the twentieth century. The classical Greeks did not have to contend with the cascade of modernity, they did not have the religious, ethnic and linguistic diversity of India and they did not have ancient histories, historical aspirations and historical grievances that Indians brought to the modern moment. Needless to say that it was Gandhi who kept this conversation centered on ethics. The Indian historian Ramachandra Guha says "Gandhi was not so much the father of the (Indian) nation as he was the mother of all debates regarding its future"[1]. While it is true that many of the stalwarts recounted above vehemently disagreed with Gandhi, 'debate' is too strong a word to associate with someone like Gandhi. We would rather regard it as a national conversation. Recounting this conversation centered on ideas and issues that others had with Gandhi[2] could serve as a prototype for us to learn from and seek ethical resolutions for a world that is increasingly shrinking in distance and in which religions, narratives, ideologies and aspirations of different peoples are seen to be in conflict with each other. We also could benefit from examining the effect of these ideas in the interim sixty seven years after Gandhi.

Gandhi and the Truth. Gandhi's mission was a quest for the truth. Gandhi's search was for absolute truth, but it was ever elusive. Relative truth was all that he had to work with. Relative truth was that which could be conceived. Such relative truth was self-evident. All that one needed to see this self-evident relative truth was some clarity[3]. The means that Gandhi used to pursue absolute truth was ahimsa, which meant radically non-injurious active universal love. For Gandhi, universal love and truth were two sides of the same coin. Truth when applied was ethics. Truth to Gandhi was God. Since truth was God, it followed that the right application of such truth guaranteed success, for God was omnipotent. This is the wisdom that the ancients had understood and is lost upon humanity in modern times. We see that Socrates makes the same argument to Tracymachus in Plato's Republic[4]. We see this in the book of Amos[5]. The Chinese in feudal age period realized that making sacrificial banquets to the Gods and the ancestors were not reliable in obtaining the favor of the Gods or ancestors. The more reliable way to obtain advantages was to take care of the well-being of the little people[6]. Gandhi subscribes to the view that it is advantageous to be ethical. In his autobiography: *The story of my experiments with truth*, Gandhi narrates through incidents in his life that when he pursued the truth he was successful in the end. Gandhi was pursuing truth and love not because he wanted to be a nice guy nor was he naive but due to his lifelong self-education through which he came to know that he would be successful in the end. The path of truth and love best guaranteed successful outcomes. More recent practitioners of non-violence like the Dalai Lama, Aung San Suu Kyi or even Martin Luther King may actually have embraced the method of non-violence as a useful technique rather than a philosophy of life that Gandhi understood it to be. For one thing Gandhi's mission was not Indian independence; his quest was for absolute truth. Moral leadership for the Indian independence movement was a consequence of his search for absolute truth. In the last sixty seven years, Gandhi has been co-opted in a piecemeal fashion by pacifists, Greenpeace activists and other interest groups. Scores of individuals followed Gandhi and became Gandhians but they have neither applied his ideas to as wide a circle as Gandhi did nor have they succeeded on a scale that Gandhi had.

Gandhi and the British. Since all his efforts at seeking constructive co-operation with the British had failed, Gandhi had come down to believing that British colonial rule was a violent and exploitative commercial and political arrangement that was embraced and sustained by gullible Indians[7]. To the British, Gandhi simply did not represent all of India[8] and they believed that India would disintegrate and that anarchy would prevail if the British left. Now that it has been over sixty eight years since the British left, we could take a moment to reflect on the correctness of their respective positions. Gandhi was certainly right in his observation that British colonialism was economic exploitation and that the British did not have India's best interest at heart. During the first 50 years of the 20th century the Indian economy grew at 1% per year[9] and the population grew at 1% in the same period, meaning that there was no net growth in individual income during this period of British preeminence in the subcontinent. After independence from the 1950s to the 1980s, when India followed a socialist model, it grew at a rate of 3.5%[10]. From the early nineties after economic liberalization until 2002, the Indian economy grew at a pace close to 6% per year[11]. The Indian economy has grown at an even greater pace after 2003 and has remained so until 2011-12[12]. The British actually acted on the notion that Gandhi did not represent all Indians and therefore they played their part in the creation of Pakistan. The British were off the mark in saying that India would disintegrate when they left. India certainly has not disintegrated in the last sixty eight years and may never do so. There however is considerable dissent within India. The rule of the law existed in India during British times. During British colonial rule, India had a functioning bureaucracy and a judiciary that for the most part was successful in maintaining order. This continued in the first two decades after independence when idealistic Indians populated the polity, bureaucracy and judiciary. Today the Indian bureaucracy is inefficient, the polity is corrupt and the judiciary is weak. Much of the groundwork for India's modern infrastructure was laid during British times. Economic liberalization in India has grown the economy but the inadequacy of India's infrastructure has become glaringly apparent. While individual Indians have been enterprising and are driving economic activity, India as a whole has not been able to bring the necessary organization of its own accord to self-administer the country effectively. The polity is not merely financially corrupt. There is profound corruption of ideals as well. In independent India, places of worship of religious minorities have either been destroyed or damaged as a result of political instigation – something that was not tolerated during the British Raj. Likewise the first government to be formed by a party headed by a Dalit (formerly "Untouchable") woman in the largest Indian state of Uttar Pradesh entered into a disgraceful political alliance with a radical right wing Hindu political party – roughly the Indian equivalent of a political alliance between the NAACP and the Christian Coalition in America. However Indian independence is not without its gains. Since independence and especially in the last two decades, India has witnessed an unprecedented inclusiveness of individuals from historically oppressed groups in positions of public leadership. Neither in

British times nor in previous ages has India experienced this sort of inclusiveness of members of the untouchable and other backward castes in the public sphere. In summation, India was better administered in British times but British colonial rule was at once both exploitative and apathetic to the well-being of Indians. This is a common theme that runs through many of the post-colonial developing nations. Colonial rule was fundamentally exploitative but relatively more effective in its administration.

Gandhi and Modernity. Gandhi comes at a point in time in Indian history when the transition begins from the pre-modern to the modern. The one thing that one notices in Gandhi's views with respect to modernity is that it is constantly evolving. Modernity as a historical phenomenon has had the effect of overwhelming pre-modern structures and institutions wherein one could say that it constitutes a transcendental moment in world history. India has been a land of innumerable castes. For much of his public life, Gandhi did not seek to overthrow the Hindu caste system. He wanted to consolidate all castes into four broad divisions of society. Gandhi was a village romantic[13] who was not entirely averse to modern technology but abhorred industrialization. Modern civilization, from Gandhi's perspective, only provided for a person's bodily comforts[14], it did not elevate his soul. Truth and ethics were timeless and the result of adhering to them would be better than all that modernity had to offer. Gandhi for his part seeks to preserve contemporary institutions - religious, social and economic from the cascade of modernity. Gandhi makes a heroic effort to stall the advent of modernity. One must regard Gandhi as the greatest of conservatives. Gandhi however is certainly right in one important respect. Modern technology reduces distance and time and thereby makes centralized control possible and easy. After Gandhi, after we have left behind the agrarian world and after we have completely embraced the modern, the rationale for centralization would be compelling and would require enormous undoing on our part to go back to our local independent communities free from external penetration or control. We see this sort rationale at work in the private sector in corporate mergers, the speedy disappearance of mom and pop stores in America and the stipulated patterns into which all newly built homes of any neighborhood in America fall due to the economies of scale. Gandhi's resistance to modernity might have been the last line of defense in the preservation of local freedoms.

Gandhi and Religions. Gandhi seeks to preserve all Religions. He would defend the temple, the mosque and the church. All religions in essence were about truth, love and morality. Adherents of different religions need to transform themselves in the light of truth and love. Modernity did not require either an abandonment of religion or its substantive overhaul. The untouchable must be allowed to enter the Hindu temple and the Muslim ought to renounce violence as neither was in the true spirit of either Hinduism or Islam. Christians ought to lead their lives in accordance with the Christian message of love. In the more than six decades after Gandhi, modernity has percolated deeper into people's lives and modernity has come into even greater confrontation with the major religions of the world. In Islam, a small section of Muslim thinkers would like halt the advent of modernity and replace it with a Taliban style interpretation of Islam and are not averse in bringing it about through violence. It is still early to say whether the wider Muslim community would gravitate to the Taliban's interpretation of Islam but they are certainly disillusioned with modern culture. In Western civilization, beginning in the 1970s notions of marriage and family had radically changed, so much so, that by 1980 it was being regarded as a matter of public concern. In this period of massive cultural change, religion has been viewed by some as the solution and by others as a retrograde impediment. In India, the people on the one hand are divided along religious lines and on the other the backward castes and Dalits (erstwhile untouchables are now called Dalits in India) are not merely fighting for their rights in the wake of modernity, some of them are also questioning the very nature and relevance of Hinduism. In Gandhi's day when religion remained largely a matter of faith, Gandhi could interpret religion in the light of truth and love. Today for the historical issues that confront humanity, interpretation alone will not suffice. Religions need to be transformed so as to address the historical issues that confront them in the wake of modernity.

Gandhi and Asia. Gandhi did not have any substantial conversation with others on Asia. However the idea of an idealized Asia is at the heart of Gandhi's world view[15]. The wisdom of Asia for Gandhi lies not in its religious and cultural symbols but it does lie in the meekest of its citizens and in the great prophets and sages of the east. To Gandhi, the renowned religious teachers of the world – Zoroaster, Moses, Buddha, Jesus and the Prophet Mohammed all belong to the continent of Asia. The Asia that Gandhi cherishes is vastly different from the rising Asia that is currently portrayed in the West. The Asia that is seen to be rising today is an Asia that thrives in globalization, rampant mercantilism and competitive capitalism – a far cry from the Asia that Gandhi would have ever imagined. Gandhi did not seem to have known much about the religious and cultural traditions of Japan and China. However during the Second World War when the Japanese militarily occupied many nations, Gandhi would say that Japan had become westernized. Gandhi regarded Western civilization as the civilization of violence in which due to a multiplication of atom bombs despair had set in and was longing for wisdom. Tragically in the very subcontinent in which Gandhi was born both Indians and Pakistanis were euphoric when their respective nations conducted atomic tests more than fifteen years ago. Gandhi believed that Asia ought not to imitate the West in making atom bombs and in Gandhi's view if Asia proceeded on the path of truth and love it would succeed in conquering the West. Such a conquest, Gandhi believed, would be liked by the West itself.

Gandhi and Violence. Non-violence was absolutely central to Gandhi's life. He remained steadfastly committed to the ideal of non-violence. To Gandhi, war was an unmitigated evil. Gandhi's insistence on the non-violent method was opposed by some Indians of his time. Among those who wanted to follow a violent course two voices have become recognizable in the subsequent historical discourse. The two individuals were Aurobindo Ghose and Subash Chandra Bose. Aurobindo was a radical in the early stages of the Indian independence movement. Aurobindo withdrew from politics in 1910 to Pondicherry in Southern India where he pursued his spiritual quest for the next forty years of his life. Aurobindo never met Gandhi and never disagreed with him publicly. We know of Aurobindo's views from the letters he wrote to his disciples. In this chapter we recount the conversations that Gandhi had with others. Though the conversation between Gandhi and Aurobindo never took place and this difference is known to the larger public only after their times, we recount it here because the substance of Aurobindo's views on violence is significant. Aurobindo had access to higher levels of consciousness through his meditations and when he viewed from these higher levels of consciousness, violence was completely justified. Since Gandhi did not have access to these higher levels of consciousness, Aurobindo believed that Gandhi resorted to an absolute insistence on non-violence. Aurobindo believed that violence itself was a characteristic of existence and as such was neither good nor evil. According to Aurobindo, non-violence was good only if one could succeed, otherwise one could resort to violence. It is the circumstance that justified the use of violence. The other advocate for violence and war was Subhash Chandra Bose. Subhash Chandra Bose seems to have been influenced substantially by European fascism. He had met with Mussolini and wanted to forge an alliance with Hitler to liberate India. Unlike Aurobindo, who morally wrestled with the idea of violence, Subash Chandra Bose does not seem to have grappled with the ethical dimensions of violence. More importantly, Subash Chandra Bose had no reservations about the people and nations that he was willing to be allied with to achieve his political objective. Bose had sought an alliance with Nazi Germany to overthrow British rule in India. Now let us contrast the attitude of these three men - Gandhi, Aurobindo and Bose, to violence. Gandhi would have no violence at all, Aurobindo would do what was necessary to destroy evil and Bose would use evil to destroy evil. The contrast in the views of these three men is best brought out in their respective positions towards Nazi Germany. Gandhi believed that Hitler was not a bad man and that the non-violent method could be successfully used against Hitler. Aurobindo was against British colonial rule and wanted its violent overthrow but he fully supported the allied war efforts against Nazi Germany. Subash Chandra Bose was willing to form an alliance with Nazi Germany. Gandhi's position reflected the purity of the truth, Aurobindo's position reflected the responsibility undertaken by the truth and Bose's position reflected the concessions made to untruth in an attempt to attain a cherished political objective. What has been the fate of non-violence after Gandhi in the subcontinent? The Indian subcontinent had its share of violence and bloodshed in the second half of the twentieth century. However none of these violent movements seem to have succeeded. Even during Gandhi's time, partition which resulted in the creation of Pakistan took place with enormous bloodshed. Subsequently, Pakistan broke up giving birth to Bangladesh. More recently the U.S. is fighting its war on terror in Pakistan and the Taliban and Al-Qaeda have been infiltrating Pakistani society and Pakistan is disintegrating further. In India, the rise of militant Hindu nationalism has polarized the Indian polity completely. The Indian government in New Delhi which has for long relied on militarily controlling the Kashmiris has found finding a lasting and meaningful political solution to the problem ever elusive. The recent war that ended in Sri Lanka between Tamils and Sinhalese demonstrates the futility of a profound reliance on violence in resolving ethnic and communal conflicts in the subcontinent. The Tamils were decimated and the Sinhalese who persecuted the Tamils could hardly hope to inspire their own citizens in rebuilding their nation after decimating a portion of their fellow citizens. The only military solution in the Indian subcontinent which is not likely to retract is the creation of Bangladesh. It is highly unlikely that Bangladesh and Pakistan will fuse together once again to form one predominantly Muslim nation that is separate from India. But then, India adhered to universal principles of right and wrong and showed great restraint in its 1971 war against Pakistan.

Gandhi and Dalits (those ostracized as untouchable in the Hindu Indian caste system are now referred to as Dalits). Gandhi had to contend with an erudite Indian Dalit leader named Dr.B.R.Ambedkar on the issue of untouchability. During the years 1932-34 Gandhi made the removal of untouchability in India his central concern. Gandhi sought to remove untouchability by purifying the caste system. Gandhi believed the so purified Hindus would not have a sense of being superior or inferior and as a result there would be no untouchability. Gandhi was prohibited from taking his program of purifying Hindu society to its logical end by historical circumstances. The call for Indian independence occupied most of Gandhi's energies for the remaining years of his life. So he was unable to devote himself completely to the task of removing untouchability. Though Ambedkar differed with Gandhi, he clearly welcomed Gandhi's leadership when Gandhi made the removal of untouchability his priority. But when the issue had to be receded to make Indian independence the priority, Ambedkar started openly and vehemently disagreeing with Gandhi. Ambedkar believed that the caste system itself ought to go and the only way to make the caste system go was to reject the religious scriptures that were at the core of the Hindu religion. Towards the end of his life, Ambedkar converted to Buddhism. In addition, Ambedkar believed in the pursuit of civil rights for the betterment of his people. Towards the end of his life, Gandhi seems to have come around to Ambedkar's position with regards to civil rights. Gandhi by then was clearly disillusioned with the obstinacy of the caste Hindus on the issue of untouchability. What is the result of their actions and where are we today? A reasonably effective affirmative action program (referred to as Reservations in India) has provided opportunity for scores of Dalits in higher education. However untouchability continues to be a menace in many of India's villages. Dalits are sometimes subjected to unspeakable cruelty, violence and sexual abuse in some of India's villages. However in the cities and towns of India untouchability is essentially non-existent. The enormous social dislocation caused by modernity makes untouchability irrelevant in towns and cities. This is not to say that the relations between Dalits and others are harmonious. The Dalits, especially the educated ones, who have become newly liberated in India's cities and towns, are simultaneously aware of both their horrific history and the continuing misery of their fellow Dalits in Indian villages. Liberal writing portrays the harsh reality of Dalit life fairly accurately but it obscures certain important facets of historical truth. For instance it assumes in true Enlightenment fashion that equal opportunity could have been provided in the pre-modern world for all people and likewise it grossly exaggerates the resources, both human and material, at the disposal of Dalits to self-help themselves. None of which creates an incentive for the Dalit to work co-operatively with others. With the result the average Dalit in urban areas develops a sort of siege mentality in which he or she sees all his or her compatriots, including well-meaning ones, as little more than enemies. Armed with such attitudes the Dalit seeks to influence and transform life in rural India. In the village it might begin with attainment of civil rights like equal rights to drinking water or temple entry or the right to walk in certain prohibited streets of the village. Alongside this quest for civil rights is a parallel effort to challenge the age old status quo in subtle but more poignant ways like wearing sandals in front of caste Hindus or using umbrellas or in some cases where a Dalit has made considerable wealth outside his village he tries to build a home that is larger than the homes of some of the prominent caste Hindus in the village. All of which rubs the caste Hindus on the wrong side. The resistance to Dalits often comes from people who belong to a layer just above them in the caste hierarchy. These are India's backward castes. Among the Indian caste Hindus, the forward castes are for the most part removed from the day to day realities of village life. Most of them have migrated out of the village and reside elsewhere. The caste Hindus could respond to the defiance of the Dalits with violence or further socio-economic oppression. So we see that, both in the cities and villages, Dalits are either socially or psychologically segregated from the rest of the population in India and they continue to be crushed in many of India's villages. What then is the way out for the Dalit? Religious conversion to Islam and Buddhism are certainly viable alternatives. Indeed these were millennial alternatives that were available to the Dalit. But the Dalits haven't taken to these religious alternatives in large numbers in our times. Despite the violence and militancy we cannot completely discredit the quest for civil rights. In the absence of this quest for civil rights, Dalits would have no way to break free from bondage in today's circumstances. There is no other alternative as things stand today. Ambedkar himself strictly eschewed violence preferring the legal course even if it took longer. Ambedkar's disciples today have not adhered to his restraint but in fairness the Indian legal system does not have the same credibility that it had in Ambedkar's day. Gandhi's approach of purifying the caste Hindus is not without merit. In this militant Dalit quest for civil rights there does not seem to be light at the end of the tunnel. At the end of the day, untouchability and the oppression associated with it must end and both Dalits and caste Hindus should come together to live harmoniously as a peaceful socio-political community in which human relationships are easy. This can never happen with a militant Dalit quest for civil rights. It certainly could have happened with the way of Gandhi, if it was pursued to its logical conclusion. Likewise with the way of Gandhi's contemporary Periyar, who sought to unite both Dalit and all other non-Brahmins into a common Dravidian fraternity, it may still be possible to attain peace with justice in India. Here experience teaches us that regardless of the approach, unity is the necessary pre-condition for finding comprehensive solutions to socio-economic problems.

Gandhi and Hindu-Muslim Division. Gandhi had to contend with the nationalistic aspirations of both the Hindu nation and the Muslim nation. While the Congress party stayed committed to Gandhi's idea of a unified India, the Hindu Mahasabha sought to create a Hindu nation which was supposed to conform to the concept of Hindutuva, in which non Hindus would be subordinate to the Hindus, and the Muslim League sought to separate predominantly Muslim areas of India into a new nation called Pakistan. Much of the impetus for Pakistan and Hindu nationalism seems to have come only in the last ten years before Indian independence. Interestingly the pioneers of both Pakistan and Hindutuva were not religious but secular men[16]. The leader of the movement for Pakistan was Mohammed Ali Jinnah and the ideological godfather of Hindutuva was Vinayak Damodar Sarvarkar. Gandhi sought to create a unified India with equal rights for both Hindus and Muslims in which neither would be dominant. India was partitioned and Pakistan was created against Gandhi's wishes during Gandhi's lifetime. The overwhelming majority of Hindus did not support Hindutuva during Gandhi's lifetime. However Gandhi himself was assassinated by someone who subscribed to Hindutuva ideology. Now after over six decades after Gandhi what has been the fate of Pakistan and Hindutuva? East Pakistan, which was separated from West Pakistan by the Indian mainland, seceded from Pakistan with Indian help to become an independent country called Bangladesh in 1971. After the U.S. war on terror, Pakistan is disintegrating further. The Pakistani Taliban, which adheres to a radical Islamic ideology, is making claims on Pakistan. The U.S. has been directly intervening in Pakistani territory as part of its effort to combat terrorism. The Pakistani army is increasingly finding it hard to control its territory. The Congress party which spearheaded India's efforts to win independence and stood behind Gandhi like a rock during Gandhi's lifetime has become corrupt. Indeed the ideology of the Congress from the early eighties onwards has progressively become indistinguishable from Hindutuva. Hindutuva now has found more mainstream acceptance. One of the two major national political parties explicitly subscribes to the Hindutva ideology. Muslims in India today are marginalized. They have been victims of communal crimes. As citizens they have for all practical purposes been subordinated to the Hindus. However, Hindutuva as an ideology is also vehemently being resisted in India. Hindutuva ideology is justly being viewed as a Hindu upper caste ideology whose purpose is to perpetrate upper caste dominance. It is inherently not possible for Dalits, Tamils, Muslims and Communists, who together could account for forty percent of India's population, to partake in this ideology. In addition, in some very populous states in the Hindi heartland, backward castes, who make up most of the populace, also view Hindutuva as being a forward caste ideology and have, in the past, been assertive in rejecting it. Hindu nationalists, for their part, have recently downplayed their core ideological message and have comfortably succeeded in forming the national government with the promise of development. However the historical issues that have been raised by the backward castes and Dalits remain.

Gandhi and Capitalism. Gandhi was undoubtedly committed to the socialist vision. He however sought to realize it by transforming the rich rather than dispossessing them. He recognized that there could be differences in the needs of the people based on their station in life; his famous quote "The elephant needs a thousand times more food than the ant but that is not an indication of inequality", captures the non-fanatical socialist spirit of Gandhi. He believed in the notion: each according to their needs and not according to the capitalist notion: each according to the market value of their deeds. He wanted rich people to exercise discretion and give away any wealth they possessed over and beyond their needs to the poor. If the rich prove to be obstinate then the laboring class could resort to non-co-operation with the rich. Since the life of the rich depended on the services of the laborer, Gandhi believed that non-co-operation can be used to make the rich act justly. After Gandhi, some of his illustrious successors like Vinobha Bhave and Jaya Prakash Narayan tried to take Gandhi's socio-economic vision called Sarvodaya to the Indian countryside. These charismatic successors of Gandhi went from village to village begging for land on behalf of the poor and the meek. Much of the land that was so obtained couldn't be used until 1968 because additional resources like equipment, fertilizers, capital and other necessities were not available. After 1968, greater organization and resources were made available and consequently Sarvodaya began yielding results[17]. Sarvodaya has successfully reduced, but has not eliminated, the socio-economic misery in many of the villages where it has been embraced. India is a nation with nearly 600,000 villages[18] and only a few thousands of them have been touched by Sarvodaya. Clearly the reach of Sarvodaya has not been comprehensive. However in Sri Lanka, it has been far more successful[19]. Now how has Gandhi's idea of each according to his needs fared? In the sixty plus years after Gandhi, there is hardly anyone amongst the rich people of India or for that matter anywhere in the world who retained only the wealth that they needed and gave the rest away to the poor. Both India and the World at large have progressively abandoned the socialist vision and have embraced globalization and capitalism.

The Alternate Gandhi. All the conversations Gandhi had with others were adherents of beliefs that were derived from religious narratives, sub-nationalist ideologies or beliefs that had their origins in Western thought. However there was in Southern India an independent thinker called E.V.Ramasamy Periyar[20], who advocated a different ethical ideal. Gandhi located himself within the Hindu narrative and reached out to everybody. Gandhi would call himself a Sanatani Hindu. Periyar located himself amongst the Dravidians of South India. While Indians were striving under Gandhi's leadership to overthrow the yoke of British colonial rule, Periyar regarded Hindu society itself to be created by alien Aryans in order to keep the indigenous Dravidians subjugated for several millennia. Periyar regarded the Brahmins who were at the apex of the Hindu caste order to be the historical descendants of the Aryans. Many of Periyar's views have their origin in two ideas that were essentially intrinsic to him, namely pagutharivu (பகுத்தறிவு) a Tamil word whose closest English equivalent would be discernment and suyamariyadai (சுயமரியாதை) which meant self-respect. To Periyar, his concept of pagutharivu or discernment was the means to know and the object that one had to uncover through such knowledge was one's self-respect. Periyar's notion of pagutharivu or discernment led him to being an atheist, being radically secular i.e. this worldly, being unsentimental, being vehemently opposed to superstition and being utilitarian[21] (as we regard being utilitarian in common usage different from the philosophical Utilitarianism of John Stuart Mill). Discernment may have had roots in his personality. From a very young age he seems to have rebelled against tradition. Once he threw himself into public service and had become acquainted with ideas of the European Enlightenment, Periyar was unhesitant in obtaining intellectual corroboration from the European Enlightenment. The other idea that Periyar espoused was self-respect. To Periyar, the essence of the idea of self-respect was that there ought to be no feeling of superior and inferior among people who were ethnically, intellectually, socially, culturally or linguistically different from one another. All reasonable, decent, ethically disposed people would agree with this understanding of self-respect that Periyar espouses. Periyar, however doesn't stop there. He goes further. Periyar includes in his idea of self-respect the notion that no people ought to participate in a narrative that had been historically condescending or humiliating to them. Nor should a historically humiliated people be part of any organization in which those who spearheaded their humiliation remain dominant[22]. Other historically oppressed peoples exhibit similar dispositions. When historically oppressed people become aware of their oppression, there is in oppressed people a deep rooted human yearning to throw off the cultural and historical baggage that they had accumulated during their oppression and culturally return to the state that they perceive as truly belonging to them. The Back-to-Africa movement to get African Americans to return to Africa was a movement to return African Americans to their roots. The Jews after hundreds of years of stigmatization and persecution in Christian Europe now identify with the state of Israel. While in other oppressed peoples it is a disposition, in Periyar it gets philosophized as an ideal, worthy enough to be pursued for its own sake. As we have already seen, he gives a name for it. He calls it, self-respect. He regards self-respect as the highest ethical ideal. In ages past, people have associated human honor with chastity and valor. To Periyar, the essence of human honor was self-respect. Such self-respect was intertwined with the integrity of one's own being. Death to Periyar was preferable to the loss of one's self-respect. Periyar was opposed to using violence to settling political differences but he believed that Gandhi's ideals were inferior to his ideal of self-respect. Periyar viewed Gandhi as someone, who through the loftiness of his method was attempting to absorb non-Brahmin South Indians in a narrative that had all along been oppressive, humiliating and insulting to them. There is this classic conversation between Gandhi and Periyar, in which Periyar accuses the Brahmins in India of dominating and Gandhi replies by saying that the intelligentsia will always dominate. Periyar remains unmoved. Even if talent sets human beings apart there was no reason for one human being to be inferior to the other. In addition, Periyar believed a historically humiliated people ought to break free from the domination of those who had dominated them. Interestingly, Periyar did not regard British colonialism as humiliation. Periyar would spell out the possibilities that could be realized by his ideal of self-respect in observing that through self-respect the whole world could prospectively come together to live as one family. History favors particular peoples over others at certain moments. Implicit in this view of Periyar is the notion that people who are historically less endowed can take the help of peoples who are more endowed if this co-operative arrangement is based on his ideal of self-respect. Periyar had co-opted the communist view that all property had to be kept common in society. During the pre-independence era, the British Government banned communist activity in India. Periyar readily gave up his communism. To Periyar, it was not merely a pragmatic choice; it was a value judgment as well. Communism only concerned itself with the material conditions of people whereas self-respect concerned itself with collective human honor. Periyar died in December 1973 and had outlived Gandhi by more than a quarter of a century. Gandhi was prominent in his lifetime and guided India's independence movement. The Self-Respect movement in Southern India found resonance only in the state of Tamilnadu and even there the outfit that went on to succeed politically - the DMK, abandoned Periyar even while remaining nominally reverential to him. Periyar's ideal of self-respect is widely cherished if not followed in Tamilnadu but his notion of pagutharivu (discernment) is not popularly embraced. Tamilnadu is a highly religious state in which it would be inherently very difficult for radically secular ideologies to penetrate and transform the consciousness of the people at large. The integrity of Periyar's ideal of self-respect nevertheless remains intact though essentially unknown to the world outside. Unlike the ideas of the European Enlightenment from which Periyar drew sustenance, his own life and thoughts, would stand the test of ethical scrutiny. Periyar was extremely civil in interpersonal relationships and abhorred the use of violence to further political purposes. He wanted all property to be kept in common and was very democratic in spirit. Periyar entirely gave away his huge inherited wealth to the party he had founded. Periyar wanted to create a Dravidian nation in Southern India so that he could transform society by making the ideal of self-respect the organizing principle of society. Periyar however did not succeed in his effort. So he spent a lifetime storming the Tamil country trying to convert receptive individuals to his worldview. Periyar has had his detractors as well. The Brahmins were understandably outraged because he sought to overthrow their preeminence. However what is less understandable is that in recent years some Dalit writers[23], partly inspired by deconstructionist ideas, have been sharply critical of Periyar. Such criticism is symptomatic of the frivolous writing that characterizes post-modern scholarship. Periyar called himself as the Buddha with the black shirt. (Periyar and his followers wore black shirts to signify the enveloping darkness that was all around them). Periyar asked the victims of the caste system to convert to Islam. Buddhism and Islam were millennial casteless alternatives to the cruelties of caste and untouchability, present right in the vicinity of Hindu India. Periyar identified himself with these millennial solutions to caste oppression and the practice of untouchability that always had existed in India. If the Dalits are so angry today, then why did they (the Dalits) not convert to Buddhism or Islam during their millennial oppression? It is intellectually dishonest on the part of Dalit writers to critique Periyar, who identified with the millennial solutions to problems of caste and untouchability that were present in the vicinity of Hindu India.

6. Expositions of the Truth

Gandhi's basic notion of truth is derived from all the major religions of the world. Such truth, to Gandhi, was inseparable from universal love. Gandhi like the prophets and sages of the ancients understood that such truth was vested with potency and absolute truth was omnipotent. However, some exposition of this truth is necessary.

Existence. Existence is a notion that finds expression in Eastern thought[1]. Existence includes space, matter, energy, time and both the individual and collective ego. Time includes the past, the present and the future. Individual ego is the distinct identification of the individual self from all else in the universe. Collective ego is the identification of a distinct collective self, separated from all else in the universe, as in nation, tribe, ethnic group, group of religious believers, group of ideological believers and the like. In short, existence is everything in the universe except God and those who belong to the realm of God - for God is selfless. For those who speculate, hypothesize, believe in or know of spatially and temporally separated parallel universes, existence includes all these universes.

The Theory of the Truth. Love infused in existence is the truth[2]. Love is latently present in all existence; such a latent presence of love is not the truth. Only when love is infused in existence do we get the truth. When love is infused all through existence it results in absolute truth. Since we do not know all of existence, we will not be able to infuse love into all of existence, and therefore we humans cannot know absolute truth. When love is infused within an existential context like the world, an epoch, a social situation or a moment in time it results in relative truth. Relative truth is within the bounds of human conception. With some clarity such relative truth will become self evident[3]. Since relative truth is self-evident, just being honest and clear about that which is self-evident is an alternate way to finding relative truth. The interplay, of infusing love into an existential context on the one hand and with clarity embracing the self-evident truth on the other, would help one accurately grasp the relative truth. When we are dishonest about the existential context we become sentimentalists and when there is inadequacy of love we tend to become bigots or misers. An existential context has a bearing on other facets of existence. The past has a bearing on the present and the present has a bearing on the future. Likewise the world has a bearing on the nation, the nation has a bearing on the community and the community has a bearing on the family. An existential context cannot be entirely insulated from the rest of existence. If we account for the influence of these existential dependencies and infuse love into an existential context and its existential dependencies then we may be able to get necessary truth. Necessary truth may be the best that we humans can get. For our purposes such necessary truth may be sufficient.

Reality. Reality is conception of existence when love may be inadequate, withheld or absent. Across cultures several methods have been developed over time to understand and manipulate facets of reality. These methods include reason, logic, civilizational narratives, political ideology, realpolitik diplomacy, correlation cosmology, astrology, theoretical science, statistics and even superstition. Broadly two approaches to reality are frequently contrasted namely Realism and Idealism. Realism is working with reality as it is and idealism is an attempt to transform reality based on some ideological criteria. Idealism should not be confused with the truth or ethics. We could have a historical ideal, political ideal, cultural ideal and the like but these ideals may or may not be ethical ideals. An ethical ideal is a means to apply the truth. Different political ideologies and civilizational narratives have different criteria that they value above all else. The Democratic ideal is individual freedom and political liberty. The Marxist ideal is a classless society. The Islamic ideal is worship of the formless God as Allah. The neo-Confucian ideal is pre-eminence of the emperor. Simply in the way in which each of these ideals has been pursued through much of history, it is not at all clear that they were comprehensively ethical. We must regard the democratic ideal as a political ideal, the Marxist ideal as a historical ideal, the Islamic ideal as a theistic ideal and the Confucian ideal as a civilizational ideal. On the other hand Gandhi pursued non-violence or ahimsa as an ethical ideal. Gandhi's contemporary in Southern India, E.V.Ramasamy Periyar propounded a different notion of self-respect. Periyar's conception and practice of self-respect can be regarded as an ethical ideal. Likewise the Christian message of love that was practiced by the pre-Pauline Jesus movement was ethical as was the Islam followed by the Prophet Mohammed.

An Integrated pan Civilizational Metaphysical Perspective on the Truth[4]. In the beginning there was nothing. That is nothingness was the lone being. Nothingness as the lone being is non-being. This nothingness or non-being simultaneously was and was not. Was this nothingness absolutely void? Or was this nothingness made up of undifferentiated chaos? Nothing could be said about this nothingness. It was beyond description. The images of this nothingness were dark and chaotic[5]. Nothingness then became aware of itself and its potentialities[6], which is omnipotence. Nothingness becoming aware of itself and its potentialities constituted the generation of consciousness. At this stage there were no other beings, so this consciousness was the consciousness of nothingness, the lone being. This nothingness, conscious of its omnipotence is the formless God. The formless God is beyond all forms. This nothingness, aware of itself, created existence and in the process became non-existence. Non-existence pervades all of existence[7]. When existence came into being opposites also came into being[8]. Within existence, non-existence manifests itself as universal love and undertakes the functions of creation, preservation and determination. The object of all creation is to elevate pertinent love. The task of preservation upholds pertinent love. Non carnal love is the criteria for all determination. Further, universal love constitutes the essence of other higher ethical abstractions like truth, ethics or righteousness, peace and the like. Truth is love infused in existence. Love is present all through existence only latently and is not always manifest. Only when love is infused in existence does the truth become manifest. Within existence, truth is always associated with light. Peace is the condition that emerges when love is used for seeking resolution. Righteousness is truth applied. Evil is truth misplaced[9]. Within existence, evil is always associated with darkness. The mythological relationship of these higher ethical abstractions like truth, righteousness and peace which are founded in universal love, universal love all by itself and evil to existential categories like time, matter, energy, place, nation, tribe and people and categories relevant to the worldly human existential context like learning, health, wealth, liberty, chastity, courage and the like constitutes the domain of polytheism. Within existence, consciousness gave way to individual consciousness and universal consciousness. Only after individual consciousness came into being do we recognize universal consciousness as universal consciousness, until then both were one and the same. Universal consciousness is the realm of God. Those who live in the realm of God are expressions of love and live selflessly. God only knows to do Good. God is untouched by evil. Individual beings are vested with individual consciousness. Individualism is an opportunity to love. To display love and to be able to respond to the love displayed, you need at least two distinct beings. Such individual beings with their respective individual egos, groups of individuals with their corresponding collective egos as in nation or tribe or community or other similar entities, matter, energy, space and time all together constitute the realm of existence. There is nothing wrong with existence. It is not possible to make ethical judgments on different facets of existence[10]. For instance the seasons of the world are a facet of existence but we cannot pass ethical judgments by saying that summer is better than winter. We can only register an individual's preference for summer over winter. However the different facets of existence work in tandem with love and are just as responsible for the triumphalism of the truth. For the growth and transformation of individuals and groups, non-existence may allow individuals and groups in existence to co-relate with evil. Non-existence pervades evil but remains untouched by it. The game of life is nothing but the descent of universal consciousness into individual consciousness and the eventual return of all individual beings to universal consciousness and nothingness. The descent and ascent of individual consciousness is a consequence of one's thoughts and actions. An individual being goes through innumerable life cycles of birth and death before they can return to nothingness or non-being. Associated with the notion of cycles of birth and death is the notion of fate or inevitability. While fate does exist, even individuals with highly evolved consciousness do not know the future in its entirety. The Buddha who attained nirvana, which is bowing out of the universe, did not know the future. He only knew his past lives[11]. Whosoever embodies love in its entirety alone can know the future in its entirety. Heaven, the good life, happiness, being a disciple of a good guru, undertaking the Haj pilgrimage, praying in Jerusalem, the inclination to practice meditation, depth in meditation, happily joining one's forefathers in the world of ancestors, nirvana and more are all ultimately rewards and incentives for service in the altar of love. Such service in the altar of love may have been performed in previous lives and may not be known to the individual. Likewise the prospects of hell, damnation, slipping in the evolutionary trajectory, enduring negative karma and the like are all at once both real and forewarnings to prohibit individuals from loveless deeds.

Religious Truth and Faith. The major religions of the world have their origins in absolute truth. How do we know that the major religions of the world are founded in absolute truth? We know it from the profundity and relevance of their message, the subsequent resonance that they have had on humankind and their transcendental origins. Absolute truth is known only to God and God is nothing but the embodiment of all possible non carnal love that exists. In this world absolute truth engenders religious truth. Religious truth could have transcendental dimensions to it that may be beyond the comprehension of humans whose understanding may be limited by the particular circumstance they inhabit. Also this religious truth is perceived and this perception of the truth is reproduced and retransmitted by fallible humans with the result we see some dissipation. In addition human selfishness, greed, pride, lust, necessity and ambition have all combined to interpret and absorb religious truth throughout history in innumerable base ways. Once we are aware that both truth and corruption have become part of religion then we can make an attempt to separate the religious truth from the corruption. Part of the reason why religion seems intractable is because religious truth operates at several different levels among which are theistic, historical, ethical, ritualistic, mythological, transcendental, metaphysical and empirical. At the *theistic* level religious truth sustains people's faith in God or extensions of God as Gods in polytheism, Gurus, Bodhisattvas, Sages and the like and frequently manifests as a personal relationship with God or other God like extensions. While the content of God is love, not all people have an equal capacity for love. Humans exhibit great variation in their ability to practice selflessness, love and truth. For the vast majority of humans who do not have the ability to live by love alone, faith is an invaluable resource by which they can sustain themselves through life and draw sustenance from when they are overwhelmed by the adversity of life. Unlike truth, love and peace, which pervade both the individual and collective realm, an individual's faith is essentially a personal matter. Wide variations exist in people's faiths. However people of faith tend to believe that there is intractable superiority in the religion associated with their faith. Different religions may be in harmony with one another but it is not possible for all of them to be simultaneously superior to each other. Indeed different religions have come into being to cater to the needs of different people and are inherently not superior to one another just as a race or nation or community is not superior to other nations or races or communities respectively. Faith, as a method, is in itself not less than love and could potentially lead one to universal love and truth. Whenever there is a conflict between faith and love it is not so much that the faithful will be let down as it is that it will become apparent to the faithful over time that the faith had been misplaced or that faith had been misunderstood and in the process the faithful would be transformed. The time needed for such a transformation in an individual may take a few years or several lifetimes through reincarnations and for a group may take a decade or several centuries. Religious orders of the world may have a role to play in human history. Religious adherents have often misunderstood such notions of destiny throughout history and have not hesitated in using it to furthering their respective personnel ambitions and political agendas. Religious truth certainly has a *historical* dimension to it and ought to become self-evident in the fullness of time. Then one can expect the confusion of the religious adherents would be elucidated. At the *ethical* level religious truth provides directives for ethical action and has attempted to preserve social harmony. The focus of religious ethical directives was not to enhance individual or collective enjoyment but to facilitate a life of service. Religions sought to achieve this directly through advocacy, incentive and regulation and indirectly through religious observations. Given that there could not have been a structural remedy to many of the inequities of the pre-modern world, when all the major religions of the world came to be, one must regard religious truth as being very positive due to its explicit preference for and insistence on service over enjoyment. For want of a better term we use the term *ritualistic* to describe religious practices vested with religious significance. These are regarded as being meritorious in the realm of religion. Specific terms or words that are used to chant prayers, pilgrimage to specific holy places, certain days of the week or year being more auspicious to pray to certain deities for certain sects, circumcision, the added value in praying in Jerusalem, bathing in the Ganges, the wearing of the sacred thread along with other similar religious practices may all be regarded as having special religious significance to different peoples. However under no circumstances should the pursuit of the ritualistic dimension of religion take precedence over ethical consideration. Otherwise some of the most horrific practices would easily obtain legitimacy through religious sanction or at a minimum, humanity would be forbidden from realizing ethical possibilities. At the *mythological* level religious truth gets expressed through mythology. Hindu, Greek and Roman cultures are among some of the most mythological cultures known to us. This is religious truth nevertheless. The ethical abstractions like love, truth, righteousness or ethics, functional categories like preservation, education, arts, valor and health among others and existential categories like matter, time, energy, tribe, nation and city are personified as individuals and their inter-relationship is expressed as myth. Unlike religious narratives which have a historically identifiable definite starting point, in myth or mythology centered cultures the historically identifiable starting point is not easily discernible. Hinduism can be regarded as a fusion between a mythological culture and a religious culture. Truth is at the origin of a religious culture and due to human weakness and necessity the corruption happens fairly early. In a mythological culture the ethical abstractions are easily ignored especially when faced with a difficult reality and what remain are the functional characteristics of the various Gods, who are propiated for favors and protection. At the *transcendental* level, religious truth is about attaining a more perfect state of being as in heaven or being freed from the cycles of life and death. Closely related to the transcendental level is the *metaphysical* level, which philosophizes the transcendental condition. When one looks at the metaphysical points of view of all major religions, one is perplexed as to how all of them can be simultaneously true. This doubt arises partly because we take permanence for granted. Nothing is permanent except non-being. Even after all beings are liberated and time ends, the universe would again be recreated from nothingness and individuals will separate from non-being and the drama of life will continue. One need not acknowledge non-being as non-being. They simply can regard it as universal love within existence. Non-being is merely an earlier state of universal love. Since nothing is permanent besides non-being and non-being or non-existence can be regarded as universal love, major religions of the world can truthfully be idealized for their respective recipients as long as they are centered on universal love. Since each religion is idealized for its recipients it need not surprise us that they seem starkly different from one another. At the *empirical* level religion lends itself to reconstruction of past events based on evidence and this is the area of modern scholarship. Modern scholarship cannot corroborate whether miracles like the Red sea parting for Moses and the ancient Jews to cross actually happened. But it can validate whether certain historical events took place. According to the Biblical account, Moses led the ancient Jews from Egypt to Israel by crossing the Red sea and wandered with the ancient Jews for forty years after which he died. Finally Joshua led them to the Promised Land after killing the earlier inhabitants. Archaeological excavations[12] since 1967 in Israel have found no evidence for this Biblical story. There are "no Egyptian artifacts"[12]; there is no evidence for "a change in population"[12] and no evidence of large scale destruction. Scholars believe that it is the inhabitants of the land of Canaan in the coastal areas near the Promised Land that moved inwards[12]. It is possible that the tribe of Joseph could have come from Egypt[12]. Scholars opine that ancient Jews were not writing objective history but were writing a story of their existence[12]. However subsequent prophets including the ones who were religiously inspired sought harmony with this story of existence that the ancient Jews had created. They did not seek to disrupt it. Objective enquiry remained unknown until the modern era, so even if they wanted to disrupt the traditional story they couldn't have disrupted it. So this brings us to the central question that modern scholarship poses to religious narratives namely 'What is the truth?' Are the findings of modern scholars true? Or do inspired religious prophets have an intuitive insight into the truth which is over and beyond the reach of those who pursue objective empirical scholarship in modern times. The answer depends on the existential circumstances in which these questions are being raised, the ethical requirements within these circumstances and the relevance of the narrative to the historical moment. Empirical enquiry is true in the sense that it is based on evidence – after all truth that is within our conception is self-evident. People have lived by religious narratives for centuries and continue to cherish them and the truth which is founded in love cannot be extended to needlessly disrupting a people's way of life. The truth has neither a preference for the narrative over the empirical nor does it have a preference for the empirical over the narrative. Wherever love is optimum there the truth will reside. Those that adhere to either perspective – the empirical or the religious, strive for consistency at the expense of love. Consistency is the hallmark of integrity but one should not lose sight of love in the pursuit of consistency. The essence of the truth is love.

Experience and the Universality of the Truth. Experience is acquired by repeatedly doing something in a certain way[13]. Experience is practical knowledge. With theoretical knowledge, we use theory to direct action. With experience, the practice becomes the de facto theory. So much so in the case of distinct peoples, some of their experience is so ingrained in their being that they are not able to change their ways. Such experiences may actually define a people and people may be able to change in only ways that their experience allows them. Nothing in world history demonstrates the delimitations imposed by human experience as the triumph and trial of monotheism. Monotheism is the belief that only one God exists and that he is formless. Therefore monotheistic religions are opposed to image worship. Judaism and Islam are strictly monotheistic faiths. Christianity too was strictly monotheistic at the time of Jesus; images however crept into Christianity later. Judaism has always been a non-proselytizing faith and people are expected to convert to Judaism based on their own inner inclination. Since Judaism is not a proselytizing religion, Judaism never confronted entire peoples with the ideal of monotheism. Therefore we cannot understand much about the ease or difficulty of distinct peoples to embrace monotheism based on their experience by studying the history of Judaism. Christian and Islamic histories however can give valuable insight on the experience and the preparedness of a people to embrace specific ideologies. Pauline Christianity was the first proselytizing religion to universally preach the doctrine of monotheism. In the Near East and the Mediterranean world where Christianity initially took root, most of the people worshipped many Gods and represented them as images. The doctrine that Christianity preached was in variance with the experience of the people that it sought to convert. Monotheism had to be interpreted and adapted to conform to the polytheistic experience of the people. As a consequence images of Jesus, Joseph, Mary, the cross and other Christian saints found their way into the church. So much so images have been a vital part of the church through much of the history of Christendom[14]. Six centuries after Christianity came Islam, which was another proselytizing monotheistic religion with global aspirations. While Islam had its founding in the deserts of Arabia it grew rapidly in West and Central Asia and Africa. Most of those who converted to Islam had been Christians prior to their conversion[15]. It is not difficult for us to see why Islam must have been so persuasive to practicing Christians. In Islam, Allah alone was God. Allah was strictly formless. In sharp contrast to the church, there were no images in the mosque. The Christian doctrine prohibited idolatry but had images in the church. On contact with medieval Islamic proselytizers, the believing Christian must have found a discrepancy between his or her professed ideal of monotheism on the one hand and great dilution in its practice on the other. This discrepancy must have made Islam attractive at a theological level. Christians, the overwhelming majority of whose ancestors were once polytheists, had been transformed in the six centuries since the inception of Christianity. In innumerable sermons they must have heard the theological case against idolatry reiterated. So by the time Islam arrived on the scene they must have been prepared to notice the theological discrepancy between the Christian ideal and the Christian practice and were ready to worship the formless God. They were ethnically the same people who were not able to embrace the formless God when Christianity arrived but were receptive when Islam arrived. Their historical experience, proscribing and yet practicing idolatry in the interim centuries seems to have created the needed strain to embrace the formless God. We also see evidence of the interplay between monotheism and human experience in the Indian subcontinent when Islam arrived. The majority of the inhabitants in the Indian subcontinent were Hindus and they were practicing polytheists. The Islamic message of monotheism was in variance with the experience of the Hindus. Needless to say the Islamic proselytizers were frustrated. Even today regions of the subcontinent that are predominantly Muslim are Pakistan and Bangladesh. Islamic invaders and migrants to the subcontinent settled through the centuries in what would become Pakistan, whereas recent scholarship argues that many of the people in today's Bangladesh were originally not Hindus entrenched in polytheism but tribals, who converted to Islam much later and much more gradually with deforestation and agricultural expansion[16]. Therefore in India prior experience with polytheism delimited a vast majority of Hindus from embracing Islam. So we see people need to be historically prepared over many centuries to accept an ideology that is alien to them. Monotheism is a theistic ideal but delimitations imposed by human experience would extend well beyond the realm of theism. A people's experience may prohibit them from practicing historical, cultural, theistic and even ethical ideals that are espoused by others. Democracy has a basis in ethics. It is better to elect one's leaders than to have one's leaders imposed on oneself. Likewise it is better for a country to have an independent judiciary and an independent press. If we look at the Freedom House report[17] for combined average ratings which includes political rights and civil liberties in independent countries then we see that besides the West, which is the home of modern democracy, countries that have had a greater historical, cultural or geographical proximity with the West have a higher rating than others – some East Asian Confucian countries being the notable exception. Even these East Asian Confucian nations don't seem to have taken to democratic institutions spontaneously and may have embraced democratic ideals because of Western pre-eminence, Western pressure, an opportunity to participate in the international economic system without a stigma or due to a realization of their dire security needs. Here again we see the historical experience of people seems to have played a part in their success with democracy. What then is the relationship between the truth and experience? We have already defined the truth as the right amount of love that can be infused into an existential context. Therefore experience must be regarded as an integral part of the existential context. We must infuse love into experience as we would infuse love into anything else that is part of the existential context. Now with increased possibilities of contact among different peoples due to advances in transportation and communication different cultures and traditions are brought in close contact with one another thereby increasing the possibility of conflict. Intellectuals in recent times have responded by claiming that all truth is subjective. Nothing can be further from the truth. One's experience and one's innate being delimits the practice of the truth but it does not distort the universality of the truth. The ethical value of democracy is universal but the inclination and ability to practice it is based on a society's experience.

Truth and Violence. How could truth which is founded in love be compatible with violence? It is a pertinent question but then truth is not merely love, it is love infused into existence. While non-violence is always preferred, in some existential situations it may not always be possible to bring about ethical transformation by non-violence alone. Violence and war may be necessary. This is because individuals in such circumstances either do not have the capacity for the needed love or they simply do not have adequate faith in love. However even in such circumstances great restraint must be shown and only strictly needed violence must be used. Also if war is to be fought it must be carried out with restraint and once the political objective is realized the war must be immediately stopped. A very good example of a war that was conducted with such restraint was India's India-Pakistan war in 1971, fought for the independence of Bangladesh. Profound violence is justified only for destroying evil. Hitler's extermination of the Jews was undoubtedly a great evil and therefore the allies were completely justified in fighting the Second World War to defeat Nazi Germany.

Truth and the Truthful Pursuit of Cherished Ideals. It is not necessary for someone to always delve into the anatomy of the truth to seek the truth. People can cherish ideals that are dear to them. They can pursue these ideals as long as these ideals are pursued truthfully and that would be the truth as much. People in the past have certainly pursued ideals they cherished truthfully. The great prophets of ancient Israel pursued the ideal of monotheism truthfully and in the twentieth century in Southern India, E.V.Ramasamy Periyar pursued the ideal of self-respect by leading a truthful public life. However as modernity makes deeper inroads into the world and as civilizations, nations, cultures and ideologies are brought face to face with each other merely pursuing cherished ideals truthfully may not be enough in averting conflicts or bringing about resolution between contending parties. We need to go to the anatomy of the truth and through it seek resolutions.

Science and the Truth. Scientific theories are conceived to explain empirical observations. The controversies in science arise when the conclusions of scientific theories happen to be politically incorrect. We see evidence for this in America. Whenever scientific theories have racist implications as in sociobiology or as in its claims that human nature is not a blank slate there is passionate refutation from liberal academics. Whenever popular writing draws on the theory of evolution to refute creationism there is a passionate response from religious conservatives. This is because public discourse in America is more an effort to uphold ideology than a quest for the truth. There is also genuine confusion in understanding the relation between science and the truth. There are two characteristics of the truth. One is that truth is pertinent love. The other characteristic is that with some clarity such truth can be made self-evident. The method of science is based on empiricism. The empirical method relies on demonstrable evidence. Anything that is clearly demonstrable is explicitly self-evident. Since we hold that truth can be made self-evident, we may regard the output of empirical science as true as long as the application of such truth would be pertinent love in our existential context. Therefore it is the application of science that must uphold the truth of science. If science is used for the benefit of humanity, it is to be welcomed as having been based on the truth. If science is used to make a plethora of atom bombs then it certainly is to be detested as falsehood. The rationale that justifies the reliance on atomic weapons needs to be reframed in a different plane of reference so that we can resolve human problems with the truth instead of having to rely on atomic weapons for security. Science in itself is only a means of understanding certain aspects of reality and in that is not fundamentally different from other modes of understanding reality like astrology or prophetic revelation. Science has so far proven to be an extremely reliable way of understanding and manipulating the physical world. Astrology attempts to predict human personality, past events and future events. To be sure astrological predictions do not have the needed statistical significance to say that it is unlikely to have arisen out of chance but the specificity of the prediction is beyond the scope of the empirical approach. For instance an astrologer may attempt to predict the precise age to which a perfectly healthy person may live something that science cannot even attempt. Likewise prophetic revelations promise us of a better future for humanity as a whole in this world and for true believers in the hereinafter. Science denies both the possibility of life after death and the prospect for transcendental existence. The advent of science has not eliminated the reliance on astrology nor has it destroyed revealed religions. Both astrology and prophetic revelation continue to influence human life. In India, which is a fatalistic culture, people, who include doctors, engineers and scientists, continue to consult astrologers and co-relate their lives in accordance with it. Astrologers develop reputation for precision and the ones who are consistently reliable are much sought after. People check with more than one astrologer to corroborate predictions in much the same way that patients with chronic illness seek a second medical opinion from another expert doctor. Date and time for marriage continue to be fixed based on astrological insight. Many Jews, Christian and Muslims regulate some of the most private moments of their lives in accordance with their conception of prophetic revelations so that they would be protected in this world and be rewarded in the next. The only reason science is as esteemed as it is, is because Western civilization has triumphed politically. There is another aspect of historical reality that is frequently overlooked by those who advocate the primacy of science. The very capacity to do science in a profound way is in itself a historical phenomenon. Almost all the major theoretical advances in science and new paradigms of thought in modern times have emerged from Western civilization. While China, Russia, Japan and India have substantial number of researchers and scientists in the world today, the significance of their collective scientific and technological output is not large. This is a result of a historical phenomenon. During the Renaissance, a passionate revival of classical learning unleashed a certain spiritedness that lay dormant in Western peoples. The intellectual consequence of this spiritedness is the application of reason in understanding the world. Indeed this is something that foreign born engineers who have spent substantial amounts of their lives both in their home cultures and Western civilization can more easily appreciate. As an example, in design discussions within engineering teams made up of Westerners and non-Westerners, Westerners are more unhesitant to question presuppositions in finding solutions to engineering problems[18]. This questioning spirit is widespread within Western culture. The only other time in Western history when such profound intellectual achievements came to the forefront was in classical Greece and it tapered off during the Hellenistic period. In the Roman Empire and during the dark ages that followed we do not see any evidence of such profound intellectual achievements. This is certainly not genetic, wherein the gene pool mysteriously became richer, because such profound intellectual output neatly correlates with identifiable historical periods. If the capacity to do science is in itself a historical phenomenon then this modern epoch of profound science could end as well. It is not so much that science will find all the truth that there is to be found as it is that the method of science may well defer to the way of love and truth.

Potency of the Truth. Some of the most revered individuals of the human race like Socrates, Amos and Gandhi have insisted that it is advantageous to be good and ethical. Based on their insight one may then say that truth which is inseparable from love and ethics has potency. Despite the profound insight of these great men, the evidence of history shows that humanity has found it difficult to inculcate and sustain a faith in the potency of the truth. In our times, post-modernist thinkers believe that there are no absolute truths and truth to the extent that it exists, is entirely subjective. They along with other skeptics may rather pertinently ask, that if truth and love were powerful then why did such truth and love with all its potency not do anything about the enormous crimes committed against Jews in Nazi Germany or against the millennial plight of the untouchables in the Indian subcontinent? We humans are placed in this world and in relation to the life of the universe lead ephemeral lives. We do not know the absolute. We are unable to comprehend why such crimes against humanity take place. Through metaphysical reflections on the transcendental truth, we know that the opposites came into being when the universe came into being. As the Taoist say, when we categorize the good as the good the non-good is already posited. If there must be peace then there must also be war and if there must be righteousness then there must also be evil. Neither the crimes against Jews in Nazi Germany nor the inhuman treatment of untouchables in Hindu India have in any way blemished the potency of the truth. Nazi Germany fell ignominiously and did not prevail committing these crimes. Hitler's horrific actions correctly continue to be represented as an expression of evil in Western civilization and in the coming future, humanity as whole will not treat it any differently. Likewise Hinduism all through its history was challenged at first by Buddhists and Jains and later by Muslims. This did not prevent crimes committed against the untouchables and others under the caste Hindu banner but provided an alternative for the victims and after the coming of Islam to the subcontinent kept Hindu society on its heels. So our basic theses that it is not advantageous to do evil holds good in both the case of crimes committed in Germany by the Nazis and through the caste system by the Hindus. However in Europe, where historical movements follow one another in quick succession beginning with Greek civilization and followed by Hellenism, the Roman Empire, the rise of Christianity, the dark ages, the renaissance, reformation, the scientific revolution, the age of discovery, the Enlightenment, Industrial Revolution and the undisputed European pre-eminence of the 19th and 20th century, it is harder to discern the potency of the truth. In China and Islam the inequities within their orders was relatively less in comparison to Hindu India and even Europe. Given that in the pre-modern world where it was inherently not possible to develop comprehensive solutions for human problems and much of the human misery could only have been reduced by individual love, we cannot suspect the potency of the truth for the conditions in China and Islam not being better than what they actually were. One can view the Mongol invasion which disrupted the entrenched status quo in Iran and destroyed the decadent Baghdad caliphate and the periodic change of dynasties in Chinese history as evidence for the potency of the truth. It is not so much that the truth identified itself with the ferocity of the Mongols as it permitted them to overrun societies where ethical possibilities were greatly diluted. So far humans have lived more often by reality than by the truth. Reality gave them short term results after which humans succumbed to the temptations of doing evil. One can view human history thus far as one in which the truth lay in the background and consistently tried to undermine the status quo in which ethical possibilities were not realized through individual transformation. The truth didn't overthrow evil because the existential circumstances of the pre-modern world didn't lend itself to such an overthrow. Even if the truth had overthrown evil, then what could it have replaced the evil so overthrown with? The only way truth could have found meaningful expression in the pre-modern world was if all humans were transformed by love and lived there lives by love alone. With the exception of some enlightened individuals nobody lived a life of love alone and as a result evil remained. However there are certain situations in history in which the transgressions against the truth were so profound that the assertion of the truth has been conspicuous and unmistakable. In addition to the eternal challenges to the Hindu caste order and the fall of Nazi Germany that we have cited as evidence for the assertion of the truth, we can find in all civilizations conspicuous evidence for the assertion of the truth in response to profound transgressions against it. Jesus preached the message of love advocating non-possession and non-violence. Jesus preached in a world where great inequities existed and comprehensive structural remedies for these inequities inherently impossible. Ideally individuals who came in contact with Jesus should have practiced his message of love. At a minimum they must have held him in reverence even if they could not follow his teachings. But they falsely accused him of a crime and wanted to have him crucified. The temple of the ancient Israelites who bore false witness against Jesus was destroyed and in addition the ancient Israelites forever lost their association with their ancient nation. The Romans, who crucified Jesus, lost their civilization and in the west lost their empire and slid into the dark ages. Towards the end of the Tang dynasty in China, the Chinese persecuted Buddhists with a view to exterminating them. The Buddhists in China had become wealthy and the monasteries were certainly becoming ostentatious. However Buddhism was founded in India and if it had comprehensively succeeded it would have restored the self-respect of all the lower caste Hindus. China throughout its history depicted non-Chinese as barbarians and in that respect was not different from the Brahminical representation of lower castes. The Chinese could have learnt something from Buddhism and could have refrained from being condescending to non-Chinese people in their national narrative. The assertion of the truth is evident in the history of the following thousand years, when China was ruled mostly by foreigners, the only dynasty that was an exception to this thousand year foreign rule was the Ming. Muslim rule in India was an opportunity for India's oppressed untouchables and lower caste Hindus to escape the harshness of the caste order. During the reign of the Muslim ruler Aurangzeb of the Mughal dynasty, rather than wooing oppressed castes and untouchables to Islam with incentives, Islamic rule turned out to be fanatical as never before. Hindu temples were erased, a Sikh guru was executed and in general non-Muslims were persecuted. Immediately after the rule of the Mughal emperor Aurangzeb, Islamic rule began its systematic decline in the Indian subcontinent. Across cultures we see whenever the truth had been violated in a very profound way, even in the pre-modern world when it was inherently not possible to have a comprehensive structural solution to the inequities of the world, whoever so violated the truth had paid a huge historical price. It is not so much that the truth was vindictive, as it is, that the truth was being upheld against all odds when the transgressions where very grave.

7. Ethical Resolutions in the Light of the Truth

In the pre-modern world, it was inherently not possible to create structural arrangements to end human inequities. Though the process we now recognize as modernity began 500 years ago, it is only in the 19th century that people in Europe began realizing its impact. The Industrial Revolution, the railways, the idea of nation state, urbanization, advances in medicine and disease prevention had brought modern life to Europe in the 19th century[1]. Earlier historical movements like the renaissance, the age of discovery, the reformation and the European Enlightenment were essentially intellectual, religious and artistic movements. The way of life of the people continued to be traditional. Only in the 19th century and that too only in Europe do we see a modern way of life emerging. It is only in the last quarter of the 20th century that the effects of modernity have, in a substantive way, reached the different corners of the world. Most third world nations now have sizable urban populations; increasingly take to modern forms of entertainment, use modern means of transportation, have some forms of modern communication and advocate modern methods of education. By the end of the first decade of the twenty first century modern methods of transportation have given us the capacity to reach the distant corners of the inhabited world in little less than a day. Modern methods of communication allow us to know of events that happen far away, instantaneously. It allows us to communicate with people in the farthest corners of the world in real time. In addition, mass manufacturing allows us to estimate, plan and mass produce high quality products that we use. Despite the geographical and historical reach of modernity great inequities exist in our midst. However, given the prowess of technology and the reach of modernity it is entirely possible to reorder life whereby these human inequities could be comprehensively ended. How can we reorder life to end the miseries and inequities in this world? There is a widely held view in the world that human intelligence, human creativity, human ingenuity and human effort can surmount any problem that we face. It is not surprising that there is so much faith in talent and effort. After all modern science and technology are products of the human mind and the historical phenomenon we understand as modernity is entirely a consequence of human ingenuity. The ingenuity and human talent that went into inventing the aircraft, radio, telephone and the computer has not been able to end hunger, poverty, malnutrition, destitution and the enormous inequities that exist in this world. Many of the global problems that we face today like war, climate change and terrorism may not have ad hoc solutions. Even if we succeed in solving some of these problems they will give rise to newer problems and it will not comprehensively make the world a better place for everyone. Intelligence, creativity, ingenuity and effort can all help but they alone will not guarantee a successful outcome. A creative idea may solve problems but these solutions will either not be comprehensive or may not endure. Or an idea not derived from ethical deliberations may be theoretically comprehensive but will be hindered along the way and fail in its implementation. Marxism-Leninism and the Peace Corps[2] are two very prominent failed ideas of the 20th century. Marxism-Leninism could never penetrate the collective consciousness of the Islamic world, India and the West and eventually lost out in Russia and is currently much diluted in China. The Peace Corps was initially meant to be a program by which America would help developing countries in nation building. In practice the scale of resources committed was grossly inadequate for the requirements of the developing world and the program fell far short of its stated objective. The greatest likelihood of creating a better world is possible only by embracing the truth. The comprehensive solution for all problems is the truth. Technical knowledge and human perspicacity will result in comprehensive solutions only if they are in harmony with the truth. Since universal love is the truth, only when knowledge and human insight are directed to the collective well-being of all, will it yield results. Indeed it would not be inaccurate to view war, climate change, terrorism and poverty as nothing more than assertions of the truth to undermine a decadent world order in which ethical possibilities are greatly hampered.

The pre-modern world was an opportunity to love and to lead ethical lives. We could have considerably reduced the suffering of the working poor, outcastes, women and aliens if we humans were capable of greater love. In other words, a better world could have been created only through individual transformation. Indeed if there had been adequate amount of love in the pre-modern world, we would not have had to reorder life in the wake of modernity. If there was enough love among humans, things would have worked themselves out naturally, even after the advent of modernity. The rich would have given away everything else that they did not need to the poor; the privileged would have come forward to take responsibility to provide all opportunities that modernity availed to the working poor. Humanity would have seamlessly embraced modernity. There neither was enough love in the pre-modern world nor do we see evidence of sufficient love in the modern world. The great lesson of human history so far is the inadequacy of love among people. However it is not necessary any longer for us to depend on individual transformation through love to end human miseries and inequities. It is entirely possible to end human miseries and inequities by making truth the organizing principle of human society. This can be done by pursuing ethical resolutions in the light of the truth and by re-ordering human life based on such resolutions.

Truth Extracted From Our Existential Context

We know that love infused into our existential context will give us the truth. We regard the world at this moment in history as our existential context. Our existential context is not separate from us; we are part and parcel of our context. So our being must be one of the subjects of our contextual consideration. Time is another facet of existence. Our moment is not isolated from previous moments in history. The past has a bearing on the present and must therefore be part of our existential context. Our being, our past and our present together make up our existential context at this moment in history. Our being, which is humanity's self, is made up of an amalgam of races, tribes, cultures, languages, religions, nations and traditions. There is identity in each one of the categories by which humans classify themselves into and there are differences among the different categories by which humans classify themselves. For instance all native speakers of German would identify themselves as German and would be different from native speakers of Swahili or Tamil. So identity and difference are characteristics of our being. As history has shown differences can be a source of conflict. When we resolve conflicts that arise out of these differences then what remains is an integrated humanity which is united. Such an integrated humanity is the identity of humanity as a whole. We do not need to do anything special to affirm the identity of humanity. If we resolve conflicts that are a consequence of our differences, humanity's identity is bound to emerge. Therefore at this moment in history, difference is the characteristic that would best expose our being as humans in existence. To those who believe in science, humanity's past includes all the stages that humans had traversed in the evolutionary trajectory right up to now. To those who subscribe to monotheistic narratives, our past begins with Adam and Eve and includes all of human history from then on. To those who attach themselves to religions originally from India, humanity's past is to be found in the sum total of the merits and demerits associated with all the deeds in all the previous lives of all the peoples that inhabit this planet. So we have several perspectives on the nature of the past itself. Which one of these perspectives is right? And more importantly how do we account for its impact on the present? It is impossible for us to account for the past satisfactorily in all its dimensions. We will therefore use one characteristic, namely experience, to talk about relevant aspects of the past that has an impact on our ability to come to terms with our times. After the cold war, Francis Fukuyama has argued that democracy and capitalism have triumphed and that this triumph of democracy and capitalism marks the end of history[3]. We may express skepticism at Fukuyama's end of history thesis. But certainly record numbers of nations have taken to democracy since the end of the cold war and the free enterprise system is the predominant economic system in the world today. So at a minimum one could say that freedom is the predominant ideal which characterizes the present world order. The present is best characterized by freedom. By infusing love into difference, experience and freedom that are drawn from our existential context we can understand the central themes that characterize the truth for our times.

Difference. There is not a shred of evidence to support differences on racial or ethnic lines. There is no evidence to say that all persons born into an ethnic group or race by virtue of their ethnicity or race can outperform all members of another race or ethnic group in any task. A belief in racial differences is racism. Racism is an untruth. The differences that have become apparent to us in the late twentieth century and early twenty first century are cultural differences. These cultural differences are a consequence of differences in the historical experiences of different peoples. Differences in historical experience of different peoples either facilitate or impede a society's ability to respond to modernity. East Asian Confucian societies like Japan, South Korea and increasingly China are able to compete foot for foot with Western civilization, which is the home of modernity. Sub-Saharan Africa and the BIMARU states of northern India have the greatest difficulty coping with modernity. However, humanity as a whole is not forthcoming in the acknowledgement of difference and understandably so. After all some of the most gruesome acts in history have been carried out by those who believed that they were different and superior to those whom they victimized. So the reality of difference and the fear of difference are an important aspect of the existential context that we live in. Since we fear differences so much, we come up with ingenious explanations for the existence of differences. One such explanation is to attribute it to European colonialism. Surely colonialism was at times exploitative and often apathetic to the well-being of the natives. Colonialism alone cannot account for all the variation that we observe among nations in their capacity to cope with modernity. A more persuasive explanation is cultural difference. Therefore the one aspect of difference that we will consider in this chapter is the difficulty some cultures have in coming to terms with modernity. We try to resolve this difference here as part of our ethical resolutions. There is another difference which pertains to the differences that arise when civilizations and cultures are affected by the dislocations generated by modernity. These differences require historical redress. We take up this kind of difference in subsequent chapters.

Love infused into Difference. We do not help ourselves denying a self-evident existential reality. Differences exist. In some measure cultural differences that have become apparent to us with the penetration of modernity are an extension of obvious differences that have always been there. Teachers are different from their students and parents are different from their children. Teachers know more than their students and therefore are entrusted to teach their students. Parents have more life experiences than their children and therefore they are entrusted to care for their children during the time period in which children are not able to fend themselves. So also societies that are not able to cope with modernity can take the help of societies that have successfully responded to modernity. However right through history we see ample evidence of the weak exploited by the strong. Therefore the process of seeking help must originate in the weak. The more endowed societies must merely express a willingness to serve others and not get involved until the weaker nation actually seeks help.

Experience. We come to modernity with our respective historical experiences. Our experience often ends up delimiting us in the choices we make. Ideologies that are substantially in variance with a people's experience soon get frustrated and advocates of these ideals have to choose between corrupting their ideals to survive and dying out. The quest for monotheism both in antiquity and in the medieval period and the advocacy for democracy in the second half of the 20th century and first decade of the 21st century tell us a lot about the impact of a society's experience on change being sought. Monotheism is worshipping of the formless God. When Christianity was restricted to the ancient Jews, it remained strictly monotheistic but when it was thrown open to the gentiles gradually images, frescoes and icons crept into the church. This is because the gentiles were polytheists before they became Christians and they brought their polytheistic experience into a monotheistic faith. Likewise several hundred years of Muslim rule could not convert a vast majority of polytheistic Hindus to Islam, a monotheistic faith, because the Hindu experience did not lend itself to formless monotheism. In more recent times there has been a spurt in the number of nations taking to democracy. Indeed record numbers of nations are democracies. But democracy in developing countries does not work anywhere as effectively as it does in the West. In part most of these developing nations have no experience with either democracy or the rule of the law but more importantly most of them have difficulty in effectively self-administering themselves. One of the reasons why most nations in the developing world have embraced a democratic form of government is ideological bankruptcy in the wake of modernity. After the fall of the Berlin wall, advocacy for democracy did not have an alternative to contend with, so it is not surprising that many nations have taken to democracy. How do people order life in the modern world? If not democracy what else? What else is available? The other reason why nations embrace democracy is Western preeminence and liberal advocacy. The inherent difficulty that a people experience in adopting political systems that are alien to them and practicing certain ideals that are foreign to them is related to the distinctness of their cultural experience. We regard such experience as a central aspect of our existential context.

Love infused into Experience. Unless foreign ideals are advocated one would never know whether a society will be receptive to it or not. So there is nothing wrong in advocating one's ideals to others. When it becomes self-evident either from history or through practice that a people are unable and therefore unwilling to practice a certain ideal because of their experience one should not persist with it. However, sometimes an opposite undesirable argument that cites differences in experience to forestall constructive change must be dispelled. This is best brought out in examining the relevance of modernity to tribal peoples and aborigines. The argument made is that tribal and aboriginal people are unable to change and are most happy when left as they always were in forests and deserts. This line of argument when pursued would have the consequence of depriving tribal and aboriginal people of the progress and possibilities that characterize our times. Just as truth is universal so also our time is universal to everyone in this world. Tribal and aboriginal people are not in any way inferior to others. Since they have lived in isolated areas, they did not benefit from the opportunity for development through contact. Consequently they have continued to remain outside the spectrum of the centers of civilization. With affectionate parental care they can and must be brought into our times. This can be done by helping them adapt their cultures to our times and circumstances.

Freedom. The world that we inhabit today is unmistakably ordered. Indeed if we did not have some sort of order, life would not be possible at all. The dominant ideological tenet that underlies the present world order is freedom. The international political order is made up of free and independent countries. The United Nations currently has 193 free and independent members. More nations in the world are democracies today than any time earlier[4].

Freedom to choose one's leaders is the hallmark of democracy. Capitalism which is otherwise known as the free enterprise system is the global economic system. Only five countries of the world today are ruled by communist parties[5]. Postmodernity and deconstruction are ideologies which not only advocate subjective freedom in identification but are suspicious of all narratives including ones that advocate reason and progress. The centrality of freedom in our discourse is evident in the quest for rights by different groups – human rights, animal rights, woman's rights, civil rights, gay and lesbian rights, workers' rights, immigrant rights and patient's rights among others. As we stand, well after the end of the first decade of the twenty first century, it must be apparent to anyone that freedom is the bedrock of the present world order.

Love infused into freedom. In our world absolute freedom is possible only if we define freedom by some transcendental criteria. Otherwise freedom must be restricted in some way or form to order life. Freedom gets restricted by laws, religious and cultural taboos, social mores and conventions, peer pressure, existential reality, historical necessity, emotional relationships and individual values among others. Freedom ought to be granted and restricted only out of love. Freedom can only be sustained by the truth. While laws, social mores and the like can be used as the means to restrict freedom, love and truth alone must be the criteria for mitigating freedom. When love is infused into freedom, so widely advocated, two constraints emerge. One is the role of responsibility in the exercise of freedom and the other pertains to the nature and end of freedom that is being advocated. As a rule nobody, either individual or group, should have substantially more freedom than what they can responsibly undertake. If they occasionally do not have a little more freedom than what they can handle they will not have an opportunity to grow and no one will know their capacity to undertake responsibility. If they have much more freedom than what they can handle then it will be self-destructive to them and harmful to others. The second constraint that emerges when we infuse love into freedom is the end of freedom itself. We see that the modern quest for freedom is an institutionalization of a ceaseless ever expanding quest for freedom as the primary driving force of history. Reaction to this quest has come from conservatives, religious groups and from traditional cultures. Often the resistance is presented as a quest for social stability, sin or even intractable ancient wisdom. None of which satisfactorily answers the proponents of freedom because all these are either subjective or pragmatic. An intellectually honest non relativistic opposition to this open ended quest for freedom can come only by worrying about the destiny of the process itself. Where does this quest for freedom end? For instance why shouldn't people appear naked in public in warmer climates where there is no climatic need for clothing? That is why shouldn't people show up for work or school with absolutely no clothes in their body? After all we were all born with no clothes. One could make the argument that the whole idea of clothing is hypocritical. The insistence on wearing clothes can be seen as restricting freedom of expression and therefore a human rights violation. The public expression of nudity has not succeeded due to the inability to mobilize sufficient number of people - not necessarily a majority - for the cause; the same could be said for incestuous relationships as well. If it is legal for man to marry another man and woman to marry another woman, why would it be wrong for brother and sister to marry each other? None of these ideas that seem obnoxious to us today can inherently be denied in the altar of freedom. If freedom continues to remain the primary driving force of history notions that seem obnoxious to us today may very well become the norm tomorrow. Indeed if this open ended quest for freedom is taken to its logical extreme then the distinction between sanity and insanity would be lost. After all, society categorizes the insane as those who are unable to conform to its norms in a substantial way. Nietzsche actually saw this coming over a hundred years ago[6], but his prescription would inspire the creation of the most horrific political phenomenon of the twentieth century in Nazi Germany. Those who worry about the destiny of freedom will not find answers by infusing love into freedom. They can gain meaningful answers only when they interrogate the historical implications of modernity on civilizations.

We had stated that truth is love infused into existence and that with some clarification such truth would be self-evident. The value of *freedom* is self-evident. The inability of some people and some cultures to undertake responsibility that freedom entrusts is also self-evident. The ability of some peoples to undertake responsibility and of others to be overwhelmed by it is a consequence of *experience*. This experience manifests itself as *difference*. If it is deemed that some people are not able to help themselves and there is no indication that those who are unable to help themselves will ever be able to help themselves, then the morally right thing to do would be for others to find an honorable way to help the helpless and this is self-evident as well.

Ethical Resolutions in the Light of the Truth

Having infused love into the three elements that characterize our existential context namely difference, experience and freedom we have the central themes that characterize the truth. We will keep these themes in the background to help guide us in our quest for ethical resolutions. Ethics is truth applied. What do we mean by applying the truth? Applying truth is living correctly. In the public sphere applying truth means living under the best possible order that our existential circumstance will allow. We have stated that the foundation of the truth is love. We cannot begin with love and truthfully call for revolution because revolutions often violently overthrow existing institutions and structures. We already have some sort of order and this order can be expressed through categories that characterize it. So we will try to arrive at what is best and ideal in each one of these categories. Before we make an attempt at spelling out what an ideal order would be, we need to take stock of our modern condition by reflecting on the development attained by different nations and peoples of the world. Then we will go back to the categories that we used for our ethical interrogation into the pre-modern world in Chapter 1 and reflect on the relevance of these categories for modernity. Finally we will look into some categories that form the basis of public discourse in our times. After having considered all the categories from the world known to us, we will then spell out newer structural arrangements that would be needed to bring out the ideal order for our times and beyond in the next section.

Development. With the end of the cold war, capitalism has emerged as the dominant economic system in the world. Some observations on the relevance of capitalism for modern development must be made. Francis Fukuyama has argued that the triumph of democracy and capitalism is the final stage in human historical evolution and such a triumph marks the end of history. Capitalism has been successful in increasing the national growth rate and thereby wealth of countries which are culturally and historically prepared to compete in the global economy but has not been able to ensure that the growth is equitable. Great inequities exist within nations and among nations. Globalized capitalism as an economic system is apathetic to individuals and nations who have difficulty competing in the market place. The varying degree of difficulty that nations encounter becomes apparent if we look at the Human Development Index (HDI[7]) for different countries. The Human Development Index is an index that is used to measure the level of development that has been attained by a nation. This index is based on educational attainment levels, life expectancy levels and the average purchasing power of an individual in a society. According to this index, countries are classified as developed countries and developing countries. Developed countries have a very high human development. Developing countries are further classified as having a high human development, medium human development and low human development. Based on the 2011 HDI more than half of the developed nations with a very high human development are Western nations. This should not be surprising since Western civilization is the home of modernity. Three Arab countries - UAE, Qatar and Bahrain, one non-Arab Islamic country Brunei, four East Asian nations - Japan, South Korea, Singapore and Hong Kong, nine former Soviet Bloc or former communist nations - Slovenia, Czech Republic, Estonia, Slovakia, Hungary, Poland, Lithuania, Latvia and Croatia, two countries in Latin America – Chile and Argentina, one Caribbean nation – Barbados, in addition to Israel are also classified as having a very high human development. The non-Western nations that have propelled themselves into this list have done so by virtue of their natural resources or by legal provisions they grant to elite foreign citizens and large corporations or by cultural advantages that enables them to effectively respond to modernity. Two of the three Arab countries and Brunei have sizable oil reserves and very small populations[8]. The other Arab country, Bahrain, also has a small population and relies on petroleum processing and refining but with crude mostly imported from Saudi Arabia[9]. With increased energy demand, oil has turned out to be one of the most prized natural resources in the world. The great demand for oil along with the high price for a barrel of oil has created enormous profits for oil producing countries. Out of the oil producing countries that are identified as very developed by the HDI, the UAE and Bahrain have some measure of economic diversification by providing offshore financial services, in the remaining two countries oil accounts for almost half their GDP. When such extraordinary wealth is lavished on small populations these nations are bound to be developed. Barbados, besides having a small population, has blue water beaches and attracts one of the largest numbers of tourists in the Caribbean[10]. In addition Barbados also derives considerable portion of its GDP by functioning as an offshore financial center. Some clarification on these offshore financial centers is due. Offshore financial centers in smaller countries provide legitimate ways to circumvent the legal and tax burdens of larger economies in which large companies and wealthy individuals operate[11]. Let us turn our attention to non-Western countries which have become developed due to their cultural advantages. The four East Asian countries that are identified as very developed have historically evolved from the same cultural process and share a common underlying Confucian cultural heritage and experience. Japan and South Korea are developed countries whose exports to the West and the rest of the world among others include cars, electronics and semi-conductor chips. While Singapore and Hong Kong are also offshore financial centers the scope and magnitude of all their undertaking is far greater and far more impressive than other such offshore financial centers. Singapore, a small island nation with little land derives

26% of its GDP from manufacturing[12]. The Hong Kong stock exchange is the world's 7th largest stock exchange[13] and Hong Kong is the world's largest re-exporter of goods[14]. In the former Soviet bloc countries the farther one goes west the higher the HDI index, indicating that the more countries are proximate to the West, the more responsive they are to Western cultural influence through physical contact and prior historical association. All the former communist and Soviet bloc countries that we have listed above as having very high human development are geographically adjacent to the West. Modern Israel is predominantly made up of Jews who migrated from different parts of Europe. In the last two hundred years, the Jewish intellectual achievements in Western civilization have been disproportionately large. Likewise Jewish enterprise has been truly breathtaking. It is not surprising that Jewish cultural and historical advantages have made Israel a developed nation. We will take up the other two countries Argentina and Chile, which are also classified as having a very high human development, when we discuss Latin America below. Now what about countries and regions that are not identified as being developed by the HDI? In the case of China it was largely a pre-modern agrarian society that was engrossed in tradition until the founding of the PRC in 1949. Even after the creation of the PRC, until Nixon's visit in 1971, China remained in essential isolation. It is only after Deng Xiaoping took over that China embraced the free enterprise system and was able to test its wits and enterprise in competition with other nations. China's growth has been rapid. This should not be surprising as other nations that had a Confucian historical experience like Japan and South Korea rapidly developed when they began functioning within the global free enterprise system. The HDI however does not yet classify China as a developed country. This is due to the vast population that China has, that needs to be uplifted. It however is only a matter of time. If China is unhindered it will soon make its way into being a well-developed country. In the Caribbean, a few developing countries which have a high human development index have done so along the same lines as Barbados, with revenues from tourism based on attractive blue water beaches and providing offshore financial and legal services. Latin America today is populated by people belonging to different ethnic groups[15]. The original inhabitants were the Native Americans. The Americas were colonized by the Europeans as was much of the world. However in Latin America some European settlers intermarried with Native Americans. Those born of mixed parentage in Latin America are referred to as Mestizos. In addition, the European colonizers imported slaves from Africa. When slavery was abolished, the freed slaves were not segregated as they were in the southern states of the United States. As a result more inter-racial marriages took place and racial balkanization was avoided. This does not mean that Latin America is ethnically homogenous. Race and ethnicity are discernible. Increasingly they are even used to drive social policy. But they tend to be fluid. In Latin America, it apparently, is not rare to find members of the same family lineage belonging to more than one race[16]. Therefore categories like race and ethnicity do not have the same meaning for Latin America as they do for the United States. It would be more appropriate to regard racial and ethnic composition in Latin America as indicators of cultural capital rather than viewing them as identifiers of biological distinction. When viewed as historical and cultural resources, the racial and ethnic composition of countries primarily influences the prospects for development in Latin America. Chile and Argentina are classified as developed countries with a very high human development and Uruguay, Cuba, Mexico, Costa Rica and Panama are regarded as developing countries but are in the top half of those which have a high human development index. Among these countries Argentina, Uruguay, Costa Rica, Cuba and Chile have a very large white population[17]. In Latin America, wherever the white population is very large, the primary cultural and historical experience of the country is bound to be European. Just as Western nations are developed so also Latin American countries with very large European populations are bound to do better in their development efforts as modernity is natural and intrinsic to them. (see Appendix 2 – Appendix 5) (Here we use the term white population only to indicate the substantial European historical origin and the distinctness of the cultural process that went into making these nations. We strictly reject any racist interpretation or racist implication in this entire discussion on development). Cuba is the only country that follows the socialist economic model and has a high human development. To be sure it has not created great wealth for itself but it has exceptional literacy and health care levels propelling its HDI score. Mexico does not have a very large white population nor is Mexico sparsely populated but it is proximate to the United States, blessed with oil and benefits from the NAFTA free trade agreement with the United States and Canada. All of which explain Mexico's higher HDI rank. In Panama the majority of the population is Mestizo, that is people with mixed ancestry, but the revenue associated with the canal aids Panama in getting a higher HDI score. In addition countries with significant Native American, Afro-biracial and black populations in Latin America tend to be hampered in their development efforts – though we must in fairness note that this is not as decisive as the presence of a large white population in aiding development. This again is not difficult to understand, as Native American and African cultures were isolated for much of history and did not have the prospects for growth through contact. In India, history and geography combine to provide some states in India cultural and historical advantages over others. The Hindu Indian caste order is a stratified feudal order in which white skinned Aryans dominated and subjugated the predominantly dark skinned Dravidians. It originated in the plains of Northern India where the domination has been historically the longest and therefore thorough. In Southern India there were lesser number of Aryans who migrated and the penetration of Aryan culture is relatively recent. The more south one goes, the more authentic the Dravidian culture is. Unlike in Latin America, in much of India, the blacker the skin color of the population the fitter a society seems to be in its ability to respond to modernity. (Again here we explicitly highlight that the skin color black being more fit for modernity in South Asia, not to suggest that black is better than white, but to break the near universal stereotype that those who are black or dark in skin color cannot measure up to those who have lighter skin in matters of intellect and enterprise). It is the South which has been the fastest growing region in India. Tamilnadu, the southernmost state in the Indian union, is a front runner in overall development[18]. Kerala, also a state in the extreme South, has the highest literacy levels and a very impressive record in social development. Overwhelming majority of software engineers who go abroad to work from India are predominantly from the southern state of Andhra Pradesh followed by Tamilnadu. The only exception to this correlation between skin color and fit for modernity is in Western India. The Northwestern states of Punjab, Haryana and Himachal Pradesh are relatively more developed states in India. Indeed Punjab and Himachal Pradesh have HDI scores that are marginally higher than Tamilnadu and for all practical purposes can be regarded as being just as developed in overall development as Tamilnadu. These regions are predominantly populated by later invaders and immigrants who came to India after the early Aryans[19]. Most of these peoples in northwestern India did not go through the interracial historical process by which the Hindu caste system was first formed in Northern India. They were co-opted into the caste order later on and that historical difference manifests itself in their ability to successfully respond to modernity. Other western Indian states of Maharashtra and Gujarat are economically more developed than almost all. In the case of Maharashtra that is largely due to the inclusion of the city of Mumbai (formerly known as Bombay) in measuring the development of Maharashtra. The cultural ethos that was responsible for the making of Mumbai is pan Indian and not that of Maharashtra and justly should not be included since we are attempting to evaluate the cultural fit of a society for modernity. In the case of Gujarat, the successful Gujarati business community that made substantial portions of its wealth outside Gujarat[20] invested heavily in Gujarat for a long time to facilitate its development. Until recently in some indicators of social development like female literacy, Gujarat lagged behind even some of the less developed states of the Indian union. According to HDI, 22 of the 24 least developed countries in the world are in the continent of Africa. This again has a basis in history. Many of the nations of Africa that have acute difficulty with development are in Sub-Saharan Africa which has all along been outside the purview of world history and therefore these regions did not have the opportunity of enriching their culture and experience through contact. So they lag behind.

Aristocracy. With the advent of modernity and consequent reduction in childhood mortality and increase in life expectancy, equal opportunity for all individuals in a society becomes a possibility that can be realized. Learning, education and a wide range of possibilities through which one could get fulfillment in life was available only to aristocratic men in the pre-modern world. Now all this and more can and must be made available to all people. Indeed one would have expected that with greater percolation of modernity, aristocracy as an institution would have been completely eradicated and the citizenry would have been homogenized. However the aristocracy has not been completely eradicated. The aristocracy has transmuted into newer forms in the modern world. There however is considerable variation between different regions of the world, in the manner in which the aristocracy has transmuted based on differences in historical experience. In America, aristocracy refers to those with generational wealth often accompanied by an Ivy League education. Given the American penchant for individualism and individual accomplishment, aristocracy in the culture at large may be regarded with mild condescension. In Europe, the aristocracy has no such restraint. Among the European aristocracy, pedigree is the marker that characterizes them. In Japan the aristocracy has transmuted into an elite meritocracy. In China, the historical scholar-gentry elite was dubbed as an intellectual class and subjected to humiliation and harsh treatment during the Mao years. After the Mao years the intellectual classes in China could very well be following the Japanese example. In India the upper caste Hindu Brahmins were never an aristocracy in the Aristotelian definition of the term. Historically they were an alien people differentiated from the masses of India by their linguistic, cultural and religious origins. Language has always defined the aristocracy in India. Before the advent of British colonialism, the lingua franca of India was the Persian language. Persian speakers were the aristocracy. Ever since the advent of British colonial rule right up to the present time, the aristocracy has transmuted into a group of proficient English speakers. While classical aristocracy is rendered meaningless with the advent of modernity, the Marxist prognosis that the workers of the world can unite, create and sustain a proletariat dictatorship all on their own is not self-evident. Modern life comes with considerable complexity and advances in communication and transportation provide opportunities for control that were hitherto impossible. Regardless of the political structure a society embraces the presence of a dominant bureaucratic and technical class is inevitable. The obverse side of the aristocracy is physical labor and that needs to be considered here as well. No matter how much a society modernizes and automates there is bound to be a need for physical labor. Physical labor is hard. Physical labor must not only be cherished but must be esteemed and celebrated. A good way to cherish labor is by expecting lower and middle management personnel to spend at least 25% of their time at work and up to 50% of their time at work doing physical labor. At a minimum at least those lower and middle managers who manage others who do physical labor must be expected to do physical work. The conditions in which physical labor is performed and the safety of the laborer must be amongst the highest priorities of a society. Technocrats and Engineers must constantly and innovatively strive to produce tools and equipment that will make physical labor rewarding. Such a transformed attitude to labor is a moral imperative, all the more so because through the ages, the condition of the working poor was abject. Now that technology provides the opportunity, the only impediment to raising the condition and status of physical labor is human will.

Economy. Francis Fukuyama argues that globalized capitalism, as is practiced in the world today, constitutes the end of history. If he is right what prospects does the world have? We have shown above in the sub-section titled Development that there is a direct connection between cultural experience of a people and their ability to take care of themselves in the modern world. Since that is the case, the prospects for struggling third world nations in general and Sub-Saharan Africa in particular will continue to be quite dim. Foreign aid and developmental assistance may help reduce human misery in these poor nations but will not comprehensively eradicate it. If we cannot convince ourselves that we can comprehensively end human miseries in the world then we must reexamine the capitalist free enterprise system to see why it is successful in creating wealth and to find out how we can make it work for all of us. One of the rationales for the free market system is that it creates an effective economic system by providing monetary incentives for preferred human actions and punishments for undesirable actions. Implicit in this rationale is the belief that humans are primarily motivated by monetary considerations. It is not self-evident that this is the case. Parents don't raise children because of financial rewards and soldiers are not willing to sacrifice their very lives for the pittance that they receive as salaries. Scores of individuals working as teachers in schools, medical assistants in clinics and hospitals, clerks and receptionists in offices and other such jobs choose occupations and perform them all through their lives knowing very well that they will never become rich. Capitalism rides on the back of a certain spiritedness, which includes the spirit of innovation that was unleashed during the Renaissance and has been a salient characteristic of modern Western civilization. If new products are not innovated then there would not be much to buy and sell in the market place. It is not capitalism in itself by itself that has produced this enormous wealth in the world but a constant stream of new products that new innovation has engendered. Then the recent increase in wealth creation in the West and the world at large ought to be justly attributed to the spiritedness of Western peoples that has been unleashed in the last 500 years, rather than capitalism. However despite all these ethical and historical issues, the global economic system is a working system. We need not overthrow it because overthrow involves upheaval and dislocation. With love we can transform the capitalist system. The capitalist system needs to do three things to transform itself overnight into an ethical system. *If labor is cherished in the culture at large, the principle of property inheritance abolished and consumption regulated so that citizens consume only what they need then the capitalist system would become ethical instantaneously.* All the advances in technology and all the innovations that can be creatively mustered will be of no consequence if consumption is not reduced to human needs because much of that which is innovated, created and developed will be consumed by some; great inequities and human misery will persist amidst great wealth for some. On the other hand if the developed nations and the local elites in the developing world reduce their consumption to their needs then the surplus resources, both human and material, would be available for the poor in the developed countries and for the developing world. This surplus is bound to be huge and if it is made available without any condescension to the poor and the developing world there is no reason why the poor and the developing world wouldn't accept it. The regulation of consumption need not frighten people who are fearful of government intervention. In countries which are capable of instituting and adhering to the rule of the law, this regulation of consumption can be brought about by a citizen's forum. The government may facilitate the process as it does with the jury system. The facts for the verdict are established by the jury, so also excess consumption can be identified by one's fellow citizens. If consumption is regulated and if the principle of property inheritance is abolished then income tax can prospectively be completely abolished. The libertarian idea of limited government and the socialist vision of sharing wealth will merge into one. Then the capitalist system will be a mere game in which all those who have money over and above their needs will be obliged to give it away to charities and projects as they see fit. The state has the resources and therefore would be in a better vantage point than the citizen in terms of its ability to form perspectives on legitimate needs of the needy and therefore can establish priorities for these charities and ensure that society's resources are properly directed. Third world nations and charitable organizations for the poor can compete for these resources and thereby benefit. This would be an institutionalization of the idea trusteeship that Gandhi advocated. This prospectively would lead to a better world in which poverty and suffering associated with it would be ended worldwide. However this can be practiced only in societies where citizens respect the rule of secularly conceived laws. In societies that do not have experience with the rule of law, classical forms of socialism are inevitable. Even when socialism is inevitable, ethical discretion must be exhibited in the manner in which socialism is established. Nationalization of industries and businesses and land redistribution may be necessary but wealthy citizens should not be dispossessed of their homes and personal belongings via government fiat even when their possession is in excess of their needs. Non-co-operation must be used to transform rich people so that they give up personal possessions that are in excess of their needs.

Ethnicity. In our times much of the ethnic conflict that exists has its origins either in ideologies of nationalism or in the presumption of the absence of difference in human intercourse.

The ethnic war in Sri Lanka that ended in May 2009 originated in the Sinhala state's attempt to impose its language on minority Tamils so that the Sri Lankan nation would conform to the Sinhala national vision. The wars that erupted in the former Yugoslavia ended with the creation of independent nation states in which different ethnic groups were predominant. The other type of ethnic conflict that happens in the world is a result of differences that has become apparent when different ethnic groups come into contact with one another. The modern world is made of independent nation states. Even within a nation state there may be many sub nationalities. One of the two basic tenets of the post-colonial world order is equality and the other tenet is freedom. The inherent equality of all nations and peoples is a self-evident truth; equality however does not mean absence of difference. People vary from each other in their mores, temperaments, values, national self-image, aspirations, sense of historical destiny, and in their culturally and historically formed traits which enables them to succeed in the modern world. Modern methods of communication and transportation, makes these diverse peoples more readily aware of each other and brings them in contact with each other more easily. The enormous opportunities unleashed by modernity have these diverse people competing for the same resources and the same opportunities. Some ethnic groups are culturally more prepared to seize these opportunities than others. While large scale Chinese immigration to Malaysia was not recent, the sheer inherited cultural advantages of the Chinese set them apart from the Malays in availing the opportunities that modernity offered. The Chinese were as a group disproportionately better educated and more prosperous than the Malays. The Malays resorted to an aggressive affirmative action plan called Bumiputra laws, which was supposed to correct the imbalance. However the imbalance continues to exist. So much so that Malaysia has started backtracking some of its Bumiputra laws[21]. We see ethnic problems erupting within India in a different setting. Sizable populations from neighboring states speaking different languages have flooded into major cities of India like Mumbai and Bengaluru in search of opportunities. Since the language of the immigrant has become the language of the street, here the assertion of the native people takes the form of linguistic sub nationalism. In the case of Malaysia, the source of the ethnic conflict was a scramble for opportunities in the modern world. In the case of large cities in India, it is cultural sub nationalism that defines the problem. After the cold war and the subsequent inclusion of many East and Central European nations into the European Union, the migration of the largely segregated Roma people from Bulgaria and Romania into Western Europe continues to be a source of considerable ethnic tension. The Roma are accused of theft, slum dwelling and an unwillingness to integrate. In each one of these strained ethnic encounters there was a presumption that both groups, the Chinese and the Malay, will perform equally when they started out which turned out to be false, there was the presumption that migrant workers from another sub culture would seamlessly integrate into these large Indian cities which did not turn out to be the case and that all Bulgarians and Romanians including the Roma will indistinguishably absorb Western mores, have Western aspirations and live like other Westerners, which did not happen. Unlike ethnic issues of the past in which difference gave way to a belief in one's innate superiority and was responsible for the oppression of others, in our times it is the denial of difference and the expectation of similarity in outcomes and behavior among different groups of people which turns out to be the cause of ethnic problems. There is no adhoc solution for ethnic problems such as these. If we begin with the notion that people are different, expect people to be different and are willing to use difference in a way that upholds the honor of all the distinct groups and contributes to the well-being of all, we would have taken an important step in ending ethnic conflict between peoples for our times and beyond. If developed nations and the local elite in the developing world cut their consumption and are willing to help nations and peoples that have difficulty with modernity and development then an equitable economic order could be established worldwide. Establishing an equitable economic order worldwide could go a long way in preventing ethnic conflicts. Only countries whose national ethos anticipates immigrants like the United States or Canada can sustain large scale migration. Large scale migration is bound to create problems for ethnic nations. If the economic incentive is removed by creating an equitable economic order, the desire and need to migrate would also reduce. Likewise if the cultural nationalism and cultural sub nationalism of all peoples are affirmed and facilitated then that would reduce ethnic conflict as well. As we saw in the case of large cities in India, the desire of the natives that their language and culture should be predominant in their cities is entirely understandable, but it is also true that these cities would never have become prominent and large without the dynamism and enterprise of people from their neighboring states. In short, natives should not have to give up their language and culture in their homeland and no one should have to migrate either for economic or even professional reasons. The more honest way of carrying out this encounter is to begin by acknowledging the existence of differences in the abilities of different groups of peoples. Then without a trace of superiority or inferiority, the society that needs help should ask for and take the help of a society that is capable of helping. In societies with diverse populations as in Malaysia, if an equitable economic order is established and if labor if cherished within the nation at large then the glamour associated with professional occupations like engineering and medicine will wean. While learning may be cherished for its own sake, there is nothing that makes professional occupations innately superior to other jobs. The human worth of the person is just the same whether one is a professional or not. In multicultural societies like Malaysia, affirmative action can be justified on grounds of promoting diversity and not on Bumiputra laws. Bumiputra means sons of the soil. Since Malays were native to Malaysia and the Chinese were immigrants who came to Malaysia in the last few hundred years, the argument goes that the Chinese have lesser rights in Malaysia. However the Chinese in the last few hundred years that they have been in Malaysia have not considered themselves as being superior. The Chinese have neither subjugated nor oppressed the Malay in all these years. They simply lived alongside the Malay and with the advent of modernity are better able to take advantage of the opportunities that modernity provides. Human history is full of migration and conquest. Can all these migrations and conquests be backtracked? To be sure in a multicultural society you must have affirmative action but the long term justification for affirmative action is promotion of diversity and not who is the son of the soil. Diversity is in itself a source of merit. There are qualities that one acquires when one grows in a home with a different culture. It is intangible and will be an invaluable resource in the work place. There is nothing to say that the examination system is perfect in identifying whether an individual is fit for a job. The examination system at best ought to be used as being indicative and not conclusive. By the same token, diversity laws may place an individual in a position of responsibility but people ought to keep their jobs only based on their ability to fulfill the basic responsibility the job entrusts. Ethnicity should not shield irresponsibility and incompetence. In Europe, any solution to the problem of the Roma must begin with the recognition, that the Roma, were a historically segregated and ostracized minority who have lived on the fringes of civilization all through their history. To have to entirely take responsibility for their lives in advanced democratic societies with a free enterprise system would be too overwhelming for them. Within the existing framework of Western institutions and structures there can be no comprehensive solution to the problem of the Roma. The problem at best can only be managed, it cannot comprehensively be solved. What is needed is a complete re-orientation of values and priorities in Western civilization. The welfare of the downtrodden must take precedence over liberty in the hierarchy of values in Western civilization. When that happens, in large measure the Roma will respond to advocacy for keeping their homes and neighborhoods clean and in refraining from committing petty crimes.

Religion. We are confronted both by ethical dilemmas and historical dilemmas in the wake of modernity. The existence of great inequities among peoples and nations is an ethical dilemma. The existence of political problems between peoples is a historical dilemma. The Arab-Israeli dispute and caste conflicts in the subcontinent are historical problems. One can argue that the social and cultural issues in America that give rise to a polarized polity are a historical problem as well. Ethical dilemmas can only be resolved by secular ethical resolution. At this moment in history it is inherently not possible to resolve ethical dilemmas religiously. Religious orders have become closely bound to cultural traditions and therefore religious resolutions will not seem to be equitable to those outside their tradition. Religious solutions however can facilitate resolution of intractable historical problems. In historical issues the contending parties are often religiously close to each other. Both Jews and Arabs worship the same formless God. So prospectively, a prophetic monotheistic vision could resolve points of contention between the Jewish and Arab narratives and try and bring both peoples together. Almost all those who engage in caste conflicts in India resort to image worship, believe in reincarnation, fate and transcendence. So a new indigenous religious order not bound to the present orthodoxy but encompassing the historical experience of the Indian people can appeal to people from all castes. The growth of such a religious order can help people transcend caste animosities. We do not know how and when such religious solutions will manifest themselves. All we can do is to wait in anticipation for religious resolution to some of the most intractable historical problems we face. In addition to the ethical and historical issues, we must also consider the notion of an individual's personnel faith. There is nothing morally wrong with the idea of faith itself. It is entirely a matter of personnel belief. However modernity is a transcendental moment and all the different peoples of the world must historically come to terms with our times. If some such transformation is in variance with people's faith then the needed historical transformation must take precedence over their faith. How are we to know that a certain historical transformation is necessary? Like the way we would know everything else – the needed historical transformation must become clearly self-evident. As an example the Taliban's interpretation of Islam cannot be defended under the pretext of faith because it restricts opportunities for women that modernity makes possible. Even Muslims who are conscious of the possibilities of modernity find the Taliban's prescriptions distasteful.

State. The independent nation state is the basic unit of the present world order. The nation state gets formulated and finds expression during the 19th century in Europe. The commonly understood meaning of the nation state is one which is vested with authority over a well-defined territory with a common culture and often a common language. As the 19th century progressed the quest for the nation state took place in the Western world when the Industrial Revolution was well underway, the print media became a vehicle for national conversation, the railways provided mobility and compulsory schooling paved the way for universal literacy. That is in the 19th century, modernity was in a substantive sense, socially and physically disrupting the old world of Europe. Therefore the nation state may be viewed as a cultural recompense for the actual or anticipated social disruption that was to be caused by modernity in the West. The culture of the pre-modern world must have corresponded with the life style of the pre-modern world and would have been difficult to preserve in its entirety when confronted with the cascade of modernity. Some cultural adaptation was inevitable. Two approaches to the creation of the nation state in Europe are identified. Eric Hobsbawn[22] argues that France did not have a single French language when the nation state was created. The French language was a result of unifying several dialects and languages. This approach where the nation state was created from a certain core seems to have been the way in which the nation state was created in England and France. According to Benedict Anderson nations are imagined communities in which an attempt is made to create a political reality that corresponds to a preconceived vision of the nation[23]. A vision of Germany and Italy preceded the creation of these nation states. Outside European civilization, countries seemingly function in the 20th century as nation states but are a consequence of entirely different historical processes. In Africa the lines that demarcate various nations on a map are merely administrative jurisdictions of former colonial powers. China was a civilization that was almost always a nation. Likewise Japan, which got its civilizational culture from China, was always a nation. An attempt to seek a unified independent political expression of Indian civilization under Gandhi resulted in the Indian nation. Countries like Egypt, Iraq and Iran have always been in the crossroads of civilizations. These countries have at times been centers of Empires and have at times been part of larger empires that were centered elsewhere. Non-European attempts at creating nations along the lines of the European nation state are hardly promising. Nasser's attempt at creating an Arab nation comprising all the Arabic speaking people has not been realized to this day. For a thousand years Islamic civilization was centered on the Turkish people. After the creation of the modern secular Turkish nation, the Arabs and not the Turks are emerging as the leaders of Islamic civilization. Nor is Turkey fully integrated with Europe. Politically and geographically Turkey is at the periphery of Europe. In the aftermath of globalization, the nation state has to contend with increasing transnationalism. As a consequence of transnationalism, people of different nations are increasingly being brought into contact with one another. With the result people tend to judge others based on their own cultural norms giving rise to conflicts. Consequently in our times the nation state is unfavorably compared to cosmopolitanism. Cosmopolitanism is the transformation of all of humanity into a state of cultural indifference, whereby we could transcend the nation and would be able to create a world government. Cosmopolitanism would be welcome in multicultural societies like Canada and America but in ethnic nations it is bound to be resisted sooner or later. It would on the other hand be better to affirm and even help preserve nationalistic cultures as long as the actions of nations and their peoples are ethical and in alignment with the necessities of our times. If cosmopolitanism is not a likely destiny for the nation state then what is to become of the nation state? Is the nation state the final political construct of history? To say that the nation state is the final construct in history it must be able to solve some of the basic existential problems that its citizens are confronted with. Unfortunately many of the third world nations are not able solve such basic problems for their citizens. These countries are not able to provide adequate nutrition, shelter, basic health care and a decent education for their children. Worse still in many of these countries the problem seems to be inherent and would persist for the foreseeable future. We must therefore conclude that we need newer structural arrangements over and above the nation state to solve some of the basic problems that many nations experience. We will take up the discussion on creating newer structural arrangements in the next section of this chapter.

Women. Women have endured enormous inequities in pre-modern times. Now we can and must correct them. Modern feminism has essentially restricted itself to securing equal rights and legal safeguards for women. While the attempt to secure equal rights for woman is laudable, modern feminism has been extremely ineffective in pursuing the protection of woman. There are whole categories of issues like prostitution, rape and the hardship faced by single mothers which are at best only rhetorically addressed by modern feminists. Modern feminists have not succeeded in bringing about a comprehensive solution for any of these gruesome problems. Indeed, morally, the existence of prostitution, the absence of societal outrage over rape and the preponderance of single mothers are more serious failures than not having proportionate number of women in high office. The reason that feminists are not able to address these issues may have to do with the first principles they start from. Modern feminists begin by accepting the primacy of freedom over all else. In a sense in the feminist hierarchy of values, freedom is more important than the well-being of women even. Since freedom is valued, prostitution and sex work is permitted under the pretext of a free woman of her own free will making a free choice. We live in a world in which we find great human misery and enormous inequity. There are scores of occupations that women can undertake based on their aptitude and inclination and lead purposeful lives. In being a prostitute or sex worker, a woman reduces herself to providing service for the weakness and irresponsibility of men. Marxist critiques attribute economic necessity for the continued prevalence of prostitution. Certainly economic necessity forces some women to become sex workers. Economic inequities certainly need to be ended if we are serious about ending prostitution. However, prostitution cannot be comprehensively ended by ending economic inequities alone. Even in Marxist societies, party leaders and men in power may be able to use their authority to bribe or coerce women into granting them sexual favors. Prostitution can be comprehensively ended only when moral outrage accompanies the legal abolition of prostitution in the same way that slavery and racial segregation were abolished in America. By abolishing prostitution are we trying to mold all the complexity of man woman relationships into a streamlined monogamous relationship using the strong arm of law? Is life so simple? No. We can make allowance for the complexity of life by saying that when marriage is by consent, when legal provision and social tolerance exists for divorce and when the husband treats his wives equally then the existence of polygamy in society is better than the existence of prostitution. Monogamy is still the ideal relationship between man and woman, we only reluctantly tolerate polygamy. Prostitution and sex work should not exist. A woman, not even one woman in the whole wide world, should have to spend an entire life time or for that matter any length of time providing service for the failings of man. It is necessary to establish the basic philosophical principle that we can consult as the guiding light for all male female interactions and relationships: *Men must be made to take responsibility for their actions and women must be given freedom with protection.* One of the most horrific crimes that can be committed by one human being against another human being is rape. Rape devastates a woman, robs her of all her sense of self-worth, shatters her dignity and destroys her self-respect. What then do we do to end rape? Is capital punishment for the criminal the answer? The entire edifice of our world view is founded on the potency of truth and love. When such is the case, to reflexively respond with capital punishment as the answer to rape amounts to suspecting the potency of love. So we will observe that it is theoretically entirely possible to prevent rape before it happens with love, but as a species we humans have not demonstrated the requisite capacity for love or even the necessary faith in love to generate the necessary imaginativeness that could be harnessed to prevent heinous crimes with love. Rape must be prevented before it occurs; it is too late after the fact. Capital punishment for anyone who attempts to rape is the only restraint that could prevent rape from taking place in the future. This capital punishment must be carried out publicly. However if the accused rapist happens to be the legal spouse of the victim, capital punishment must be reduced to a less severe punishment. Yet another issue that modern feminism is not able to comprehensively end is the plight of single mothers. Divorce in a tangible way works to the disadvantage of the women because in overwhelming majority of the cases women end up raising the children. The man just takes the child out one day a week and pays some money as alimony. To be sure, there may be some instances in which the couple simply cannot live together and there is a need to separate. Or in cases when women are victims of domestic violence, which involves a repetitive pattern of either physical or emotional abuse, the couple must necessarily separate and the perpetrators of such violence ought to be punished. Or when the integrity of the marriage is compromised by infidelity then there may be justification for separation. In divorce cases, except in cases of adultery on the woman's part, when all else is equal the court system must be sympathetic to the woman's side. To bring about all these changes, feminists can begin by championing the well-being of women; they should not axiomatically assume that anything that promotes freedom necessarily results in the well-being of women.

Outcastes. Democratic societies that engage in passionate deliberations about historically oppressed people generally provide opportunities for very able members of historically oppressed groups to occupy some of the highest offices in their respective countries. Democracies are extremely inept in bringing about a comprehensive solution for all members of historically oppressed groups. Marxist societies are relatively better at bringing about a comprehensive change but are insensitive to the experiences and difficulties of historically oppressed peoples. In the coming future, the preeminent national and global priority must be the well-being of the downtrodden. The well-being of the downtrodden must take precedence over economic growth, technological advancement, scientific progress, religious quest, cultural nationalism, artistic expression and almost everything except the truth. Truth is pertinent love and therefore nothing can be better or greater than it. Associated with the well-being of outcastes and other historically oppressed groups, is the case for affirmative action and for reservation in college admission and employment. Affirmative action or reservation can be justified only to promote diversity in multicultural societies[24] and to speed up the process by which the laboring classes and historically oppressed people enter the modern world in traditional societies. The pursuit of affirmative action could result in social justice. Social justice provides opportunities in education and employment for people from disadvantaged groups so that they may be able to realize their potential.

Vegetarianism. If adequate nutritious vegetarian food is conveniently available for all people there can be no justification for eating animals, birds, fish and other creatures. In addition, animals must be treated with compassion. Zoos must reflect the natural habitat of the animals and must have lots of space for animals to roam freely. All cruelty against animals must be stopped. For performing in the circus, animals must be humanely trained. Circuses should not travel around because that would contribute to the caging of animals. The animals, which perform in the circus, can be made to reside in a natural habitat with lots of space to roam around freely. Researchers should not use animals in harsh and painful experiments. Education must be provided for pet owners so that they are competent in caring for their pets. Sterilization may be used for domestic animals like cats and dogs to ensure that they do not overpopulate – especially when there is no one to take care of them.

Labor. Labor is something that we need to grapple with even after the advent of modernity. In the pre-modern world back breaking labor was the norm for much of humanity. With automation and the use of other sophisticated technology the intensity of labor can be greatly reduced. We however have not reached a stage where labor can be totally eliminated. We may never reach such a stage. It may not even be desirable for us to completely eliminate labor altogether. Even if we eliminated physical labor altogether through technical innovation, will we be able to provide white collar work for all the people? Even if we were able to provide white collar work for all the people, we need to ensure that such work is socially purposeful, enhances an individual's self-worth and is within the capability of the individual performing the job. An agricultural laborer, a skilled lathe operator, a teacher, a design engineer or a government official may derive satisfaction from the work they have accomplished and responsibilities that they have undertaken in ways that a shop keeper or clerk may not. In the globalized capitalist system of our times, innovativeness and acquisition of sophisticated skills that are valued in the market place are the most prized traits in employment, business and in remuneration. But the difficulty with this approach is that innovativeness is intrinsic to the individual and everyone may not have the aptitude to obtain sophisticated skills. As a consequence even when jobs are available in the market place we often have unemployment. A comprehensive approach to ensure that everybody is purposefully employed is to taboo the use of certain technologies all through the economy. Automation must however be willingly used at all times for dangerous and unsafe jobs.

Entertainment. Nothing in this world of ours highlights the ethical problems of our times as people's attitude to entertainment. Ethics is about right action. We can do one of many things at any given moment – work, pray, spend time with our family, play a game, go to a night club or theatre, read, study, volunteer our time for a higher cause or for that matter do almost anything. Responsible people typically prioritize before they act. Ethics establishes the ideal criteria for such prioritization. Our world is beset with enormous inequities. In the world of ours, sustenance of civilized life is possible only through interdependence. If parents do not care for their children then children will become orphans. If school teachers are ineffective in teaching their students then many of the students will have difficulty in functioning in the world when they grow up. So also in a world with great inequities, if those who are endowed with advantages do not care for those who happen to be helpless and downtrodden, then the world will be a harsh place to live. The condition of the world determines the ethical object of life. In the world of ours, with such enormous inequities, then the object of life, properly, ought to be one of service. Service in our world is an expression of love. Sacrifice for a meaningful purpose constitutes a profound expression of love. If the principal object of life on earth is love and service then what is the place of entertainment in the human scheme of things? Regardless of the condition of the world, a life of uninterrupted service is bound to be monotonous. The object of entertainment then is only to provide spite from the monotony of work. Everybody may not be able to lead a life of service like Mahatma Gandhi or Mother Teresa[25]. People vary in the nature of their consciousness, personality, inclinations, temperament, circumstance and talents. So based on our respective nature and circumstance we must undertake duties and responsibilities in life so that we are useful to those around us. This view on work and recreation is in sharp contrast to current attitudes on entertainment that are prevalent. The object of life, we are told, is to enjoy oneself and everything in life from work, to learning, to marriage ought to be "fun". In a world full of inequities, it is unethical to give such precedence for fun and enjoyment over work and service. Let us look at learning as an example. Learning need not be fun, it ought to be effective. At the philosophical level we insist that love is vested with potency. Therefore we should be kind and use love as a tool for imparting knowledge because that is the most effective method and must resort to other methods only when our faith in love wavers and our capacity for love is inadequate. But there should be no confusion on the purpose of the endeavor. The object of learning is to learn, not to have "fun". Since the object of life is service, in the wider culture we must value and celebrate those who lead a life of service and must show tolerance for people who vary in their capacity for service. Through advocacy, education and emphasis we can try to inculcate the value of service in society.

Sexuality. Great variations exist among the major cultures on human sexuality. Some ancient cultures persist with arranged marriage while developed liberal first world countries are embracing gay marriage. In human attire we see the difference between the bikini of the West and the veil of Islam. Many of these vast differences must be attributed to the differences in the experiences of different peoples. Each one of the major civilizations of the world needs to be historically transformed from within. This is a task that remains to be done. When this happens the different cultures will be brought closer, or if differences still persist, human relations would have become easier whereby true understanding between cultures could be realized. Therefore in the realm of sexuality it is best to defer judgment. Quite independent of the historical transformation of the different cultures we must treat gays, lesbians and transgender people with compassion. It is wrong to blame people who are sexually oriented differently from birth. It is not fundamentally different from blaming somebody for their ethnicity or skin color. Sex for the purpose of procreation is noble and ought to be welcome. Sex for pleasure or carnal love is morally no different from other forms of recreation or entertainment. It ought not to have a special place in human discourse. Sex also need not be the subject of human advocacy.

Ideology. Doesn't truth over time become an ideology? It certainly has. All the civilizational narratives were once truths that fairly early in their respective histories became narratives. If that is the case will not fallible human nature transform the truth once more into another narrative? What sense does it make to seek ethical resolutions if we are inherently not capable of sustaining it? These are very pertinent questions. Modernity is a transcendental moment in world history. As space and distance shrink and as cultures are brought in close contact with one another, if we did not seek ethical resolutions, every ideology and every cultural narrative will start making universal claims on its own behalf. Indeed we already see evidence for this in globalization, Hindu nationalism and the rise of the Taliban. Violence may be used as a means to realize these claims. The prevalence of modern weaponry both conventional and nuclear could make it horrendous for humanity. Elucidating the truth for our times and circumstances will refute the erroneous claims of various narratives and ideologies. Now will those who adhere to different ideologies and narratives be willing to embrace the truth? Truth that can be conceived, when elucidated, must be self-evident to everybody. Inertia, a sense of pride in one's own tradition, a sentimental attachment to existing beliefs and above all ignorant pursuit of naked self-interest may certainly prohibit nations and cultures from embracing the truth. To those who resist the truth, the potency of the truth will in itself be an impediment to their persistence with untruth. Since historical circumstances now will allow us to seek the structural remedy for the inadequacy of love, the assertion of the truth is bound to be profound if we persist with untruth. Now having shown the need for resolution at this moment in history let us turn to our original question namely - Will truth not degenerate into another ideology? Even if all nations and cultures embrace the truth now in a short while the truth could degenerate and it may become an ideology. After all, all the major cultural narratives were truths in their inception and degenerated fairly early. Once we have created an ethical order we need a way to sustain it. Sustenance happens in time and time is defined by movement. Some nations have historically evolved ways to sustain order. Chinese thought identified patterns of change that was found in nature. The Chinese pair of opposing forces, the yin and yang, was philosophized as the culmination of the process of change. Ideologies like Taoism, Buddhism and Confucianism co-existed in China. No resolution was sought. Political necessity and China's heuristic understanding of the process of change possibly determined the degree to which a specific ideology would be embraced at a given period. Necessity and the process of change preserved order in China. In India, religious ideologies were engaged in passionate millennial struggles. These struggles constituted the central dynamic of Indian history. Millennial contentions established the basis of disorder – and thereby order - in India. In the modern West, pluralism sustains the democratic order. We see evidence for this in the two party system in America. Conservative and liberal are hardly intellectually consistent philosophical positions. They are just as much a coalition of interest groups. The conservative pro-life advocates are also against gun control. Conservatives defend life inside a womb but are unwilling to ban the guns that could potentially kill a life when it is outside the womb. Liberals on the other hand will permit killing an unborn child but want gun control to protect those who are alive. Both political parties, Republican and Democratic, are platforms by which the American democratic order is preserved. The country that embraces the truth before it is too late will succeed and can consolidate its gains by preserving the truth. Preservation of the truth will be in accordance with its experience.

Self-Respect, Parentalism and the Structure of Peace

Almost all the resolutions that we have proposed for an ethical order could be realized with existing institutions and structures. But the need for greater co-operation between nations and peoples in the face of vast differences that exist between them requires newer ideals and newer structures. However, before we identify relevant ideals and appropriate structures to help us cope with difference we must reiterate the existence of difference and dispel attempts to blur it.

The international order is made up of sovereign independent nations. In the present world order, all the nations and peoples of the world regard themselves as being equal to each other. Equality and freedom are the two great ideals of our times. Largely as a consequence of liberal ideas espoused during the last three hundred years, equality in the wider culture is assumed to be an equal capacity to perform. However the reality is that countries and cultures vary in their ability to cope with modernity. There is an obvious gap between liberal conception and conspicuous reality. Various reasons are suggested to explain the gap. We will take up some of the frequently cited reasons and try to respond to them.

The most frequently cited reason for the present economic and social misery that we see in quite a few third world countries is colonialism. The argument is made that colonialism was exploitative and the effects of colonialism have been so deep that they prohibit developing nations from progressing. Colonialism was certainly not a benevolent enterprise. One could persuasively make the case that it was exploitative. Minerals and raw materials were certainly taken from the colonies to the colonizing imperial nation for consumption. The colonizing powers were apathetic to the economic well-being of the colonies. They did not mean for the colonies as they had meant for themselves. However the issue that concerns us here is whether this exploitative colonial process was so deep that it holds back a former colony from becoming a developed country. As late as the year 1800 only the new world and Siberia were significantly colonized. (Many of the third world countries in the new world were formerly colonized by Spain and Portugal. At least the larger of these countries got their independence by the 19th century. Many of them were populated by white immigrants from Europe, who intermarried with indigenous peoples. In these countries one could assume that the colonized and colonizers were not fundamentally a different people and therefore a case could be made that the impact of colonialism in inhibiting development essentially weak). Otherwise in the year 1800, European colonialism in the continent of Asia and Africa was mostly restricted to the coastal regions. It was only after the comprehensive defeat of the Indian princes in the Great War of 1857 does all of India comes under English domination. Likewise it is only in the year 1881 do we see the scramble for Africa. By 1945, immediately after the end of the Second World War and the creation of the United Nations, decolonization acquired enormous political and moral impetus. Therefore we can see the countries of Africa and Asia were substantially dominated by European powers only for a period of 65 to 90 years. Human civilization has existed for at least 5000 years. Was a mere 65 to 90 years of colonial rule so profoundly devastating that these former colonies cannot take care of themselves in the modern era? Along with colonialism came the material advancement of modern civilization and that certainly must have been very disruptive to traditional cultures in Asia and Africa. But then modern technology is so seductive that no nation has been able to say no to it in a comprehensive way. If the colonized countries embrace technology by consent then what separates countries is the ability to come to terms with modernity. Not all former colonies are miserable and even among those that are miserable they are not uniformly miserable. Great variations exist. As we have shown above in the section on *'Development'*, there is a near one to one correspondence between development and pre-modern cultural experience. Singapore, Hong Kong and South Korea were all colonized but for all practical purposes today they can be regarded as being developed. On the other hand most nations that have a low human development according to HDI are African. The notion that colonialism is responsible for holding nations back from development is not borne out by evidence.

Yet another popular view has to do with time available to modernize. The West had four hundred years to get to where it is now but most of the less developed poorer nations have been independent only for about fifty or sixty years. According to this line of reasoning, with time, the less developed countries will be more familiar with modernity and therefore will be able to embrace modernity effectively. Countries in coastal Africa were far more familiar with modernity because they were colonized much earlier than the African hinterland. Countries in coastal Africa, however, are not significantly more developed than the African hinterland. India was colonized and was easily more exposed to modernity than China but today in almost every conceivable yardstick China is ahead of India despite China having a little larger population to cater to. Indeed regions of the Hindi heartland in Northern India referred to as the BIMARU states are not appreciably more developed than Sub-Saharan Africa. The case for more time for development is arguably best negated in Latin America. As we have stated in the section above on Development and have shown in Appendix 2, 3, 4, and 5, in Latin America there is a close relationship between the ethnic composition of a society and the level of development it has reached. Almost all the countries in Latin America declared their independence from their colonial masters between 1810 and 1830. That is, they had nearly 200 years of independence and yet great variation exists among them in their levels of development.

Then there are those who deny that third world nations continue to experience difficulties. They are euphoric about globalization and insist that it is effective in spreading wealth around the world; in their perspective China and India are seen to be rising and the claim is made that Africa's prospects are promising. In addition, we are told new innovative methods would bring comprehensive relief for many of Africa's miseries in the not so distant future[26]. In the case of China, this line of reasoning is not inaccurate. It is a country with a Confucian ethos and if it is unhindered, like other Confucian nations it will succeed. In the case of India, as we have shown in the section on development, great variation exists. India has its Africa and its Western civilization within it. We cannot be any more hopeful of India than we are of the world as a whole. In the case of Africa it is true that a few countries have statistically registered noticeable increases in growth rates recently. Among these, countries that have a significant measure of economic diversification are South Africa, Tunisia, Morocco and Egypt[27]. South Africa had a harsh, cruel and humiliating apartheid system and the perpetrators of the apartheid system were racially white and culturally of European origin. Initially the post-apartheid South African government[28] under

Mandela showed great magnanimity, forgave the white oppressors and was inclusive of them in the reconstruction of their nation. With subsequent governments corruption has become rampant and the administration has become inefficient. Among the reasons that allow South Africa to continue to be clubbed together along with the more developed countries of Africa are the residual effects of administrative structures created during the apartheid years and the varied cultural experience of its diverse population. Tunisia, Morocco and Egypt are located in North Africa and are not Sub-Saharan nations and have come into being as a result of very different historical and cultural processes. This difference manifests in their ability to better respond to modernity. Among the rest of the countries in Africa[29] that are not poor and have posted high growth rates are oil rich countries that have benefited from earlier rises in oil prices. There are also some poor countries that have posted noticeable increases in growth rates in Africa and these are able to do so because they are poor and start from a smaller base. In these poor countries even a significant increase in mineral prices or long overdue basic restructuring of the economy or a combination of both would result in noticeable increases in growth rates. Otherwise, the recent euphoria that Sub-Saharan African nations are showing promise does not have a basis in fact. Likewise, we are told new innovative methods and technologies will comprehensively heal the sick and solve many of the miseries faced by people in Sub-Saharan Africa and in other parts of the developing world in the not so distant future[30]. However the reality is somewhat different. The only infectious human disease that has been comprehensively eradicated worldwide so far is smallpox. The eradication of smallpox[31] was spearheaded by the World Health Organization with enormous support and assistance from the two superpowers of the day namely the United States and the

Soviet Union. If only one infectious disease can be comprehensively eradicated worldwide through the efforts of two super powers and an international organization then we need, not less but greater, direct effort from the advanced countries of the world to end human miseries in the developing world. A new vaccine or a new delivery systems or for that matter any new technology does not exist in vacuum. To actually succeed it must have organization, focus and resources – all of which are beyond the capacity of a developing county, particularly one in Sub-Saharan Africa.

It is argued that progress and development do not result in happiness and therefore must not be used as yardsticks to measure the state of nations. According to this perspective all non-Western peoples are regarded as having been happy in their pre-modern setting. The savage is idealized as the 'noble savage'. That is a savage was happy and perfect in his primordial setting. Happiness is however a subjective thing. People find happiness in all sorts of activities. Family, friends, nature, ethics, religion, success, entertainment, charity and the good life have all been sources of human happiness. Happiness can neither be quantified nor can we set objective standards for it. However the value of certain aspects of progress and development are self-evident. It "is better"[32] to be healthy "than"[32] to be sick. It "is better" to be fed "than" to be hungry. It "is better" to live longer "than" to die early. If people felt that it was better to die than to live and if life was not worth living then far more people would be committing suicide. So also it "is better" to be literate and educated "than" to be illiterate and uneducated. It is in these basic issues of life, health, nutrition, literacy and education that we see huge disparities between developed rich countries and the less developed poorer countries. According to an Oxfam International Briefing Paper published in

January 2014, the personal wealth of the richest 85 people in the world is worth more than the combined wealth of the poorest 3.5 billion people in the world[33]. According to the United Nations World Food Program (WFP) one in eight people - 842 million around the world - go to bed hungry every night and in Sub-Saharan Africa one in four – 222.7 million - go to bed hungry every night[34]. According to the United Nations Millennium Development Goals Report 2012, 783 million people or 11 % of the world population lack access to safe, clean drinking water and 2.5 billion people lack access to basic sanitation[35]. The same study says that nearly 40% of all people in the world who lack access to safe, clean drinking water live in Sub-Saharan Africa. According to the United Nations Educational Scientific and Cultural Organization (UNESCO), an estimated 773.5 million adults are illiterate today[36]. According to the World Population Prospects, The 2012 Revision released by the Population Division of the United Nations Department of Economic and Social Affairs (UN DESA) life expectancy in Japan is the highest of any country at close to 83 years and the lowest life expectancy of any country is Sierra Leone at 44 years for the period between 2005 and 2010[37]. Advanced countries tend to be nearer to Japan in life expectancy and the Sub-Saharan countries tend to be nearer to Sierra Leone. Infant mortality rate (IMR) is defined as the number of deaths of infants under one year old per 1,000 live births. Again according to the United Nations Population Division, infant mortality for the period 2005-2010 is lowest for Hong Kong Special Administrative Region (SAR) of China, a developed region, at 1.9 and highest for Sierra Leone, a poor country, at 127.2[38]. If life expectancy, health care facilities, access to nutritious food, access to clean water and literacy levels were the same between nations and they differed – let us say - only in their modes of transportation, wherein, in rich countries they used cars and in poorer nations they used bullock carts then we could say that the slower pace made life happier in poorer nations. It is intellectually dishonest and morally wrong to argue that poorer countries are happier with inadequate food and water, preventable diseases, lower life expectancy and illiteracy.

The most popular liberal explanation for the poverty of poorer countries is that they continue to be exploited by rich countries. We must investigate this exploitation theory. There are two direct ways in which this sort of exploitation takes place. One is in the mining of minerals possessed by third world countries and the other is usage of cheap labor for manufacturing in third world countries under appalling conditions for consumption in richer countries. In both cases the direct beneficiaries are Multinational Corporations (MNCs) which are based in rich countries. One could certainly argue that these are exploitative relationships; however our objective here is to find out whether these relationships are responsible for the continued poverty in many third world nations. Many of the poverty stricken third world countries often don't have the requisite technology to mine the mineral or to add value to the mineral so mined. So they have to turn to MNCs for assistance. Poor Third World nations need to import necessities like armaments for defense, food, medicine and oil from other countries for which they have to pay in hard currency. The poor country can get hard currency only by exporting something of value to the rich countries. If the only thing that a nation has to export is its minerals then the poor country becomes very dependent on MNCs who are capable of extracting these minerals. The vulnerable situation of the poor country would certainly embolden the MNCs to set terms and conditions that are entirely favorable to the MNC. Often poor third world countries are corrupt and do not have the rule of the law. So the MNCs can bribe the local elite in poor third world countries and get even more concessions. All of this is certainly exploitative. But if a poor third world country has other sources of generating hard currency like a manufacturing base or a capacity to offer useful services then that could enhance the prospects for the third world country. This does not mean that the third world country will not be exploited. It very well may continue to be exploited but it will not be desperately poor. In the modern world, unless it possesses oil or high quality diamonds, no nation can sufficiently provide for itself by its mineral wealth alone. Here we see that poor third world countries are certainly exploited but the cause of poverty is not the exploitation but the inability of the poor third world nations to diversify, produce goods and services of value beyond being an exporter of minerals.

Now let us take up the case of exploitation that is a consequence of MNCs setting up manufacturing facilities in third world countries. The ostensible motivation for the MNCs is the cheap labor in third world countries. But in addition many third world countries are corrupt and do not have stringent enforceable environmental or labor laws that one finds in advanced countries. So MNCs can bribe corrupt officials in the third world and force laborers to work long hours in unsafe conditions. This too is exploitation. Even this exploitation is possible only because third world leaders and bureaucrats are ready to forsake their national interest for their own personnel self-interest. However exploitation is only one part of the story. Most third world nations are far behind developed nations in terms of technology. MNCs are vehicles by which technology can be transferred from advanced countries to less developed nations. In the present world order, one way a developing nation can acquire advanced technology is through MNCs. When MNCs set up a manufacturing facility in a developing country, especially in rural areas, the local infrastructure improves. The manufacturing facility provides employment opportunities for people and ancillary units spring up in the vicinity to support the manufacture. None of this contributes to poverty in third world countries. MNCs are not enlightened entities which have noble purposes. The object of the MNCs is profit and the MNCs may very well have been exploitative but they are not responsible for the abject poverty in third world nations.

Abject poverty and enormous misery is prevalent in poor third world countries mainly because they as a people are independently not able to take care of themselves. We see a close co-relation between a people's prior historical and cultural experience and their ability to take care of themselves. Why then do we see such passion in denying an existential reality? The reason is fear. Human history is littered with records of peoples who have been suppressed and subjugated by others. African Americans were bought, sold, whipped and persecuted as slaves by white slave owners. The Dravidians, untouchables and backward castes were humiliated and ostracized in India by alien Aryans. Hitler systematically tortured and exterminated Jews in Nazi Germany. Dark images of persecution and suppression come to mind when we think of the historical consequences of human differences. We however do not help ourselves in denying an existential reality. If we are outraged by the suffering in the world and are serious in bringing about positive change then we must face reality.

Not all differences that exist in people have resulted in oppressive and exploitative relationships. Differences need not always frighten us. There is in nature a ubiquitous institution that is characterized by differences. This institution is the human family. Children cannot help themselves and parents care for them, love them, nurture them and provide for them. The family as an institution works admirably well. The world can be modeled on the family. Why can't the nations of the world live together as a family does? Why cannot developed nations care for nations that struggle with development like the way a parent cares for their children? If we are able to honestly convince ourselves that a parental relationship will not become exploitative, oppressive and humiliating then we can strive to create a new world order in which the whole world can live as a family.

People frequently tend to sustain themselves with a sense of superiority. Beauty, pedigree, wealth, learning, intelligence, talent, courage and success have all been used by individuals both to affirm their existence and to look down upon others. While such condescension is unfortunate, this kind of superiority exhibited by individuals does not result in institutionalized social oppression. On the other hand when the superiority of a people over another people becomes the organizing principle of society then institutionalized oppression is inevitable. The Nazi's in Germany believed that the Germans were the pure Aryan master race and were destined to subjugate others. Nazis also believed that the greatest threat to the Aryan nation was from the Jews. These beliefs of the Nazis were the organizing principles of the state in Hitler's Germany. As a result Jews were exterminated in Nazi Germany. The Hindu caste system in India was formed as a result of the Aryans in India subjugating the indigenous Dravidians. The Aryans believed they were superior to the Dravidians and the superiority of the Aryans constituted the organizing principle of human life in Hindu India over the millennia. The caste system was cruel to untouchables and other castes that were considered lowly. Likewise when the organizing principle of society explicitly insists on equality then the opportunity for such oppression is greatly reduced. In Islam all believers were one before God. There was no difference among them. Islam's insistence on the equality of all believers had facilitated relatively harmonious ethnic interactions among believers through the centuries. After the civil rights movement, America passionately embraced multiculturalism and as a consequence, today people from different races and cultures co-exist with each other in relative amity. As is evident, the one powerful tool that the world has at its disposal is the organizing principle of society.

What is the one ideal above all else that could be made the organizing principle of human life so as to ensure that a parentalistic world order would not become oppressive, exploitative and humiliating? It cannot be liberty because it is liberty that is the problem. Liberty has given all the third world nations independence and many of these nations are unable to take care of themselves and it is for that reason we need to create a parentalistic world order in the first place. Can it be equality? Equality among all nations and all peoples is an irrefutable truth but equality can easily be misconstrued as the equal capacity to perform, which evidently is not true. Can it be non-violence? It certainly can be non-violence. If a parental order were to be created through conquest and warfare, it would be no different from imperialism. The mighty and powerful nations can simply invade weaker countries under the guise of parentalism. So non-violence certainly must be one of the ideals for our consideration. There is another ideal that was espoused by Gandhi's contemporary EV Ramasamy Periyar and that is the ideal of self-respect, which is worth consideration[39]. We will refer to this as Periyar's ideal of self-respect to distinguish it from other notions of self-respect that were espoused by others like Hegel, for example. To Periyar, the ideal of self-respect meant that nations and peoples ought not to participate in narratives that made them inferior. Periyar believed that with his ideal of self-respect the whole world could live as one family. Let us contemplate on how the world could live as one family. At specific moments in history distinct peoples could rise and be powerful and influential because the contemporary historical circumstances would favor them. At such moments, the disadvantaged nation or peoples could seek and obtain the assistance of the nation or peoples that have advantages, provided, the basis of their engagement is founded in and sustained by Periyar's ideal of self-respect. That is the dynamics of coming together must vehemently refute the notion of superiority and inferiority among peoples and nations of the world. As a consequence, the story that they tell themselves about their interaction and interdependence, which is the narrative, must vehemently deny any notion of superiority and inferiority. Specifically a people ought not to participate in narratives that lowers them, humiliates them and makes them inferior. Periyar was never for using violence to settle political disputes so implicitly Periyar's ideal of self-respect encompasses nonviolence as well. Therefore Periyar's ideal of self-respect is the one ideal above all else that ought to be made the organizing principle of world government if we want the nations of the world to live as one family.

The needy countries can obtain the help of developed countries only if these developed countries are prepared to help. A rich and developed country merely offering to help will not suffice. To help a poor country, a rich and developed country has to be transformed from within. There are three elements which constitute this transformation. First the developed rich country must reduce consumption in its own country, so that citizens don't consume any more than that which each of them needs. Second the principle of property inheritance must be abolished. Last physical labor must be cherished. The surplus that would result due to reduced consumption can be made available to poor less developed countries and to the domestic poor. This money should not be given away as handouts to corrupt third world leaders. The rich countries must ensure that the money is well spent in poorer countries and on the domestic poor. There must be accountability. The poor countries for their part must begin by facing the truth. Different nations rise at different moments in history. The inability of a nation to take care of itself is not a dishonorable thing. The wheel of time and the innate impartiality of the truth will ensure that all incapacity and difficulty is temporary. However human suffering is real and it must be ended. If a rich developed country is transformed from within then a developing nation need not hesitate in taking help from the developed country as long as the poor country initiates the process of seeking help and the ideal of self-respect is adhered to at all times during the interaction. The symbolism and the narrative associated with the interaction must reflect the pre-eminence of the ideal of self-respect.

Initially the poor country can take ad hoc help from a developed country. The developed nation can provide financial assistance to pertinent development projects that are honestly run. It can take responsibility for specific tasks like eradicating preventable diseases; provide clean drinking water, running the airline of the poor country and even completely undertaking the administration of a specific government department like education, transportation or health. If this process works well and the nobility of intent of the developed nation becomes self-evident and the narrative of the developed nation is not condescending or humiliating to the developing nation then the developing country may entrust the entire responsibility of governance to a developed nation. Even then the head of state of each nation must be its own citizen. The highest office that a foreigner may occupy is that of head of government. So also the culture of the developing nation must be primary in its land. Parentalism must not be an excuse for cultural imperialism. The developed nation must function in a spirit of service.

So far we have just discussed the way in which one nation that needs help finds another nation that is willing to help. This process of a nation seeking help from another nation can be extended to the whole world wherein all the nations of the world can live as one family under one government. In short this process can pave the way for a new world order to emerge. Here we will layout the ideals, structure and essential characteristics of this new world order. To realize this new world order Periyar's ideal of self-respect must be made the foundational ideal. That is no nation should participate in a narrative that is condescending to it. Also we need to recognize two types of relationships that would characterize this new world order. One is a parental relationship between a developed country and a developing country. The other is fraternal relationship between two developed countries. One nation in the fraternal relationship would be the senior partner and the other a junior partner, just as the relationship between an elder brother and a younger brother in a traditional family. However for the continent of Asia, which has well defined pre-modern structures, we envision a two tier parental relationship. This two tier approach is necessary in the continent of Asia where the political issues are not always contemporary but historical as well. Based on historical relevance and cultural fit for modernity one core nation from each civilization can be in a parental relationship with other nations that need help from that civilization and likewise this one core nation can be in a fraternal relationship with other nations from the same civilization that are relatively better able to cope with modernity. This will constitute the first tier of parental and fraternal relationships. The core states of each civilization in turn will come together to form an international fraternity of responsible nations which make up the second tier fraternal relationship. One appropriate nation of the second tier fraternal nations can provide a focal point for all decisions that need to be taken. Without such a focal point the unity and purpose of the world government would fritter away. Indeed one of the structural problems that inhibits the current United Nations from not being able to comprehensively find solutions to problems of peace, hunger, malnutrition, illiteracy, infant mortality and environmental degradation is that in the ultimate analysis, no one nation is responsible for the world at large. The head of government of this appropriate nation in the second tier fraternity of nations can be regarded as the head of world government.

Civilizations

8. An outline for a discourse on Civilizations

Scholars have identified civilizations as distinct historical entities. The most significant work of recent modern scholarship that is based on the concept of civilizations is Huntington's clash of civilizations thesis. Since it is recent, scholarly and draws on the previous works of other scholars on civilizations, we will use Huntington's work on civilizations as the starting point for our discourse on civilizations. Huntington defines civilization as - "A civilization is thus the highest cultural grouping of people and the broadest level of cultural identity people have short of that which distinguishes humans from other species. It is defined both by common objective elements, such as language, history, religion, customs, institutions, and by the subjective self-identification of people"[1]. Huntington has identified seven or eight possible civilizations in the world today[2]. They are Western, Latin American, Orthodox, Islamic, Sinic, Hindu, Japanese and possibly African. We are not interested in civilizations that have existed in antiquity but are no longer with us now. Indeed in this book we have used the term *'major cultural traditions'* to mean major cultural traditions that are with us now. In addition we also use the more widely used word *civilizations* to mean *major cultural traditions*. In this book we define our major cultural traditions by the distinctness of their origins and not as the "highest cultural groupings" by which people are differentiated. Based on the distinctness of their origins we have identified four major cultural traditions that are with us namely Indian, East Asian Confucian, Islam and Christendom.

In this book we refer to our major cultural traditions in two important ways. One is in Chapter 4, where we juxtaposed the nobility and relevance of the ideals that characterized our major cultural traditions at their inception with the reality of their practice right through history. The other occasion for us to refer to our major cultural traditions is in this and in subsequent chapters. Here we attempt to highlight the central historical challenge that modernity poses to each of our major cultural traditions. In attempting to understand this challenge we seek to delve into the very nature of these cultural traditions so as to gain insights which we can use to chart the way forward for humanity. The reference to major cultural traditions in this book is consistent with our requirements. Therefore we have often had to treat the East Asian Confucian cultural tradition as being synonymous with China. Japan which obtained its Confucian culture from China is a distinct variation of the Confucian culture and has a rich and colorful history. In the 20th century Japan's recovery after the war and its economic success have been truly phenomenal. Likewise Vietnam and Korea (both North and South Korea) are nations, who are culturally rooted in Chinese culture, historically tied to China and have retained their cultural distinctiveness. Yet the centrality of China to East Asian Confucian culture is inescapable. China is the source of Confucian culture and even Buddhism went to Japan and Korea through China. China's population is more than ten times that of any other country with the Confucian ethos. China borders nations from all other major cultural traditions. In similar vein when we have to refer to Christendom in this book we tend to refer to Western Christendom. Traditionally there were two strands of Christianity. They were Catholicism and Orthodox. Orthodox was the religion that came into existence in what had been the eastern half of the Roman Empire where Greek was the main language and

Catholicism was the religion that was followed in what had been the western half of the Roman Empire where Latin was the main language. The main center of the Eastern Church was Constantinople and the main center for Catholicism was Rome. The city of Constantinople fell to the Turks in the year 1453. When Constantinople fell, Moscow became the main center of the Orthodox Church. The center of the Orthodox Church relocated itself among an ethnically and linguistically different people. Later when the Soviet Union came into existence, the state persecuted all religions and promoted atheism. The historical continuity of the Orthodox Church was hampered and a geographical continuity did not exist. On the other hand, though in the West, Catholicism was also challenged by the Protestant Reformation, with time and not a little bloodshed, the contending parties learnt to co-exist with each other. In addition, the West is the home of modernity. Christianity also went to many other parts of the world along with colonialism. In many of these countries Christianity is fairly recent in origin and is often a variation of Western Christendom. Western Christendom then is the cultural tradition within Christianity that has the greatest continuity and encompasses within its ambit the onslaught of modernity and therefore it is reasonable for us to use it as our reference for Christendom. We have split Africa between Islam and Christendom and have made no space for pre-colonial African cultures. Likewise we have not included Native American culture, Polynesian culture and the like. This is in no way a judgment on the worthiness of these cultures. Each culture is supremely worthy; just as all peoples are supremely worthy. All of these cultures remained substantially isolated from the rest of the world and therefore were unable to benefit and grow through contact with other cultures. Therefore these cultures had not attained a level of development that even closely approximated that of our major cultures in the pre-modern world. We have not been able to give greater consideration to these cultures in this book because such consideration is not directly pertinent to the discourse in this book. Truth was the subject of consideration in the previous section. We were concerned in the previous section about the nature of truth and its relevance for modernity. Civilizations are the subject of consideration in this section. Here we intend to explore the intrinsic nature of our four major cultural traditions from the perspective of the historical challenges posed by modernity. Historical issues are not necessarily ethical issues. Each cultural tradition is a product of different experience and has to confront different historical issues when it is confronted by modernity.

In the case of India, the modern moment also coincides with it attaining political independence and democracy. India like many other nations with an ancient history is beset with inequities. There however is an important difference in the case of India. India's multitudes also have a communal identity. They are divided on the lines of caste, language and religion. They do not merely want an end to inequities that they find around them. They also want to unearth and debate their respective histories. They want the miseries that they have endured at the hands of others to be placed on the table, interrogated and meaningful resolutions found. In short they want justice.

In the case of China, it has remained in relative isolation right through its history. It was surrounded by inner Asian tribes. These inner Asian tribes were culturally less developed than China. These inner Asian tribes sometimes dominated China and sometimes China dominated these tribes. As a consequence China has no experience dealing with other nations as equals[3]. Modernity now has effectively brought China out of its isolation. It is physically no longer possible for any country to remain in isolation. With the result, the great challenge that China faces is that it has to come to terms with nations that are, as a matter of principle, equals.

Some of the modern liberal notions of progress are antithetical to Islam. Islam is a religion of the book and has a well-defined set of laws. Muslims believe that these religious laws must be obeyed as they are the word of God. When Muslims become aware of a liberal, especially permissive, way of life in Western civilization they find it repulsive as it is completely antithetical to their way of life. So Muslims generally tend to be more receptive to advocacy that calls for a return to a more authentic form of Islam. On the other hand a few westernized Muslims want their countries to seamlessly embrace liberal values. The great challenge that Islam faces is in finding the right mix between progress and tradition on the one hand and in choosing decency over decadence on the other.

It is hard to imagine that Western civilization also would be affected by modernity as it is the home of modernity. Modernity has had its detrimental effect on the West as well. The great challenge that Western civilization has to ponder over is the destiny of freedom that it has so passionately embraced. Some of the benign consequences of this quest for freedom like abolition of slavery, women rights and decolonization were inevitable in the wake of modernity. (We have discussed this in chapter 2). The result of freedom is not entirely benign. As a consequence of freedom, the institution of family is greatly weakened in Western civilization. In a world where great inequities exist, is it just or ethical to provide freedom for some to consume way more than what they need? Many Western nations have passed laws permitting gay marriage. By extension would it be justified for brother and sister to marry each other? Will nudity in public be regarded as freedom of expression? In short where will this quest for freedom end? Answering this question is the great historical challenge that modernity poses to Western civilization.

All our major cultural traditions are historically challenged by modernity. Are there certain features in the evolution of civilizations that makes them vulnerable to modernity? The English historian Arnold Toynbee argues that all civilizations went through similar stages of historical evolution[4]. Then why is it that they are all differently challenged by modernity? In each one of our major cultural traditions, it is the circumstance in which they came into being that manifests as the source of the modern challenge. It is the nature of the origins and not the manner in which these cultural traditions evolved that gives rise to the different ways in which civilizations are challenged when confronted by modernity. We shall see below that the central issues that each of these civilizations face in the wake of modernity is closely tied to the nature of their respective origins.

In India, the Hindu caste system essentially was the outcome of contact and conflict between two peoples, the Aryan and Dravidian, each adhering to a different civilization. Today modernity has rendered the caste system historically absurd. The dislocated Backward Caste and Dalit (the term Dalit is used by erstwhile untouchables to identify themselves) people, who mostly constitute the civilizational descendants of the early Dravidians are asking fundamental questions about their historical oppression. The Hindu – Muslim veneer which defined politics in the subcontinent during the 20th century is tearing itself apart. Pakistan is disintegrating and in India even the though the Hindu nationalist party won a major electoral victory recently it did so on the promise of development and not on a vision of Hindu revivalism. The historical issues raised by the Dalits and Backward castes remain and needs to be addressed.

One of the earliest facets of Chinese history is the concept of Emperor. The Chinese Emperor was superior to all others on earth. This concept of Emperor existed even before all of China was politically unified as one country. In the feudal age period the Emperor ruled the capital and performed rituals to appease heaven. His extended family ruled the rest of the country. After the country was unified, the Emperor actually ruled the entire country. Even when China came under alien dynasties, the superiority of the Emperor, though of alien origin, was upheld. The modern international system renders such notions of superiority absurd. While great variation exists in the power and influence of nations and their leaders, at least in principle no nation is innately superior to another nation. Nor are the leaders of one nation superior to the leaders of another nation.

Islam is a religion of the book. Islam is also a religion of laws. Islamic laws are the word of God and followers have to obey it. In practice however Islamic teachings have been interpreted to meet existential needs. However there are limits to the degree to which interpretations can be made. Modern liberal culture is diametrically opposed to Islamic teaching and Muslims recognize it. Here again we see it is nature of the origin of Islam, namely the inviolability of God's law, that alerts Muslims to the decadence that surrounds them.

Christianity took root in the Middle East and it was brought to Europe. The cultural origin of Christianity was Jewish. The pre-Christian culture which Christianity confronted in Europe was Greco-Roman. The Pauline transmission of Christianity to the gentiles ended up destroying the Greco-Roman culture without replacing it with Jewish culture. So much so, to this day, the cultural origin of the Christian West is not discernible either as Jewish or as Greco-Roman. Nor can we say that it is a fusion between the two cultures. Indeed the culture of the Christian West merely had a few residual elements from Jewish and Greco-Roman cultures. When modern liberal ideas spread in Western civilization they did not have an organically evolved cultural core to contend with. With the passage of time these liberal ideas were embraced by the general population with relatively less resistance. In other parts of the world, especially outside Christendom, modern liberal ideas have largely been restricted to cities and even in that it is often restricted to sophisticated elites.

In all the four major cultures, the conflict with modernity surfaced roughly within a matter of a decade, beginning in the 1970s.

Above all else, India is a nation of communities. Indians identify themselves on the basis of caste, language and religion. Since independence right up until the year 1980, amity and peace existed among India's diverse populations. The central government was primarily concerned with issues of national security, territorial integrity and development. Up until that time the activities of right wing Hindu nationalist organizations were kept in check. After her election victory in 1980, Mrs. Indira Gandhi had decided to play with the politics of religious identities for electoral advantage. She started explicitly identifying with the Hindu religious tradition, openly following Hindu religious practices and eagerly visiting Hindu temples including the Bharat Mata Mandir in Haridwar instituted by the Vishwa Hindu Parishad, an extreme right wing Hindu Organization. She even met with the then chief of the RSS, an extreme Hindu right wing organization. As a consequence of all this she set in motion the political quest for Hindu nationalism or Hindutuva. In addition, towards the end of her term, she used the Indian army to attack the Golden temple, which is the most revered Sikh shrine. Needless to say India was polarized on religious lines.

Subsequently, India's backward caste Hindus and untouchables, who were becoming aware of their painful histories, refused to bandwagon with the Hindu nationalist project reasoning that it was Hinduism that had been oppressive to them all along. So much so the complete political fabric of India is now divided. The recent euphoria over economic development hides the reality of dissent that lays dormant in todays India.

The historic event that brought out China's reaction to modernity was Nixon's visit to China in 1971. Even after the founding of the PRC in 1949, China remained in essential isolation. By 1971 the Chinese leadership must have realized that modernity brought nations and people closer together and made them aware of each other and that integration with the rest of the world was inevitable. However China still had its emotional ties with its civilizational narrative which was founded on Chinese superiority. It offered an invitation to Richard Nixon only after - *"Knowing of President Nixon's expressed desire to visit the People's Republic of China"*[5].

From about the year 1600 we could say that Islam as a civilization was in the process of historic decline. Islamic states, which once conquered European lands and later engaged in rivalry with European powers, increasingly found themselves taking sides in European wars. This process continued during the cold war years as well. The first time an Islamic society took on a superpower, after Islam's substantial slide relative to the West, was during the revolution in Iran, which overthrew the Shah in 1979. The American embassy in Tehran was occupied by Iranian students and its staff taken hostage. The Iranian Revolution constituted an opposition to a liberal way of life. The revolutionaries sought to return their country to an Islamic way of life. Especially shocking were some of the restrictions imposed on women in the immediate aftermath of the revolution.

In the West the traditional family continued to be the central institution in society during the modern era right up to the 1970s. Towards the end of the 1970s the disintegration of the family was being regarded as a matter of public concern[6]. Up to the 1970s, the quest for liberty was essentially seen as being positive as in the freeing of slaves, procuring women's rights, decolonization, desegregation and promotion of democracy. That is to say, well after slaves were freed or well after women began obtaining their rights or even well after decolonization nobody regretted it. Whereas even now well after the family started disintegrating people tend to regret it. The disintegration of the family, perhaps for the first time, made the quest for freedom as the primary driver of history appear blemished in people's eyes in Western civilization.

We now need to get further insight into the essential being of the four major cultural traditions so that it may help us chart the course for humanity in the coming future. We seek to comprehend the nature of the four major cultural traditions from the perspective of the central issues that confront them in the wake of modernity. The nature and circumstance of each cultural tradition is different at this modern moment. Therefore we believe that the best way to understand them is through four essays, one on each civilization, on a topic that is pertinent to each civilization, in the wake of modernity. The next four chapters in this section will be made up of these four essays.

9. India: A World within the World

What is India? India is a nation that would baffle any observer. India is an ancient civilization. Almost all the major religions of the world have a sizable following in India. It is a polyglot nation in which many tongues are spoken. Indians divide themselves into countless castes. There are great disparities in wealth among its citizens. Yet India is also a modern nation. It has a written constitution, which legal experts continue to consult. It is a parliamentary democracy. English is the language of the educated classes. English usage continues to be very important in business, law and education. In the modern era Indians have passionately embraced science and technology. Cricket is the most passionately followed game in India. The ethos of the Indian army continues to be founded on British military tradition[1]. More recently India has embraced the free enterprise system. To top it all, India's Hindi film industry is called Bollywood, intentionally so named to rhyme with Hollywood. There is nothing uniquely Indian in any of these things. Parliamentary democracy, modern science, modern industry, the English language and the game of cricket are all of English origin and Hollywood is evidently American. Structurally what we witness in India is a continuation of the British Raj with some amendments made to account for the transition of international power from Britain to America. The major difference now is that Indians are at the helm of the Raj instead of Englishman.

What does this persistence with anglicization in independent India suggest? Are Indians so depraved a people that even after colonial rule ended, they would continue to yearn for the colonial ethos? Or alternatively is Western civilization a universal civilization to which all others ought to convert to and that India merely happens to be the earliest convert because it has had greater opportunity for contact through colonialism. China's embrace of the free market system after Deng's reforms and the supposed democratic aspirations of the now derailed Arab spring might have given some credence to this line of reasoning. Or is it the case that India does not exist at all and is largely a British creation. Winston Churchill rather disparagingly observed "India is merely a geographical expression. It is no more a single country than the Equator"[2]. Was Churchill right or was he wrong? We can better understand India by reflecting on Indian history and Indian metaphysics.

Several themes are evident in Indian history. One such theme has to do with the nature of order. Order in India has always been centered on a linguistically differentiated minority. The language of this minority becomes the preeminent language of India in each epoch. The earliest recognizable pan-Indian social order is the Hindu caste system. In it the Brahmins and by extension the Aryans were the linguistically differentiated minority and their language, the Sanskrit language, was the preeminent language. The Muslims created political order through a series of dynasties following one another. Muslims were politically dominant for five centuries. During this period Persian, which was one of the main languages of the Islamic world, was the preeminent language. The British created their empire, which came to dominate much of the 19th century and the first half of the 20th century. The British, by a conscious policy, created "a class of persons Indian in blood and colour, but English in tastes, in opinions, in morals and in intellect."[3] This class of English speaking Indians along with their

English masters constituted the linguistically differentiated minority on which British colonial rule was based. Later the English speaking Indians inherited independent India and the English ethos continued even after independence. Likewise for all practical purposes the English language continues to be the pre-eminent language in the subcontinent. This conception of order does not mean that other orders did not exist in Indian history. Even when Muslim rule and British colonial rule existed, the caste system ordered life among the Hindu population. The overarching order which was vested with the greatest power and had the prospect for the greatest control and influence is referred to here as order. It is this order that was always centered on a linguistically differentiated minority

The other theme that comes through in history is that India has been promptly punctuated by all the major historical trends in the world. When the ancient civilizations sprang up on river valleys, India had the Indus valley civilization. The German philosopher Karl Jasper writes that the period between 800 BC and 200BC was one of great intellectual and spiritual ferment in Greece, India, China and the Middle East. He refers to this age as the axial age. The Hindu Upanishads, the Buddha and Mahavira were from India during the axial age. When unified empires rose in different continents between 550B.C.E. and 27 B.C.E[4], the Mauryan Empire unified much of India around 286 B.C.E. After its classical period, when Islam expanded outside of its traditional lands, it established its rule in India just as it was dominant in the Mediterranean. When in the 19th and the first half of the 20th century the world was under European colonial domination, India experienced British colonial rule. When the different nations of the world were independent after the Second World War, India too was independent. We see evidence of this theme in recent Indian history as well. In the

1950s when capitalist democracy and centralized communism were ideologically pitted against one another, Nehru's India was equally idealistic both in being a socialist democracy and in being at the forefront of the nonaligned movement. In 1971 when idealism in international affairs gave way to realpolitik and Nixon went to China to forge friendship between Capitalist America and Communist China, India, a democracy entered into a friendship treaty with the Soviet Union. In the early 1990s when the cold war ended and the world began embracing *laissez-faire* capitalism India also liberalized its economy. Other civilizations also are affected by trends in world history but they tend to skip a step or do something way ahead of time. For instance Europe never had a river valley civilization. Likewise, after political unification in antiquity, China persisted with its notion of unified empire through much of its history unlike other civilizations. Even in recent times we see that other civilizations are not as integrated with international historical trends as India. While other nations were interacting with one another and were members of the United Nations, China remained in essential isolation until Nixon's visit in 1971. During the cold war years Western Europe did not exhibit the same level of ideological intensity that one found in America, China, Latin America, Africa, India and the Soviet Union.

 Yet another theme pertains to the historical aspiration of the Indian people. The India of antiquity latently yearned for a unified nation of its civilization called Bharat in the lands that its people traditionally inhabited. This yearning is akin to the yearning of Jews for Israel. In the Hindu Brahminical literary tradition, it finds expression in one of the plays written by India's most famous playwright Kalidasa called Shakuntala. We are told that all of India will be called by the name of Shakuntala's son Bharat. The Hindu epic Ramayana presupposes the existence of a unified nation of all of India in Bharathavarsha or Bharat. The golden age of Bharathavarsha in North Indian religious tradition is called Ramarajya – a period when God will rule on earth. The other Hindu epic Mahabharata depicts that great civil war that all Indians fought among themselves. The name Maha**bharat**a contains the word Bharat. While in Brahminical texts Bharat existed only in myth and destiny, it existed in fact under Buddhism. The Buddhist Mauryan Empire lasted 92 years and encompassed all of India except the three southern most kingdoms which constituted the Tamil country. This Buddhist Mauryan empire was called Bharat.

The next theme that we take up is the evolution towards Bharathavarsha, a unified nation of all of India, which can be witnessed in Indian history. India was rarely politically unified until the early 13th century. From the 13th century onwards the centripetal forces propelling India towards a unified state started getting momentum. It was the Muslims who put India on a permanent path towards political unification. Much of the northern plains of India were unified for 300 years under different Muslim dynasties and for another 200 years under the Mughal dynasty. Then under the British, all of India was unified for 90 years and this is followed by an independent India which has remained unified with English institutions, English ideas and an overarching anglicized culture now for 68 years. Based on what we know of India in the last seven hundred years we must conclude that it is the foreigner[5] who has provided India with the impetus to unite politically on a more or less permanent basis.

Another theme that is characteristic of India is that when a civilization ascends and its reach becomes global, the most ethical expression of its ascendant civilization is to be found in India[6]. While modernity had its origin in Western civilization, ethics was deliberated in the public sphere only in India under Gandhi's leadership in the modern era. Nehru's rule of India was in some way a continuation of the spirit of Gandhi in the political and administrative realm. In the same way in some future date when historians ponder over Islam's interaction with other cultures they are bound find its idealistic best in India. The relation between Muslims and Hindus in India was always difficult. This is partly because their religions were so different. Hindus are image worshipping polytheists and Muslims worship the formless God. Islam is a proselytizing religion whereas traditional Hinduism does not accept any converts. However one great religious teacher named Kabir found harmony between the two religions. Likewise Muslim rulers could never penetrate the consciousness of their Hindu subjects. In the middle of the 16th century an enlightened Mughal Emperor called Akbar succeeded in winning the confidence of the Hindus. Emperor Akbar took Hindu Rajput wives, had Hindu courtiers in his court and made a Hindu prince as his most trusted general. In addition he founded a syncretic religion based on the best elements of all the religions of his empire and even became a vegetarian. Just like Gandhi and Nehru in the modern world, in the future Kabir and Emperor Akbar may be regarded as the highest ethical expression of Islam's interaction with others.

Now let us state the central concern of Indian metaphysics. Metaphysical systems in India sought to transcend the realm of existence and sought something that was better and permanent. They found this in non-being or non-existence. Hindus believe that non-existence permeated all of existence.

Let us once again take up our original question – What is India? We will answer this question by relating the themes that we have highlighted above in Indian history to the central concern of Indian metaphysics. India is, above all else, a nation of communities. Order in India is centered on a linguistically differentiated minority. This minority defines what it is to be Indian. We could have a Brahminical India, a Muslim India or an English India based on the minority that is at the helm. India does not have an identity of its own. Until the 13th century when the civilizations of the world were in essential isolation, Indian metaphysics grappled with the notion of non-existence and cherished the idea of a politically unified India. During this period the Hindu caste system was the basis of order but it was constantly challenged and considerably undermined by Buddhism and Jainism. After the 13th century when civilizations ascended and started penetrating other lands, these ascendant civilizations started defining and ruling India.

India grappled with the notion of non-existence when the civilizations of the world were in isolation. Just like non-existence which has no identity of its own, India also does not seem to have any identity of its own. Historically India is defined by something as arbitrary as language. Non-existence pervades all of existence. Existence is made up of time, space and ego. Indian history is promptly punctuated by all the major trends in world history and this can be viewed as non-existence pervading time. The different civilizations exist mostly in geographically contiguous lands and they have distinct identities. When these civilizations ascend they reach India, India offers its land to these civilizations and takes on the identity of these civilizations – the taking of identity may be achieved either by offering the foreign civilization ultimate political power or a pre-eminent cultural and historical space. This can be viewed as non-existence pervading geographical space and civilizational ego. Therefore we can say that historically India pervades existence like the way non-existence pervades existence in metaphysics. Also from metaphysics we know that non-existence manifests itself within existence as higher ethical abstractions like love, truth and righteousness. So also when each civilization ascends and grows outside its traditional lands, the highest ethical exposition in its ascendancy finds expression in India. India then is the historical expression of non-existence.

We find evidence of this universal character in modern India as well. Different states in India and the different peoples within India can be viewed as being identical to their counterparts in the world today. The English speaking Macaulay Indians are akin to Western civilization. They are modern, live in urban areas, generally lead a middle class life and have considerable lateral and vertical mobility for advancement in life. The state of Tamilnadu, which has a unique ancient culture and one of the most industrialized regions in the country with a penchant for manufacturing, can be viewed as India's China. While China resists democracy, among all the people in India the practice of democracy is most ill-suited to the Tamil temperament. The Deccan states of Karnataka and Andhra Pradesh can be viewed as India's India. More than half the Information Technology professionals in India come from Andhra Pradesh but Andhra Pradesh is relatively underdeveloped, poor and great inequities exist among its people. In this respect it is very much like India. Indian software-engineers work all over the world but India is also home to great socio-economic misery. Bangalore, India's I.T. hub is the capital of the other Deccan state, Karnataka. Both Andhra and Karnataka have conspicuous dissent in their states. In Andhra, the Telegana region has broken away from Andhra Pradesh and has become a separate state within the Union of India. This again is similar to India which was a victim of partition at the time of its independence and encountered secessionist movements from within after independence. Karnataka has sizable minority populations like Marathi speakers, Muslims and Tamils whose identities may be in variance with the mainstream Kannada population. In some cases these minorities are viewed as being subversive. This is not again different from India which views Communist activities, Khalistanis in the Punjab, Tamil nationalists and Muslims with suspicion. The manner in which these two states reflect India is a little different. They reflect slightly different facets of India but that they are expressions of India nevertheless. The BIMARU states of Northern India which lag behind the rest of India in overall development can be compared to Sub-Saharan Africa. As in Sub-Saharan Africa, there is some misplaced euphoria over developmental prospects of the BIMARU states of Northern India. Such optimism does not take into consideration that these regions start from a lower base and therefore even long overdue basic structural changes to the economy or a cyclical rise in the prices of indigenous natural resources results in noticeable improvements in economic indicators. The Western Indian states of Maharashtra and Gujarat may be compared to larger countries in Latin America like Brazil and Argentina. These two states are industrialized and are relatively more developed than many other states in the Union of India and in that are similar to Brazil and Argentina which are industrialized and relatively more developed than other developing countries. However Latin American countries, though conservative by Western liberal standards, are generally free of the communal violence that one finds in Maharashtra and Gujarat. Kerala with its Communist inclinations, impressive social development indicators and relatively poor economic indicators is like Cuba and West Bengal can be compared to some of the culturally rich East European Countries on the periphery of Western Europe like Romania for instance. Punjab can be compared to Iran. Pre-revolutionary Iran was a relatively developed place in the Islamic world and so has Punjab been in India. Like the Iranians, the Punjabis are a flamboyant people. Just as Iran has been at the crossroads of Indian and Islamic civilizations, the Sikhs have been the moral fulcrum between the Hindu and Muslim communities of India, always tilting away from the unjust of the two. Pakistan can be compared to a militant Islamic society and Bangladesh can be compared to moderate Islam that can be found in South East Asia – the difference is that Bangladesh does not have the rich mineral resources that these South East Asian countries have, it is burdened with a large population and does not have an enterprising Chinese minority to drive the economy. Indian Muslims are like mainstream Arabs. India's Dalits can be compared to African Americans. Hindu nationalists are like the Christian Coalition in America. Many of the North Eastern states can be compared to historically isolated cultures of the South Pacific. The Indian subcontinent then is a world within a world.

10. The Chinese Mind

China must seem mysterious to any onlooker. Why would a country ruled by a Communist party embrace free market economics? How is communist ideology compatible with the Shanghai stock exchange? The inconsistency is not limited to the ideological realm alone. Modern China's interaction with other nations is filled with paradox. During the Vietnam War, the Chinese sided with their fellow communists in North Vietnam against the American backed South Vietnam. Then in 1979 China turned against Communist Vietnam and fought them. Until the late 1950s, India and China had an especially close friendship. In 1962, the Chinese fought the Indians in a border war. Likewise the Soviet Union was very friendly with China in the 1950s. In 1969 the Chinese and Soviets were engaged in a series of clashes along the Sino-Soviet border. Red China despised America during the 1960s but in 1971 China welcomed and publically received the American President Richard Nixon. Why this paradox? There is inconsistency in the actions of other nations. But usually they can be explained on the basis of ideology or realpolitik. But in the case of China the contradictions in its actions are more profound and readily noticeable that we must seek explanation elsewhere.

Are there certain characteristics uniquely Chinese that makes China think and act in a different way? Scholars tell us that when Chinese students and Westerners are asked to observe and to record their observations, Westerners tended to look at dominant themes whereas the Chinese looked at the entire picture. Similarly when Chinese students and Westerners were asked to classify objects, Westerners tended to classify them on the basis of categories whereas the Chinese classified them on the basis of functionality[1]. As an example Westerners classified the animals together whereas the Chinese classified the monkey with the banana because monkeys ate bananas. This tells us that different ways of thinking can be attributed to Westerners and Chinese people. However we are not interested merely in differences in thinking for academic purposes. Nor do we seek to identify differences, so as to facilitate easy interaction among people, as travel books try to do. In this section we are trying to grapple with the central concern that our major cultural traditions are confronted with in the face of modernity. How are we to know the central concern the Chinese are grappling with? Only from their actions can we know the central concern that China is grappling with. The actions of the modern Chinese government are made up of profound contradictions. They cannot be explained either by Communist ideology or realpolitik. Unlike in the erstwhile Soviet Union where Communist ideology was overthrown along with the Communist party, the Chinese have significantly diluted Communist ideology but have not overthrown the Communist party. Can we argue as Francis Fukuyama does, that by the last quarter of the 20th century the movement of world history was towards democratic capitalism and China was just another country in this international trend? An international trend becomes apparent only with the individual actions of different countries. Nations make choices for varied reasons. The key question is did Communist China undergo a transformation of the sort that the erstwhile Soviet leadership underwent before the Berlin wall fell. If it did then why did it not abandon the Communist party? We must look for rationales for China's actions in its history, its narrative and the ideologies associated with its narrative. Such an understanding is what we refer to as the Chinese mind.

There are five different facets of the Chinese mind. Firstly the Chinese have an intense sense of self. Secondly they believe that change is the only constant in life. Thirdly there is great emphasis on discipline in Chinese culture. Fourthly the Chinese perceive reality heuristically. Finally their concept of ethics is profoundly intertwined with reality. Now let us take up each of these facets one by one.

The Chinese traditionally believed that the whole world was under heaven and that China was at the center of this world. The undisputed leader of all of China was regarded as the emperor and this emperor ruled with the mandate of heaven. They also believed that the rulers of all other nations derived their authority from the Chinese Emperor. Non-Chinese were regarded as barbarians. This sense of self is a deeply held Chinese belief and is similar to Muslims believing that the formless God alone is worthy of worship or Western liberals who believe that representative democracy with universal suffrage alone is the ideal form of government. This is a belief that China sought to sustain even in the face of historical adversity. When China was conquered by non-Chinese inner Asian tribes, as the Mongols and the Manchus did, the concept of heaven's mandate was extended to the non-Chinese. The non-Chinese rulers were accepted as Emperors. During the opium wars of the 19th century when the Chinese were forced to acknowledge British sovereignty, such acceptance was seen as humiliation. Accepting British sovereignty would imply that the British monarch did not derive his authority from the Chinese Emperor. We see evidence for Chinese centrality in more recent times as well. International relations in the modern world are based on the equality of all nations. In theory, no nation is superior to any other nation. The head of state or the head of government of no nation is inferior or superior to his or her peers in other nations. But this is a notion that is antithetical to China's historical self-perception. During the Mao years China remained substantially isolated from the world. In fact, China had an ambassador in only one country in the world in the year 1969^2 and that was in Egypt. As a consequence in matters of protocol the supreme leader of China, Chairman Mao, could avoid dealing with his counterparts from other countries on the basis of equality. Later when Deng Xiaoping took over he was called strong man and was shielded from the requirements of protocol even when he retained ultimate authority over China. During these years an appointed Chinese President, who in the Chinese conception was hierarchically lower than the supreme leader of all of China, functioned as the head of state in matters of protocol in China's interaction with other nations. After Deng Xiaoping no single leader was accepted by the Chinese as the undisputed leader of all of China. After Deng's death the term paramount leader which is now used to designate the undisputed leader of all of China is seldom used and power is generally held collectively[3]. This sense of Chinese superiority especially as it pertains to the undisputed ruler of all of China is an important characteristic of the Chinese mind.

The next characteristic of the Chinese mind is that of change. The oldest book of Chinese civilization is the Book of Changes. After which, during the Han dynasty the Chinese thinkers took to co-relative cosmology[4]. Co-relative cosmology is the process by which one looks to nature to understand the process of change. Change in nature is observed and from this process the metaphysics of change is expounded. The seasons of the world – spring, summer, autumn and winter following one another may be an example of an observation that one makes about nature. Through a process of making such observations, the ancient Chinese found that the process of change culminates in opposites finding expression. This is philosophized in Chinese thought as the opposite forces of yin and yang finding expression, where yin is the dark feminine force and yang is the bright male force. Chinese thought encompasses the opposites. Both elements of a contradiction have their respective places. Lao Tzu's Tao Te Ching has many references to such contradictions. Since change is philosophized and has a right to be of its own accord, a perspicuous Chinese could co-relate events with his understanding of the process of change to ensure favorable outcomes. In some ways this is similar to a Hindu or even a Buddhist seeking astrological insight when he or she is struck by the calamities of life. To be sure modernity is a powerful force and science exerts a powerful influence on China as it does in India but that does not mean that all Chinese have entirely severed their links with alternate methods of knowing that were produced by their millennial civilization. The Chinese may have embraced market economics both during and after the Deng era based on a heuristic understanding of the process of change that they have inherited from their millennial past. We see antecedents for such political choices in China's medieval history. In the 13th century Genghis Khan set out to conquer empires and peoples by unleashing terror, violence and war. Genghis himself didn't conquer China. China was conquered by his successors using the same aggressive tactics. After the conquest, Genghis's grandson Kublai Khan took to Chinese ways and ruled China benevolently. It is not accidental that the then unprecedented terror, aggression, war and violence were followed by great benevolence. It is a profound expression of the Chinese mind. In other cultures ideologues try to strive for consistency. In China change is sought for its own sake. Everything has a place in time. The Chinese then are not being pragmatic nor are they hard headed realists when they change their stance in politics. They are giving expression to their metaphysical understanding of life.

There is great emphasis in East Asian Confucian thought on discipline. Even before China was called China, discipline was emphasized in China. Chinese civilization was referred to as the Way of the Li (Li meant ritual). Ritual was then used to inculcate discipline among the people. A ritualist says that the difference between the ritualist (that is the Chinese) and others is that while the ritualist (the Chinese) would do what ought to be done, others would do as they please[5]. When China was searching for an appropriate ideology during its passage from the feudal world to empire, Confucius reiterates this ancient wisdom of discipline through ritual. Other East Asian Confucian societies who have inherited their culture from China emphasize on discipline and order as well. The nail that stands out gets hammered is a well-known Japanese proverb. In other cultural traditions discipline may be cherished for its usefulness but in East Asian Confucian societies it forms the foundation of its cultural tenets. Therefore we include the emphasis on discipline as one of the characteristics of the Chinese mind.

Another aspect of the Chinese mind is that it perceives reality heuristically. This heuristic understanding of reality is akin to rationality for the Western mind. The Chinese not only comprehends reality heuristically, but such comprehension of reality may sometimes be inseparable from the response to reality. These heuristics may sometimes manifest themselves as proverbs. "The Chinese"[6] tend to "make"[6] these "proverbs up as they go along"[6]. We see evidence of this both in policy pronouncements and public perception. As an example Deng Xiaoping's "Its glorious to be rich" is a heuristic that served as a policy pronouncement. Likewise when Churchill stated that China was a civilization that was in search of a nation the Chinese responded by saying that America was a nation that was in search of a civilization[7]. This was public perception of reality intertwined with a response to that reality and expressed as a heuristic or proverb.

The last concept of the Chinese mind is their conception of ethics. Ethics to the Chinese is intertwined with reality. We have already stated elsewhere in this book that it was inherently not possible for a state to embrace political ideologies based on ethical criteria in the pre-modern world in the same way many modern nations have taken to socialism or democracy after becoming independent in the 20th century. Empires typically identified with religious ideologies and propagated them to the masses. It was the role of religion (or quasi-religious doctrines like Confucianism) to transform the individual and make the world a more habitable place. Since the empire was central to Chinese civilization and since it was inherently not possible to practice ethics with empire in the pre-modern world, in China the conception of ethics is generally intertwined with reality. The preeminence of the emperor is an ideal that the Chinese hold as absolute and has been pursued right through history like the way the ideal of freedom is pursued in the liberal West and the monotheistic ideal has been pursued in ancient Israel and Islam. The comparison of such idealism between China and the others stops right there. In Islam and ancient Israel the monotheistic ideal was accompanied by a system of laws which adherents strove to maintain or skillfully interpret. In the West, liberals have passionately sought to extend the ideal of freedom. Whereas in China there has been far less effort expended in adhering to dogmas in a consistent way. The Chinese conception of ethics is generally tied to attitudes. In eternal China individuals are rarely blamed for lack of intelligence or competence and are often taken to task for arrogance, non-conformity, irresponsibility and lack of effort on the individual's part. The Chinese value what is hard and difficult. The most esteemed occupation in traditional China was that of the scholar-bureaucrat followed by the farmer, artisan and only finally the merchant. This is understandable because the scholar bureaucrat is necessary to help administer the empire, the farmer sweats and labors harder than the artisan while the merchant merely wheels and deals.

There are implications for the Chinese mind and we will explore them here. Outsiders tend to think that the Chinese enjoy a wide range of flexibility in political choice. This is not entirely true. The Chinese are delimited by different considerations. Besides the pre-eminence of the emperor, the Chinese are not tied to any doctrinal ideological considerations and therefore have certain amount of tactical flexibility. Since it does not have an indigenous ideological system[8] that it identifies with, philosophy is China's most passionate import. In the pre-modern world the object of such import was Buddhism. In modern times it might very well have been Marxism. Once it imports a philosophical system it does not strive to adhere to it in a doctrinal way, as others do making accommodations only for reality and experience. China embraces the philosophy and changes it as an end in itself giving expression to different facets of the philosophy at different moments in time. Currently it is fashionable among neo-liberal intellectuals to talk about the end of history. China for its part had ended its history fairly early in its imperial trajectory. While empire of continental scope came into being in Europe, India and the Middle East at roughly the same time as in China, it persisted in China through much of its history. In other parts of the world it was more intermittent. Equal opportunity was almost impossible in the pre-modern world and became a possibility only after modernity had sufficiently penetrated a society. China had instituted the examination system even in antiquity and as it must have proven difficult to sustain, circumvented it with considerable nepotism. Ritual was used to inculcate discipline and peer pressure was used to order society. In each one of these things – in the persistence with empire, in the examination system, in creating a mechanism for self-regulation of society we see great resolution on the part of the Chinese. Since the object of resolution was order, they needed some mechanism for historical movement; otherwise the very reaction to the order would have turned against the order in a dialectical way. They obtained the mechanism for historical movement philosophically from their understanding of the process of change. Having resolved the historical questions fairly early in the history of their empire they used their understanding of the process of change to dispose of events. They would follow a course of action and for no reason at all would after some time follow another course of action. This does not mean that China did not have to face existential problems. Chinese like others were also confronted with threats to the empire from others and like all others elsewhere their first priority was protecting their empire from these threats. However in addition when they had the margin of choice, which they did, they imported philosophical systems that attracted them from other parts of the world and explored variations in the imported system. Besides they used their understanding of the process of change to order life and preserve their empire.

For a practical understanding of the Chinese mind it is worth pondering over the seminal foreign relations event of the People's Republic of China (PRC) namely Nixon's trip to China in

February 1972[9]. During the 1960s the rift between the two Communist giants China and the Soviet Union started widening, culminating in a series of armed military clashes along the Sino-Soviet border in 1969. Nixon wanted to pit Communist resources against one another so that they would not be available for worldwide expansion. Nixon's objective is fairly clear to us now but why did China respond favorably to Nixon's overtures? It is hard to imagine that the Chinese could have been intimidated by a few border clashes. After all they were dedicated Communists who began with little more than a few rifles and went on to claim the Kingdom of Heaven. They had taken on America during the Korean War when America had an outright nuclear superiority and were aware of the Soviet unwillingness to run risks during the Cuban missile crisis. So the argument that they sought strategic reassurance from America is untenable. It was more the case that the Chinese were co-relating with a heuristic on the process of change that their ancient civilization had uncovered. America and China had no diplomatic relations then and their initial communication was carried out through intermediaries. True to itself, in these initial exchanges, China welcomed the President of the United States to visit China and had offered to publicly receive him but it refrained from inviting him. The American President held office according to the Chinese narrative at the discretion of the undisputed supreme leader of all of China. China didn't see it fit to invite the American President. The American President had to come to China on his own accord. They would only welcome him and were willing to receive him publicly. After these early contacts, the Pakistanis arranged for Nixon's National Security Adviser Henry Kissinger to go to China on a secret visit code named Polo I. In their secret meeting Chou En-lai and Kissinger agreed that at a predetermined time both China and America would announce a predetermined message to their respective populations of the then upcoming Nixon visit. This predetermined message stated that the Chinese Government on "Knowing of Nixon's *expressed desire* to visit the People's Republic of China . . . has extended an invitation to President Nixon . . . President Nixon has accepted the invitation with pleasure"[10]. In other words Nixon asked to be invited to China. Why was China so unwilling to extend an invitation to President Nixon? After all in the last forty years China took part in the international system as an equal member and it has invited scores of leaders from other parts of the world to its soil on state visits. To the Chinese mind, Nixon's visit marks the end of millennia of self-imposed isolationism. It was asked to be part of the international system by the head of state of the richest, developed and most powerful country in the world – the United States of America.

To prepare for Nixon's visit to China, Kissinger embarked on a second trip to China code named Polo II. In China, in the room that Kissinger was staying, the Chinese had put a note that was derogatory to the United States. It is hard to imagine that a people who are as self-disciplined as the Chinese would have accidentally left an offensive slogan in sight of their principal ideological adversaries when they sought to make up with them. Kissinger thinks that this was most likely due to factionalism within the Communist ranks. It is certainly true that factions existed within China and Mao himself actively urged the proletariat to rise up against the bourgeoisie and later during the Cultural Revolution Mao inspired the Red Guards against intellectuals, bureaucrats and party officials. But in all these revolutionary uprisings the impetus came from Mao. These uprisings were not spontaneous outbreaks of people's movements but were pre-meditated by Mao. A policy of profound historical significance, as was rapprochement with the

United States, could not have been initiated without Mao's consent. If Mao consented to publicly receiving Nixon in China then it is untenable that a faction in Communist China would have placed statements that were derogatory to the United States within Kissinger's sight. If the Chinese wanted cordial relations with the United States they wouldn't be testing the limits of American patience in their initial contacts with America. Derogatory comments are bound to irritate adversaries and certainly not appear endearing to them. The derogatory comments were an end unto themselves. It has its origins in China's heuristic understanding of the process of change that they intuitively understood and applied as events unfolded.

In conversations with Kissinger, Chou En-Lai quoted a Chinese proverb which stated "The helmsman must guide the boat by using the waves; otherwise it will be submerged by the waves"[11]. This proverb describes modern China's understanding of reality with respect to the world around it in general and the Nixon visit in particular. China was the boat; the Chinese leadership was the helmsman, the prospect of complete nuclear annihilation was the equivalent of being submerged and the Nixon friendship overture was the geopolitical momentum that represented the waves. The reference to this proverb gives us an indication of China's reliance on proverbs and heuristics to comprehend and respond to reality.

After Kissinger's visit and before Nixon's arrival, the Chinese received the Ethiopian Emperor in China with great fanfare and adulation[12]. Why did the Chinese who were so lackluster in their public posture towards Nixon's visit show so much enthusiasm in receiving the head of state of a poor African nation? To China ethics is intertwined with reality and manifests itself in attitudes. Arrogance the Chinese understand portends disaster. To demonstrate that they were not arrogant they played host to a grand reception for the Ethiopian head of state. The Chinese were protecting themselves against the consequences of arrogance that their actions during Nixon's visit could have implied. In Kissinger's second visit he was taken on a boat ride for what the Chinese called contact with the masses. In contrast when Nixon's motorcade sped through the streets of Beijing they were bare and empty with no people at all. The Chinese pair of opposites found expression in their public contact with these two American leaders. Finally for Nixon's short meeting with Mao he was ushered in all of a sudden without any prior notice. Kissinger writes that Mao's remoteness during the visit was a show of majesty. This was once again a reiteration of the supremacy of the undisputed leader of all of China.

In the previous chapter we concluded that India was the historical expression of non-existence. Knowing what we know of the Chinese mind we need to ask the question: What is China? China has an intense sense of the self, which is the national ego. In addition, China understands the process of change from nature. We commonly understand nature as being made up of matter, energy and time. Matter, energy, time and collective ego are all facets of existence. Therefore we could say that China is the historical expression of existence, albeit a disciplined one. In recent years with the rapid economic growth of India and China there is a great temptation to compare them. In addition there are even attempts to pit them against one another as rivals. Nothing can be further from the truth. Except for the fact that both India and China are two ancient civilizations and both of them have spiritually drawn sustenance from eastern metaphysics there is very little in common between them. Indeed it would be more appropriate to compare America with China. Both America and China are large countries.

Both countries have traditions of isolationism. Both countries regard themselves as being apart from the world. The Americans believe in American Exceptionalism, whereas the Chinese believe in China's cultural superiority. Both countries have an appetite for large scale undertakings. Both nations excel in operational effectiveness. In both countries idealism is mixed with sizable doses of realism. Both countries have political traditions in which the office of head of state and head of government is vested in an individual person – President in the case of America and Emperor in the case of China.

11. The Ethical and Historical Dimensions of Islam's Interaction with Modernity

Modernity challenges Islam in the way it challenges other civilizations. Let us first recount Islam's interaction with modernity. Islam had its origins in the seventh century in Western Arabia. For a thousand years after its inception Islam remained the most ascendant civilization in the world. Even when Muslims were militarily overrun - as it happened during the Mongol invasion, the invaders were sufficiently impressed with the message of Islam that they converted to Islam. The decline of Islam coincided with the rise of European powers in the seventeenth century. By the nineteenth century the last of the major Islamic empires – the Ottoman Empire was regarded as the sick man of Europe. The rise of Europe was as real as the decline of Islam. Intending to reverse these trends, Muslim intellectuals pondered over the reasons for Europe's rise and their own decline[1]. The reasons they attributed to European success were superior weaponry, superior military tactics, industrialization and education. Clearly the intention was to emulate these European advantages. In this respect Islam did not differ from other non-Western countries. Russia during the time of Queen Catherine took to ideas from the European Enlightenment. Indians in the nineteenth century showed greater inclination towards modern education in English rather than learning in Sanskrit or Hindustani. After the opium wars the Chinese came to realize that the Chinese empire faced its greatest threat since its inception in the year 221B.C. They also realized that it was meaningless to try to defeat the Europeans and that one had to learn from them. The degree of Western material, technological and scientific advancement was so large that other nations didn't need to be persuaded to follow European ways. Some found European material civilization appealing while others found it useful and necessary.

The twentieth century was characterized by the rise of independent nation states. The nation state was itself a product of nineteenth century European political evolution. In the twentieth century the European idea of nation state caught on among the political elites of the Islamic world. At the end of the First World War, the Ottoman Empire gave way to the creation of modern Turkey which was a secular state. Later Muhammad Ali Jinnah spearheaded the effort to create Pakistan, which was to be the nation state of Muslims in the subcontinent. The Egyptian leader Gamal Nasser had dreams of pan Arab nationalism. There is nothing Islamic about the nation state. Politically until the twentieth century, Islam was characterized by multiethnic empires. During the cold war Muslim nations took sides - some with the Soviet Union and some with the United States. During the entire period of Western ascendancy up to 1979 Muslims like the Russians, the Chinese, the Indians, the Japanese and the Africans were not only receptive to Western science and technology but were also open to Western political concepts and ideologies. Though Islam continued to be cherished, it was no longer the lone source for organizing politics and society[2].

The Iranian Revolution in 1979 was a watershed moment in modern Islamic history. From that moment onwards Islamic societies began looking to Islamic sources with greater interest. But here again Muslims were not the only ones who experienced such transformations. Roughly during the same decade all our four major cultural traditions began transformations that were civilizational in nature. In 1972 China ended its millennial isolation with the Nixon visit, in the West the disintegration of the family had become widespread by the 1970s and in the early 1980s political impetus was provided to disrupt India's socio-communal amity in a manner that would force Indians to rethink their civilizational history.

Bernard Lewis, arguably the West's most distinguished scholar on Middle Eastern studies, has argued that the militancy and radicalism that is growing in the Muslim world is a continuation of the millennial rivalry between Christianity and Islam. Lewis calls it the clash of civilizations[3]. This implies that Muslim societies are unaffected by time. However even a cursory look at the evidence does not provide support for such a perspective. Within the framework of its law and tradition, Islam has been very receptive to ideas from other civilizations. While the West was reeling under the dark ages it was the Muslims, who sought and preserved the knowledge and wisdom of the ancients. It was the Muslims who took the number zero from India to Europe. Again Muslims helped popularize the numeral system that we use today. Also certain strands of Sufi in Islam were willing to synthesize prophetic monotheism with eastern metaphysical ideas from Hinduism. The only civilization that Muslims did not borrow ideas from was pre-modern Christian civilization. That was because Western Christendom was in the dark ages and culturally did not have anything to offer the Muslims and the Byzantine intellectual contribution was mostly theological. The suggestion of millennial rivalry as the reason for the current fervor in Islam is therefore a view that is not tenable.

How then are Muslims so passionately able to turn to Islamic sources for their ideology? Isn't modernity a historically transcendental moment? How can a pre-modern ideology suffice in coping with the requirements of modernity? To some extent the answer lies in the content of the Islamic message. Islam certainly predates modernity. Islam as a civilization reached its apogee in the middle ages. However for those who are prepared to look at Islam in context, its message must seem quite progressive. In the pre-modern world when social hierarchy was the norm, Islam advocates the equality of all believers and never had a formal caste system[4]. In other civilizations back breaking labor was the norm for the vast mass of humanity that was engaged in agriculture. Islam encourages trade and commerce and is more an urban civilization[5]. The Muslim diet has proportionately greater meat content than rice or wheat[6] and to that extent has been less reliant on back breaking agricultural labor. Islam advocates charity as a religious duty. Charity mitigates some of the inequities that characterized life in the pre-modern world. In some ways the Islamic message may have been more considerate than some of the modern alternatives. The Islamic ban on usury is one such case. The Islamic message clearly surpassed the modern world in some important aspects of women's welfare as in its absolute intolerance for prostitution and rape. One aspect for which Muslims societies get criticized for in our times is the imposition of the veil on women. Certainly the insistence on wearing the veil is a retrograde phenomenon. Muslim intellectuals[7], point out that there is no support for insisting on the veil, in the Quran. At any rate the veil is not worse than foot binding that was practiced in China and is definitely less harsh than the practice of sati which was followed in India - where a woman was burnt alive in the funeral pyre of her husband. The Islamic message is concretized in a system of laws. Therefore there is lessor discrepancy between the content of its message and its actual practice. This partially explains how Muslims are able to go back to the Islamic message.

In this context it would be useful for us to reexamine modern notions of progress. Are modern notions of progress really progressive? The nations of the world that are flag bearers of progress are also beset with many social ills. The disintegration of the family, teen pregnancy, the rise of single parent homes and the prevalence of narcotic drug usage are all social ills that are prevalent in the more progressive countries of the world[8]. Many of these social ills have started surfacing within the last fifty years. One may be tempted to argue that in going back to Islam, Muslims are trying to protect themselves from these social ills. That again hardly suffices as an explanation. An unmarried teen age girl becoming pregnant is unknown in the Islamic world, single parent homes are if anything a rarity and the family continues to be for the most part the bedrock of a Muslim's life.

What then do Muslims find obnoxious in the modern idea of progress. After all progressive ideas have ended slavery in the 19th century and gave independence to the nations of the world. They advocate equality for women and promote representative form of government. Progressive ideas have advocated the welfare of minorities and other historically downtrodden people and generally promote and encourage diversity.

We live in a world which is shrinking in distance at a breathtaking pace. The general Muslim population is vividly aware of events that take place in other civilizations. Books, newspapers, magazines, television, movies and the internet all depict other cultures pictorially. Immigrants take back tales of the world to their native lands. Muslims are aware of the liberal ethos of the Western world and find that it is in variance with their own values. The greatest area of discrepancy between the West and Islam is in the realm of human sexuality. Muslims then are taking a stance against the permissive sexual mores that are prevalent in the Western world. They are particularly opposed to all forms of sex outside marriage. The intellectual origins of their opposition to sexual permissiveness have its roots in the Islamic notion of sin. Since it is Islam that informs them that sexual permissiveness is not progress, it is not at all surprising that they are passionately turning to Islam for their ideological tenets. The vast majority of other eastern peoples who live in India, China, Japan and South East Asia are also not enamored by the sexual permissiveness of the Western world. Permissive liberal Western culture is appealing only to a section of the Westernized elite among Eastern peoples. However other Eastern cultures are far older than Islam and therefore had culturally inherited social ills of their own. These Eastern cultures realized on contact with modern ideas of progress that their cultures had to be purged of these retrograde practices. China comprehensively did away with foot binding and India ended child marriage and the practice of sati. India regards the continuing misery of untouchables as a horrific social menace and socially conscientious Japanese recognize the hardships faced by the Dowa and are working to end it. Islam too did have the institution of slavery. But the condition of the slave in Islam was mostly better than that of the free poor. At any rate in the nineteenth century the Ottoman Empire started a process of systematically curtailing slavery. This eventually led to abolishing the practice almost completely. So when faced with modernity Islam did not have to confront social inequities on the scale other civilizations had to confront. Consequentially Western liberal notions of progress do not have the same appeal to Islam as it does to other cultures. Therefore when Muslims started becoming aware of the sexual permissiveness in the Western world and its possible percolation in to their own world, they were at once both concerned and sufficiently self-assured enough to take a stance against it. Other cultures may not be as self-assured as Muslims in the social realm because of the social baggage that they brought to the modern moment but they are just as self-assured in other ways. The Chinese continue to value the concept of yin and yang and co-relate with the process of change that their ancestors had insightfully conceived. The Japanese arrive at decisions based on their centuries old system of consensus rather than through Western style deliberations. Indians believe in the primacy of their metaphysical systems, consult astrologers and continue to arrange marriages for their children.

The stance against sexual permissiveness is at the heart of Islam's concern against modern liberal ideas of progress. Islam takes this stance based on the message of Islam and its conception of sin. How will the world respond to Islam's stance against sexual permissiveness? The world can respond using both ethical and historical criteria. Needless to say the ethical criteria should take precedence over the historical criteria.

First let us recount some of our earlier ethical observations on sexuality for the modern world. The world of ours is filled with inequities. This is the reality that we face. In this world the ideal thing to do is to love and serve. A life of service alone is bound to be monotonous. Therefore we need recreation and entertainment to give us spite from the rigors of purposeful living. Entertainment however should not be an end in itself. Sex for procreation is necessary to propagate the human species. Besides that sex is no different from other forms of entertainment. Just as entertainment should not be an end in itself so also sex should not be an end in itself. Therefore any advocacy for greater more permissive sexuality cannot be ethically justified. In the spectrum of human sexuality, towards the opposite end of sexual permissiveness is fidelity in sexual conduct. Sexual fidelity is part of the relationship between a person and their spouse, lover or partner. Insistence on sexual fidelity ought not to be the business of the state or society. The only thing that must concern the state in matters of sexual infidelity is a willingness to grant divorce to those victims who seek it. Sexual infidelity is punishable under Islam. But to punish infidelity four witnesses are necessary and that is a practical impossibility. In effect Islam taboos sexual permissiveness but makes it very difficult, almost impossible, to punish sexual infidelity. The Islamic position on sexual permissiveness is more or less the same as the secular ethical position we have spelt out here.

In so far as sexual permissiveness is concerned, it is Western civilization that must self-examine itself. As we have shown above liberal advocacy for sexual permissiveness cannot be ethically justified. Sexual permissiveness raises another deeper issue that is never part of any public discourse or conversation and that is the destiny of freedom. Where then will this liberal quest for freedom end? Does freedom include the freedom to walk naked in the street? Does freedom include the freedom for a son to marry his mother or the freedom for a brother to marry his sister? We cannot provide an ethical answer for it. We need to get historical answers and these answers have to come in the fullness of time. When these answers come, Islam will have no reason to be opposed to the West.

Muslim opposition to a progressive liberal world view has understandably created fears in the minds of Westerners about Islam, especially as Islam happens to be a proselytizing religion. Will Muslims violently attempt to impose an Islamic cultural matrix on Westerners? If Muslims try to impose their religion forcibly on the West, it would certainly be wrong. There is no sanction for such a course in the Quran. Islam asks Muslims to fight a holy war only to destroy evil. Violent methods are not to be used to impose Islam on unwilling people. Indeed even if Muslims launched such an effort it is not likely to succeed. Islam is a monotheistic religion in which believers worship the formless God. On the other hand Westerners have all along been image worshipers. Even though Christianity was founded in the Middle East and has a monotheistic narrative, Christians are generally tolerant of images, icons, frescoes and paintings in their churches – a far cry from the strict abhorrence of images that characterizes Islam. In addition Christendom has been systematically secularizing its culture in the last five hundred years. The central issues of public discourse in Western civilization are entirely secular. The principal areas of public discourse revolve around the economy, national security, equality and the politics of liberty. People today in the West are not concerned about whether God has a form or whether he is formless. If people were primarily grappling with aspects of theology then the strict monotheism of Islam will have a certain appeal for them. It is not possible to make large population centers embrace religions that are fundamentally in variance with their experience. However there is nothing wrong in Muslims suggesting Islam as a solution for the West's problems as long as there is no compulsion to convert.

In addition, there is one area in which many Islamic societies experience difficulty in the modern world and that is development. However when development issues are statistically compared between nations, Islamic nations as whole do not look as bad as other developing regions partly because of oil wealth, partly because of the handsome handouts poor Muslim nations receive from more prosperous states and to some extent the message of

Islam which is relatively progressive. However if we look closely at other indicators of development like non fossil fuel related industrial output or the number of technical and scientific papers published in respectable journals then they lag behind[9]. Islamic nations can certainly benefit from a more direct administrative, technical and economic assistance from more developed countries.

No discussion on Islam's interaction with modernity can be complete without reference to the most volatile issue that Islam had to confront with in the last hundred years namely the Arab-Israeli problem. The enormous suffering endured by the Jews through the millennia has few parallels in world history. Gandhi refers to the Jews as the "untouchables of Christianity"[10]. Both Islamic and Jewish narratives anticipate the creation of Israel. Jews through the millennia have cherished the prospect of returning to Israel in their bosom. On the Islamic side too there is tacit affirmation for the existence of Israel. The Prophet Mohammed initially had made the Muslim faithful turn towards Jerusalem in prayer[11]. On finding, in Medina, that the Jews were not well disposed to Islam he made Mecca the holiest city in Islam[12]. In other words the Prophet Mohammed would claim Jerusalem and by extension Israel for Islam only if the Jews participated in his order. If the Jews did not participate, he is not interested in claiming Jerusalem for his people. Jerusalem in Prophet Mohammed's conception is associated with the Jews. If both Jewish and Islamic narratives associate Jerusalem, and by extension Israel, with the Jews then what is the cause of this bloody contention in the Middle East. In one word the answer is "Zionism". Zionism is a secular project. During the nineteenth century when the concept of nation state took root, Zionism became the vehicle for Jewish aspiration. Its object was to create a homeland for the Jews in Israel and to resettle Jews scattered all over the world there. Zionism differs from other forms of modern nationalisms in one important way. Other nations make a claim for modern nationhood based on the territory they currently occupy. Zionists make a claim for nationhood based on lands in which they presume to have lived nearly two thousand years ago. The Zionist state has been created and sustained by the Anglo-American political and military pre-eminence of the twentieth century. Needless to say, the Arabs in Palestine resented it because they had to give up land and therefore resisted the formation of the nation state of the Jews. That Arab resistance continues up to the present day. They could rather pertinently ask: Why should Arabs give up lands in which they have lived for centuries? If instead of Zionism, the attempt to create the state of Israel stemmed from a genuine religious enterprise, it could have obtained Arab consent with relative ease. A genuine religious enterprise by definition would have to be ethical and it would have made an appeal along religious lines. Such an appeal may very well have persuaded the Arabs to accept Israel. In this way the great ethical impediment to the creation of Israel, namely the lack of Arab consent, could have been overcome.

12. Secular Historical Reflections on the Second Coming

The second coming is the most important event in the Christian faith. It is the Christian belief that Jesus will come back to this world, destroy evil and would establish his righteous rule on earth. This righteous rule of Jesus is to last a thousand years. Here in this chapter we will be concerned with the secular historical aspects of the second coming and will not concern ourselves with the theological or ethical aspects. This is not to say that the theological and ethical dimensions of the second coming are not important. They certainly must be important. But the theological aspects do not lend themselves to collective secular human enquiry and to the extent possible we refrain from using religious language drawn from specific religious or cultural traditions to talk about the ethical domain in this book. (We have dealt with ethics in the section on Truth in this book). Despite our not considering the ethical or the theological aspects of the second coming here, we must note that the theological aspect of the second coming is not unrelated to its ethical dimensions. Christian ethics advocates individual perfection in the altar of love. Christian theology insists that even the imperfect can be redeemed through faith. Theology at once allows believers to bypass ethics and at the same time assures them of a world order in the imminent future in which ethics will be pre-eminent. This is a position that can only be sustained by one's personnel faith and is beyond the scope of secular human enquiry. On the other hand, the historical dimension of the second coming can be a subject of secular human enquiry. Using secular enquiry we can identify historical problems for which we are not able to provide meaningful secular answers. These are problems that appear real to us but their resolution seems intractable. These are problems that can only have transcendental, other worldly, religious solutions. It is such solutions that we attribute to the second coming in this book. We also limit our discussion of the second coming to the historical needs of Christendom as we have already discussed the central historical issues pertaining to our other major cultural traditions in the previous three chapters.

Christianity has had the longest continuous history only in the West, where the church functioned relatively independently with lesser direct interference. While the Eastern Orthodox Church has also had a continuous history, its geographical center was moved from Constantinople to Russia around the time when Constantinople fell to the Turks. Unlike the West where the Church had relative independence, in Russia and Byzantium, the Emperor (Czar in Russia) by tradition could overrule the authority of the Orthodox Church[1]. The Christian population in the Middle East and North Africa has been relatively small for a very long time. Elsewhere Christianity either did not have a continuous presence or was not demographically substantial. Therefore, though Christianity had its origin in the Middle East, we for all practical purposes regard the West as the home of Christendom.

The most intractable problem that confronts Western civilization is the destiny of freedom. Freedom has been the most cherished ideal in Western civilization for the last three hundred years. Freedom also has been the prime mover of Western history during this time. This preeminence of freedom in the Western world has also coincided with the spread of modern life. Modern life is characterized by great advances in manufacturing, transportation, communication and medicine. Mass manufacture enables large quantities of goods to be produced with great precision. Advances in transportation make travel and migration much easier and therefore people do not have to be restricted to their place of birth. Communication advances ensure that people can come to know of distant events with relative ease. Modern medicine has substantially increased the human life span. One of the consequences of all this is that it has increased both opportunity and mobility for humans. The call for freedom resonates with increased opportunities and greater mobility. If machinery could substitute human labor then there would be no need to possess slaves. Since modes of transportation were revolutionized, people, who until then were segregated, came into contact with each other more frequently. It was no longer physically possible to segregate people. As the Apartheid government in South Africa eventually found out – it was very difficult to operate a modern economy in a racially segregated society[2]. The dish washer, refrigerator, microwave oven, electric toaster, canned food, washer, drier and vacuum cleaner have all significantly liberated the women from domestic chores. Increased life expectancy has resulted in smaller families. Smaller families with fewer children and lesser domestic chores have freed women to pursue careers of their own. Likewise European colonial powers could not cherish freedom as an ideal in their domestic discourse and deny the very same freedom to their overseas subjects. Nor did these European colonial powers have the resources to keep restive populations perpetually under their control. Therefore freedom for slaves, freedom for women and freedom for colonized people were all, in time, generally welcome as being progressive. Advocacy for freedom was in a sense advocacy for the inevitable.

In time this quest for freedom has acquired a life of its own. Freedom besides being a source of good has also displayed its negative effects. Drug abuse, teen pregnancy and the disintegration of the family are some of the most pernicious effects of unabated freedom in Western civilization. In addition free societies also promote rampant consumerism. In a world where there are enormous inequities and great suffering it is out rightly wrong to promote such consumerism. As a result one thing is becoming certain and that is freedom can no longer be regarded as entirely a virtue which once facilitated the transition to modernity.

There is an even greater problem with the onward march of freedom and that pertains to its destiny. Where will this quest for freedom end? Is nudity in public an expression of freedom? Today it is legal to use marijuana not merely for medical purposes but also for pleasure. Will the consumption of other more potent drugs for pleasure also be legalized? Already the libertarians in America are making a case for unrestrained legal availability of all drugs. In many Western countries including the United States gay and lesbian marriages are legal. Some day will a case be made to legalize incestuous relationships as well? Some feminists have argued that women are socialized to being women and that there is nothing innate in their being that makes them behave like women. A similar argument can be made someday in the future, where one could argue that we are merely socialized to conform to incestuous taboos. In the run up to gain public acceptance for homosexuality, endearing letters written by the American President Abraham Lincoln to his male friends were shown as evidence for the prevalence of homosexual tendencies in previous eras. Now how much more ammunition will those who someday may seek to legitimize incestuous relationships have - Will not every act of natural affection that parents give children and siblings show each other, be held suspect? Human civilization has existed for over five thousand years in most places and most times without democracy and with much less freedom. Can human society function for even a single day if brother and sister can marry each other or if parent and child can marry each other? The destiny of freedom is a difficult and seemingly intractable question to consider. Therefore there is a tendency to put it off. The subject that societies choose to consider in the public sphere must be the ones that are likely to have the greatest impact on them. The more profound the impact of an issue the more urgent must its public consideration be. If a society merely considers only easy questions, it then is quite possible that it might miss the most pertinent questions and be lulled into believing all is well when it is not. Avoiding difficult questions is an irresponsible course. At least when we engage with difficult questions we have the possibility of arriving at answers. But if we don't engage at all we will be doomed when these questions become realities.

Alternately the case may be made that a society ought to be pragmatic and consider only issues which have practical relevance. The destiny of freedom may be viewed as an esoteric question which only select people like philosophers should worry about. Indeed the destiny of freedom was the domain of philosophers. Nietzsche was concerned about the destiny of freedom over a hundred years ago. It is only when problems caused by freedom started manifesting themselves are we making the case that we must consider it with the seriousness it deserves. The problems which are a consequence of unrestricted freedom like disintegration of the family, teen pregnancy and drug abuse are social problems experienced by people here and now. The next step in the trajectory of unrestricted freedom obviously seems nightmarish. There is nothing esoteric about these problems.

Another point of view that is advanced is that more urgent priorities like debt, deficit and unemployment must take precedence over cultural issues which tend to distract our public conversation. Unemployment is certainly an issue that requires immediate redress but in almost all the developed countries of the West there is some form of unemployment assistance that is available as a buffer. The impact of debt and deficit, for all their harmful effects, are experienced by a society only with the passage of time and not at the moment of borrowing or spending. Cultural issues that arise from the malevolent effects of the progress of freedom that we have highlighted here would easily be more devastating than the harmful effects of the debt or the deficit. Economic woes like debt or deficit will at best bankrupt a nation, destroy its credibility and leave its citizens impoverished. Many nations in history have been impoverished and we do see in our times quite a few third world nations are impoverished and their citizens living in abject poverty but we cannot conceive of a single nation in the world that can function with legitimized incestuous relationships.

Are those who express concern over the destiny of freedom fear mongers who simply seek to stir people up about possibilities that may never become a reality? Based on past experience we cannot make such assumptions. A hundred years ago most people would never have thought that pre-marital sex would be socially acceptable and yet it is the norm in Western civilization today. Towards the end of the Second World War, Gay marriage would have been unthinkable. Today homosexual marriage is legal in some nations (almost all these nations have been predominantly Christian and most of them are Western). What is to stop notions that are obscene to us today like incestuous marriage, bestiality or public nudity from becoming a reality tomorrow? Or would Western civilization treat them as an expression of multiculturalism and seek to legitimize it. If so then the one value

– multiculturalism, which has worked well in Western civilization in the last twenty five years has the prospect of becoming profoundly stained.

One could acknowledge the ugly destiny that is in store for the historical advancement of freedom, but may choose to cross the bridge when the time comes rather than worry about it now. This would be an extremely irresponsible course. Before we build a building we draw up a plan. We never start construction on a building without a plan. Before a business venture is founded a business plan is created. The founding fathers of the United States stated that all men were created equal in the Declaration of Independence even though slavery was practiced in the United States at that time. Though the political circumstances at the time did not permit the abolishing of slavery, they were hoping that slavery would eventually be completely eradicated in the United States. In other words they had some conception of the future when the United States became independent. In so far as the destiny of freedom is concerned we are grappling with issues that may arise as a result of an ongoing historical process. If we postpone judgment now we would be willfully facilitating the realization of the ugly consequences of the advancement of freedom. The ideal of freedom is so central to both Western history and to our conception of modernity at the present time that we cannot and must not avoid considering any malevolent impact that it may have in the future.

Can Western civilization protect itself from an ugly destiny that freedom could someday take it to? Before we attempt to answer this question we must consider what caused the problem in the first place. We have already described the cause of the problem when we provided an outline of civilizations in Chapter 8. Let us recount it here once again.

Christianity had its roots in the Middle East. The cultural origin of Christianity was Jewish. Paul broke Christianity's cultural link with ancient Judaism. Pauline Christianity, when it went to Europe, destroyed the Greco-Roman culture it found there but it did not replace it with Jewish culture. So much so, to this day, the cultural origin of the Christendom is not discernible either as Jewish or as Greco-Roman. Nor can we say that it is a fusion between the two cultures. Indeed the culture of Christian Europe merely had a few residual elements from Jewish and Greco-Roman cultures. When modern liberal ideas spread in Western civilization they did not have an organically evolved cultural core to contend with. In addition, liberal ideas were intrinsic to Western civilization. With the passage of time these liberal ideas were embraced by the general population with relatively less resistance. In other parts of the world, modern liberal ideas have largely been restricted to cities and even in that it is often restricted to sophisticated elites. Other cultures are delimited by their previous historical experience in accepting liberal Western ideas. Besides in our other three major civilizational traditions – India, Confucian East Asian and Islam - they have an organically evolved cultural core which prohibits liberal ideas from penetrating their respective cultures.

When modern civilizational scholars classify civilizations often we find that Christendom has more representatives than any of the other three civilizations. As an example Samuel Huntington identified seven or eight civilizations of which three or four belonged to Christendom namely Western, Orthodox, Latin America and possibly Africa (one could say Africa is partially Christian and partially Islamic). The next highest was Confucian, with China and Japan, with just two representatives. East Asian Confucian culture is five thousand years old, much older than

Christendom, and therefore must have had greater scope for variation within its ambit and should have had more representatives in any civilizational classification. That however is not the case. The reason that Christendom has more representatives in civilizational classifications of the sort Samuel Huntington proposed is because it is unified only in what it destroyed and not in what it had created. Civilizations have had substantial interactions with others. Some even imported religions from other civilizations. However in none of them except Christendom did their population become an altogether different people - almost completely different from their native or foreign cultures. China also had imported Buddhism from India but it did not allow Buddhism to destroy or replace Chinese culture. China co-opted Buddhism with its culture essentially intact[3]. Islam confronted and overcame a highly developed civilization in Iran. Even today the civilizational identity of Iran is unmistakably Islamic though a Persian substratum is discernible. Hindu Indian civilization is a product of two peoples Aryan and Dravidian adhering to two civilizations and speaking two different languages. Yet even after four thousand years of their interaction, in the twentieth century in the Southern Indian state of Tamilnadu, the Self-Respect movement was fairly successful in weeding out Aryan elements from Tamil culture. Freedom alone without the absence of an organic civilizational core would not have created the historical problems for the West that we have highlighted here. India is a democracy and the different Communities in India debate political, historical and social issues passionately but that has not thrown Indian civilization into disarray (though political and social life in India is characterized by unprecedented communal divisiveness!). Nor are the historical and social problems the West confronts, a consequence of development.

Japan is just as much an advanced industrialized first world country but it does not confront the profound historical dilemmas the West faces.

So what then is the solution for the Wests historical dilemmas? We cannot suggest that the answer lies in medieval Christianity. Westerners did not leave medieval Christianity through religious conversion. Had they left behind medieval Christianity through religious conversion at one previous moment then we can suggest a return to Christianity as a solution for their present historical dilemmas. They however left behind medieval Christianity through historical evolution - by a slow process that was primarily facilitated by ideas of the European Enlightenment. So our thesis that there is something inherent in Western history that is responsible for the dilemmas of the West is a reasonable one.

Likewise the West cannot take the civilizational matrix of another civilization. India and China are not aggressively proselytizing cultures and hitherto their cultures have been embraced only by kindred people who lived in geographical proximity to them and as we have made it amply clear in the previous chapter that the West will not be able to embrace Islam.

For Western civilization to protect itself from a horrific destiny that could descend on it, it needs a way of life. Democracy is a political system that is created to order political arrangements in a country. Capitalism is a way to organize economic life in a society. Neither democracy nor capitalism constitutes a distinct way of life. The West needs a civilization born anew[4]. Nobody knows what this civilization can be. A civilization is not merely a set of arbitrary cultural practices. A civilization is a spiritually integrated way of life. From a secular perspective such a civilizational solution for the West seems intractable. Therefore we refer to it as the historical aspect of the second coming. The one thing the West can do is to see what it can do now to ensure that the second coming will be favorable to it.

However we should not fail to note that the West's cultural dilemmas are historical issues and not ethical issues. We cannot blame the West for cultural ills like permissiveness in sexual life. Nor can we hail it as progress. Sexual permissiveness is not more evil than other heinous crimes like murder or rape. By the same token as we have stated in the section on Truth, that when sexuality is not for the explicit purpose of procreation it is no different from other forms of entertainment and all entertainment is only for recreation. Recreation cannot be justified as an end in itself in a world with great inequities and enormous social misery.

Destiny

13. The Way Forward

So far in this book we have arrived at some conclusions. These pertain to the Truth. We have also gained some insight into each of our four major cultural traditions. We will use our understanding, so obtained, to chart the way forward for humanity.

When we sought ethical resolutions for the modern world in light of the truth we came up with a structure for peace. The structure of peace we proposed was parentalism. Parentalism runs the risk of humiliation and exploitation. To realize parentalism without exploitation, humiliation and dishonor, it is absolutely necessary that Periyar's ideal of self-respect becomes the preeminent ideal that binds humanity. Without self-respect parentalism would be nothing but slavery.

Using the framework that we have laid out for the Structure of Peace we will try to chart the way forward for the nations and peoples of the world. We do not know the choices that leaders will make and the varied paths different societies will traverse. Nor do we seek to accurately anticipate all the twists and turns history will take. What we seek is a way forward which nations and peoples of the world could use, not as heuristic, but as a guideline to realize the Structure of Peace we have spelt out in this book.

We begin by identifying nations and peoples who either explicitly or implicitly could make ideological claims on modernity. Then we examine the historical relevance and ethical correctness of these ideological claims. In addition, we try to give useful suggestions to these nations and peoples for their onward journey. Finally towards the end of this chapter we provide a concrete way in which the Structure of Peace that we have laid out could be realized. We currently have a world order and this world order has an ideological basis to it. The nation that, for the most part, takes responsibility for the current world order is America. So we have included America. China is a rising power and has a historically evolved worldview, therefore we include China. India is obviously not making any unique ideological claim on modernity that is historically intrinsic to it. But we have shown in this book that even when other civilizations rise beyond their geographical spheres they not only encompass India but the most ethical expression of their rising civilization is to be found in India. Therefore we have included India, so that we can make some observations on whatever India may have in store for humanity. In this book we have presented parentalism as the Structure of Peace. Parentalism, we have also stated, ought to be realized only through Periyar's ideal of self-respect. Tamilnadu is the home of Periyar and Tamils have been the only people to have shown some receptiveness to Periyar's ideal of self-respect. Therefore we include Tamils. Islam is a comprehensive ideology and Muslim societies are increasingly gravitating to Islam as an ideology to help them cope with modernity. Therefore Islam is included. We have included Israel because it is politically at the crossroads between Islam and the West and certainly has the prospect of being the flash point in some future conflict. It is necessary we understand how Israel can facilitate resolution of such a conflict. Such resolutions would have a bearing on ideological claims made on modernity by others. Therefore we have included Israel. We have included the third world as they are bound to be the greatest beneficiaries if our world view is realized. In addition we also include Asia Pacific countries as some of these countries are world leaders in modern development, encompass enormous cultural diversity among them and in the past have put forward an alternate approach to development and therefore are worth considering.

America. America is without doubt the most powerful country in the world today. It is the richest nation with the highest GDP. Militarily America has the capacity to destroy the world many times over. Politically America sets the agenda for humanity. The U.S. dollar is the most used international currency. American Universities are disproportionately predominating in ranking among the top Universities of the world. America continues to be home to most of the technological innovations in the world. Despite its awesome power, Americans perceive two types of threats or challenges. On the external front Americans feel threatened by the environment, radical Islam and the rise of China. On the internal front Americans are challenged by the disintegration of their way of life and the national debt. Increasingly, Americans find these challenges difficult to comprehend even - leave alone finding a solution to them. In this book we have presented an alternate, indeed timeless, approach to problems using the potency of love and truth. America can use such an approach to finding solutions to these seemingly intractable problems. All America needs to do is to do what is right. Righteousness or Ethics is nothing but truth applied. Ethically, the single biggest problem that exists in the world today is the gross economic inequities that exist between nations and peoples of the world. It is caused partly by the inability of nations and peoples to take care of themselves and partly by the excessive consumption of a few. Structurally it is caused by the independence of helpless nations and globalized capitalism. We cannot blame anyone for helplessness, but globalized capitalism, as it is practiced in the world today, is the global face of evil. All other forms of evil like war, untouchability, racism and crimes against woman are either only local in nature or directly affect only some members of specific groups of people. Since America is the most powerful nation in the world, it must step forward to solve this problem. America needs to do three things to transform its capitalist system overnight into an ethical system. *Labor must be cherished in the culture at large, the principle of property inheritance must be abolished and consumption must be regulated so that citizens consume only what they need. Then the American capitalist system would become ethical instantaneously.* Physical Labor is hard and must not be treated with the frivolousness and condescension that it has been through the ages. Sneering at inherited wealth is quintessentially an American characteristic. America values individual achievement and personal responsibility and cherishes the ethic of the self-made man. In abolishing the principle of property inheritance we are extending the much cherished American ideal to all of society including to one's own children. Frequently in America's domestic discourse on the economy any attempt to increase the rates of taxation gets met with stiff resistance. Americans like smaller governments with lesser taxes. The recommendations we have made above not ought to have any impact on taxes as we only recommend that consumption be reduced to necessities. The regulation of consumption also need not frighten freedom lovers in America. America can regulate consumption through some sort of a citizen's forum like the jury system in America. Fellow citizens drawn from the wider community can help individuals regulate their consumption. Each person who is picked to have their expenses inspected by their fellow citizens (like those picked for a tax audit) should defend each expense they made, as having been necessary, to their fellow citizens who regulate them. If consumption is so regulated and the principle of property inheritance abolished then what does society do with the profits and surpluses? Individuals who make these profits cannot spend it on themselves nor can they leave it behind for their children. They simply have to give it away. The government can establish priorities for giving it away so that all the money does not end up in Museums or Art galleries. The government must ensure that much of this surplus is directed towards the domestic poor and helpless nations. Individuals and companies who made this money can have discretion on how this money will be given away. Nonprofit organizations and third world governments can compete for these resources. Since individuals who made this money decide who gets the money there will be accountability for the money given away. Since American citizens would have been regulated so as to ensure that they consumed only what they needed, nobody can accuse Americans of exploitation. As a consequence America would have unprecedented goodwill in the world. Third world nations can make an honest appraisal of their situation and may realize that they have cultural disadvantages that hamper them in establishing an effective self-government. Then they can ask America for help and America can help run specific government departments like education or health either through the auspices of the United Nations or even directly. America's national narrative beginning with the Declaration of Independence[1] through the abolishing of slavery right up to the civil rights movement and the active promotion of multiculturalism has systematically refuted the notion that people are innately superior or inferior to one another. With the election of President Barrack Obama as America's first black President, America has further disassociated itself from any notion of superiority or inferiority among people as part of its national narrative. Notions of superiority and inferiority among people along racial lines were introduced in the early 18th century by British colonialists well before the American colonies became independent. Periyar certainly allows for subjectivity in the conception of self-respect but to one who looks at it reasonably, America's national narrative would not seem to be an affront on the self-respect of any nation. Therefore third world nations need not stop with taking technical and administrative assistance from America. If and when third world nations are convinced of the nobility of intent of America then they can even be forthcoming in ceding authority over their government to America. America may carry out this same task through the offices of the United Nations but it must take responsibility for the outcome. America can encourage other Western nations and other East Asian Confucian nations to reduce consumption to their needs. If these countries comply then America can delegate some of the technical responsibilities that America has undertaken to them while keeping overall Administrative responsibility with itself. In the case of Asian nations which have well defined pre-modern structures they will be well advised to take the help of more able nations from amongst kindred peoples before seeking American parental help. This will ensure that the parental order will be sensitive to the cultural and historical experiences of these countries. Why must America take responsibility for other nations and other peoples? Other nations and peoples may be poverty stricken, endure epidemics and preventable diseases and may face enormous social misery and yet all of this will disappear in the fullness of time. Absolute truth operates in innumerable ways and therefore has in its potency to solve these and more problems. These people may be helpless but they are not dependent on America or any other nation. America needs to help other nations and other peoples for its own sake. America and other Western nations need a way of life. If history is any indication, the coming of a new way of life is always accompanied by great upheaval. If America took responsibility and successfully helped all helpless nations and peoples in a comprehensive and equitable manner then it would be a profound expression of truth and love. The potency of truth and love can, in all likelihood, be expected to circumvent the upheaval that would accompany the coming of a new way of life. For the same reason the rise of China, radical Islam, the environment and the national debt will not threaten America. How much time does America have to comprehensively end inequities in the world? America and the rest of Western civilization had all the time. Western civilization was more comprehensively aware of the value of an equitable economic order and social justice than any other civilization. Amos, Hesiod, Socrates, Plato, Aristotle, the Christian message of love and Thomas More have all reiterated this message through the ages. America has time until it is too late. President Barrack Obama spoke about – "the fierce urgency of now" - during his first Presidential election bid. The issue that America needs to act upon with "the fierce urgency of now" is the gross inequities that exist in the world today. No task is more urgent or more necessary than ending the gross inequities in the world and if President Obama takes it up and America succeeds in this effort, he would go down as one of the great Presidents in U.S. history.

China. China's rise in the last three to four decades has been truly spectacular. China like other East Asian Confucian nations has demonstrated to itself and the world that it can compete on even footing with Western nations in all areas of modern life. China plays its cards too close to its chest and therefore it is difficult to say what China's long term aspirations would be. China's historical view of the world is one of China at the center of the world with all other nations of the world as tributaries. This vision is laid out explicitly by Mencius. Mencius articulates this vision by quoting Confucius: "There are not two suns in the sky, nor two sovereigns over the people"[2]. This is understood to mean that all the rulers of all the nations of the world derive their authority from the Emperor of China, who is none other than the undisputed ruler of all of China. The vision for humanity that we have laid out in this book is one of parentalism, where nations that are better able to cope with modernity could help nations that have difficulty functioning in the modern world. Since China is a large country that is successfully able to function in the modern world and it has a historical self-perception of being at the center of the world, one may be tempted to think that China is in some ways the most appropriate nation to be the head of a parentalistic world order. Nothing can be further from truth. It is certainly true that China has successfully come to terms with modernity and therefore can play an important role in the affairs of the world but we cannot ask China to head a parentalistic world order because China has represented the nations of the world with condescension through the millennia. It has depicted them as *barbarians*. Even in the modern era it is not entirely clear that China has completely disassociated itself from its millennial perception of self-superiority. If the rest of the world participated in a parentalistic world order with China at the helm then it would be an affront to the self-respect of the nations of the world. Periyar does not allow that. No nation is inferior or superior to any other nation in the world. The poorest nation can continue to be poor, helpless and miserable but it ought not to participate in an order in which it has been deemed inferior. The honor of the nations of the world is greater than all the material benefits that these nations can have. However China can still use its enormous potential and play a useful role in world affairs. The world is beset with many evils like hunger, sickness, hatred and war. Though other nations will not be able to accept China as helmsman in world affairs, China can strive to remove evil root and branch in this world. The world will be profoundly thankful to China for such efforts.

India. In so far as the Indian subcontinent is concerned, the truth is upholding[3] Gandhi above all else. Gandhi may not have been as formally inspired by religion nor was he as formally associated with any particular tradition as Jesus was, but in so far as the moral content of his life is concerned, Gandhi is comparable to Jesus. The ancient Israelites bore false witness against Jesus and the Romans unjustly crucified him. As a consequence the ancient Israelites lost their temple and their nation. Also, as a consequence, the Romans lost their way of life and in the west lost their empire and slid into the dark ages. Just as Jesus was upheld by the truth so also we now see unmistakable early signs of Gandhi being upheld in the Indian subcontinent. The truth does not seem to be influencing events based on Gandhi outside the Indian subcontinent. This is understandable as Gandhi's cause was the cause of India. In the subcontinent, we can first see evidence for this in the fate of Pakistan. During Gandhi's lifetime, the powerful Muslim leader, Muhammad Ali Jinnah opposed Gandhi's idea of a unified India and created Pakistan - a separate nation for the Muslims of the subcontinent. What happened to Jinnah's creation? Pakistan since its inception has been on a downward spiral. It has been plagued by military coups and assassinations ever since it was created. In 1971 the eastern half of the country seceded from the western half to form the nation of Bangladesh. Now, on the one hand Pakistan is under assault from radical Islamists and on the other America is running bare foot through Pakistani territory as part of its war on terror. Pakistan is disintegrating by the day and the process doesn't seem to be reversible. Gandhi was for a non-violent struggle. In this, Gandhi was primarily opposed in his day by the militant Indian nationalist leader Subash Chandra Bose. Bose's famous dictum was 'You give me blood and I will give you freedom'. Bose tried to get the help of Axis powers to get Indian independence from Britain. He was willing to use military means but he failed in his efforts. Not only did Bose fail in his time, more recently, a militant leader of the Sri Lankan Tamils named Vellupillai Prabhakaran drew inspiration from Bose embarked on an armed struggle against the Sri Lankan state employing extreme violence and met an even more horrendous fate. Indeed when the history of independent India is written, the only armed struggle so far that would have had an enduring political outcome would have been the Indian effort in creating Bangladesh in 1971. But then India adhered to universal principles of right and wrong in going to war and displayed restraint during the war. This may prompt us to ask: If Gandhi is being upheld then how is it that India is seen to be on the rise and gets bracketed along with China as a fast growing economy? After all, Indians have strayed away from Gandhi in every possible way. Indians have even voted and democratically handed political power to a political party, the BJP, which subscribes to an ideology - referred to as Hindutuva, which had inspired the killers of Gandhi. Indians were certainly wrong in voting for a party that subscribed to an ideology that had inspired the killers of Gandhi. The truth will assert itself in India as it now is being asserted in Pakistan. The truth has merely delayed its assertion in India. Why? After independence and especially in the last two decades, India has witnessed an unprecedented inclusiveness of individuals from historically oppressed groups in positions of public leadership. Neither in British times nor in previous ages has India experienced this sort of inclusiveness of members of the untouchable and other backward castes in the public sphere. Truth and love have to take note of such a profound inclusiveness of historically oppressed people before profound transgressions against the truth are repelled. What forms will the assertion of the truth take in India? There are two ways in which the truth may assert itself in India. Let us explore and see what these two ways might be. Gandhi explicitly had said that he was a soldier in defense of Hinduism. In voting for a party whose ideological roots had inspired the killers of Gandhi, the Hindu people of India have expressed greater faith in the killers of Gandhi than Gandhi in the defense of Hinduism. Secondly empowering a political party that adheres to an ideology that had inspired the killers of Gandhi was a democratic act. The majority of the citizens of India through their elected representatives had handed over power to the BJP for the first time in 1998. In May 2014 the BJP has won an even more resounding election victory. The will of the majority is not greater than the truth. A group of people cannot gang up together and do as they please and hope to get away with it. In a court of law they may be able to get away with it but that is not possible in the altar of the truth. Democracy is not greater than the truth. So in the Indian subcontinent we can expect the truth to do two things with near certainty. One is that the defense of Hinduism, as we know it, is bound to fail. The other is that democracy will not endure in India. If democracy is to fail then what is to become of India? Indians will be wise to start thinking about the contours of a post democratic India right now so that they can at least save the Union for posterity. It is not so much that Gandhi was God but that the truth that Gandhi strove for with such earnestness was indeed God. Though Gandhi strove for perfection in his life, some of his contemporaries and many later commentators have spotted inadequacies and imperfections both in his ideas and in the way he lived his life. Apparently the all-powerful truth finds him sufficiently perfect to uphold him.

Tamils. Just as Gandhi is being upheld by the truth so also Periyar, separated from the ideals of the European Enlightenment, is being upheld by the truth. Periyar spoke the truth in public life, gave his entire wealth to the propagation of his beliefs, eschewed violence and refrained from seeking high office. In short Periyar lived the truth in his public life. However unlike Gandhi and Jesus he did not advocate the path of love and truth. His path was an unsentimental secular rationality. Indeed it is testimony to the majesty of the truth that Periyar is being upheld despite him being a secular atheist and an unsentimental rationalist. In the case of Periyar, he is being upheld to the extent he is because he lived the truth in public life and located himself amidst the Dravidians of India. Other nations and cultures have their downtrodden people but in the case of the Dravidians, an entire civilization has been condescended and relegated for all of known history. Periyar would have sneered at any attempt to seek co-relation between the nobility of intent or the truthfulness of one's life and the attainment of favorable outcomes as superstition. Nevertheless the evidence is clear. Periyar wanted the Muslim leader Jinnah to include the demand for Dravidasthan, an independent Dravidian nation comprising the four southern states along with the demand for Pakistan. Jinnah brushed him aside. As we had seen above, Pakistan has been floundering since its inception and the enormity of India's resources were stacked up against Pakistan all the while. Periyar declared India's Independence Day on August 15th, 1947 to be a day of mourning. In independent India, Periyar's ideal of self-respect does not have any prospect for realization – priesthood in Hindu temples continues to be the prerogative of ethnic Brahmins, Sanskrit continues to be the language of liturgy in Hindu temples, untouchability has not been comprehensively ended and caste based political parties have sprung up in Periyar's home state of Tamilnadu. While his declaring Indian Independence Day as a day of mourning would be repugnant to Indian nationalists and patriots, in so far as the prospect for the realization of his ideal of self-respect is concerned, Periyar has been proven right. After independence, Periyar consistently backed an idealistic Indian nationalist leader Kamaraj ahead of both the DMK, which then contested elections on a secessionist plank and the Communists. In consonance with Periyar's inclinations the people of Tamilnadu seem to be apathetic to secessionist aspirations. Periyar was opposed to participating in electoral politics. Two political parties the DMK and the AIADMK, that trace their political roots to Periyar, have successfully captured political power in the state of Tamilnadu but have compromised on their ideals and are perceived to be corrupt by both true Dravidian believers and the general population of Tamilnadu, thereby giving credence to Periyar's foresight. When Sri Lankan Tamils came to Periyar with their plight he welcomed them back to Tamilnadu, he did not advocate an armed struggle. Needless to say the armed conflict came to a disastrous end. There is only area in which Periyar is not being upheld by the truth and that pertains to his secular atheism and unsentimental rationality. Tamil culture is a religious culture and Tamils are a religious people. Such radically secular atheistic rationality has no roots in Tamil experience and the majority of the Tamil people are not able to embrace it. Besides the fact that Gandhi and Periyar are being upheld by the truth, there is another aspect of reality that Tamils must confront and that is the recently concluded war in Sri Lanka in which the Tamil Tigers were comprehensively defeated at Nandi Kadal lagoon. The place Nandi Kadal is telling and the truth seems to be giving a cue to Tamils.

Nandi in Hindu mythology is a bull that obstructs the path to the supreme Hindu God Sivan. Sivan is synonymous with love in Hinduism. Nandi Kadal means an obstruction that is as large as an ocean that has come upon Tamils due to the inadequacy of love. Vellupillai Prabhakaran's Tamil Tigers fought the injustice of the Sri Lankan state with single minded ruthlessness and extreme violence. Prabhakaran's Tamil Tigers were no doubt fighting injustice, but if they were allowed to win then that would be a victory for the way violence. As Gandhi is being upheld in the Indian subcontinent by the truth, there can be no final victory for unrestrained violence. But by the same token, the truth cannot choose the Sinhala over the Tamil because the Sinhalese perpetrated extreme violence and injustice towards the Tamils. Therefore the truth is giving a cue to Tamils by ending the war in Nandhi Kadal lagoon. If Tamils restarted their struggle with love and commit themselves to journeying with love and restraint then the truth would open doors for Tamils. Tamils are indeed a martial people with a great martial tradition but they should not even think about war. Even if they are ever forced to fight a war, they must proceed with great circumspection and restraint and immediately stop as soon as the political objective is realized. They must not harbor notions of revenge and must seek to transform people. Tamils justly have and continue to regard Prabhakaran as a patriot who was deeply committed to the cause of his nation. In addition, in the annals of war, Prabhakaran has shown unprecedented integrity in the protection of women. Even when his women were raped by his enemies, Prabhakaran and his men, to their lasting honor, would not forcibly touch any women, including those of their enemies. Certainly Tamils must celebrate Prabhakaran as a national hero and a patriot. But going forward patriotism alone is not sufficient. Tamils need to begin with the truth, wherever possible journey with love and make truth once again their destination. Therefore in the future Tamils must avoid Prabhakaran's extreme reliance in pursuing an armed struggle. Likewise, in so far as idealism is concerned, the future of Tamils lies in pursuing Periyar's ideal of self-respect. So far Tamil self-respecters have tried to pursue the ideal of self-respect as pure idealists. They do not want to touch anything even remotely associated with their historical humiliation. Therefore they avoid everything in formal religion and practice a form of secular rationality. This sort of secular rationality can be practiced only by people with a certain temperament. The vast majority of Tamils are not able to embrace it. Tamils are a religious people and the historical experience of Tamils does not lend itself to this form of secular rationality. Even though it is inherently not possible for Tamil self-respecters to root their ideological system in Gandhi, Tamils would be wise to take a page from Gandhi. Gandhi after all was one of the most successful politicians of the 20th century. Gandhi described himself as a practical idealist. Tamils too can move from pure idealism to practical idealism. Pure idealism will be of interest only to idealistic people whereas all people will find value in practical idealism. Indeed the purity of the ideal must be in the background as a guiding light and it is the practicality of the ideal that must be presented to the public. Tamils must deconstruct Hinduism and keep those aspects of Hinduism that are Dravidian in origin and leave of those aspects of Hinduism that are Brahminical in origin. In doing so, Tamils will not be participating in a narrative that had historically humiliated them. Therefore all of religion need not be thrown away. However, before we delve into aspects of Hindu Indian culture that are Aryan and Dravidian we must reiterate that notions of seeing Hindu Indian culture as being made up of two peoples (which we now know as Aryan and

Dravidian) with two different literary and cultural traditions precedes modern European scholarship by at least a thousand years. As an example, Tamil Saivam, the religion of the Nayanmars, despite being responsible for the enormous social misery and great humiliation of Tamils has ironically regarded the Tamil literary tradition as being distinct and separate from the Vedic tradition and even seems to have regarded both these traditions as being morally equivalent[4]. None of the present Gods that constitute the Hindu pantheon is of Aryan origin[5]. Puja as a mode of worship is again of Dravidian origin[6]. To be sure there are many aspects of Hinduism that are of Aryan origin and therefore humiliating to Dravidians. These ought to be changed but they must be presented to the public for their practical value. To begin with Non-Brahmins must be made priests in Hindu temples. Indeed we do not need an ordained priesthood at all. Devotees themselves can be priests in Hindu temples. Decorating the Gods with flowers or following some simple temple rituals is hardly a complex task and almost anybody can perform them. In this day and age when Obama, a black man, is the President of the most powerful country on earth, must we continue to reserve priesthood in Hindu temples for ethnic Brahmins? If Non-Brahmins are made priests in Hindu temples automatically the practice of Yagna (Yagam in Tamil) would be ended in Hindu temples and the Sanskrit language would not be used as the language of liturgy in Hindu temples as it is only the Brahmins who know Sanskrit and perform Yagnas – thereby further enhancing the ideal of self-respect. Rather the local language of the people must be made the language of liturgy in Hindu temples. Then people would understand the prayers that are being recited. While Tamils should not hate Brahmins as a people, Brahmins are certainly different from Tamils in their ethnicity, language affiliation and civilizational belonging. Expression of identity is not prejudice. However Tamils must ensure that Brahmins, neither substantially nor through symbolism, dominate them in anyway. Indeed a good way for Brahmins to help the cause of self-respect in India is to discard the poonool or sacred thread, which confers a superior status to them according to tradition. Dravidian self-respecters who are atheists today need not lose heart. Secular atheism is difficult to follow, but a successful attempt at de-Brahminisation of India is bound to revive transcendental atheistic religions like Buddhism or Jainism so as to preserve the eternal spiritual wisdom of India. If Buddhism is to take root then one would hope the austere Theravada Buddhism would be a nice antidote to our consumerist culture and therefore be preferable. Tamils need not keep this message of self-respect to themselves. They can transmit it to the world. Pursuing the ideal of self-respect, developing nations can honorably seek the assistance of developed nations and this can ultimately lead to the formation of a world government in which nations of the world can live as a family. The way to create unity is by spelling out the truth, walking in love, valuing non-killing and pursuing the ideal of self-respect. First Tamils must create unity among themselves before they create unity in the world. In recent years the Dalits (erstwhile untouchables) have broken away from mainstream Dravidians and some of the Dalit writers, inspired by deconstructionist ideas popular in the liberal academy, have attacked Periyar. Tamils must respond to these attacks point by point. One of the reasons that these writers cite for attacking Periyar is that the Dravidian movement is an elitist movement. It is true that many of the early leaders of the Dravidian movement were privileged non-brahmins and even later many of the leaders were from non-Brahmin communities that had been historically better placed in the Hindu caste order. But then as long as these groups enthusiastically engaged themselves in the political process, the Dravidian movement did not fundamentally compromise on its ideals. By the early 1990s these communities became far less enthusiastic in the political questions of the day and caste identities had replaced ideology as the principal factor in the politics of Tamilnadu. With the result the political party that had been the ideological mouthpiece of the Dravidians, the DMK, had struck a disgraceful electoral alliance with a militant rightwing Hindu political party – the BJP in 1999. Different communities in India have been shaped by vastly different historical experiences. Individuals of talent may be born in any community and must justly be recognized. However an individual's capacity to function is not the same as a group's capacity to function. The capacity of different groups to function as a whole varies based on their historical experience. In modern India, ideologically based political movements, which did not have the enthusiastic support of communities that were relatively better placed in the caste order, have effortlessly compromised their ideals on taking political power. One just has to witness the sharp distinction between the Dalit leader Mayawati's BSP and the Marxists in relation to the BJP, the radical right wing Hindu party. Mayawati entered into an alliance with the BJP whereas the Marxists have steadfastly been opposed to the BJP. The Marxists draw their constituents from both intellectuals and trade union workers. Intellectuals tend to be from communities who were better placed in the caste order and have helped the Marxists from straying away. This shouldn't be surprising as it is these communities who had greater opportunities in the pre-modern world and therefore have had some experience with idealism. So also it is with the Dravidian movement. Periyar, if anything offers to the Dalits the services of these relatively endowed groups at the best possible terms to the Dalits. Indeed the great historical legacy of Periyar is to have transmuted the falsehood of the European Enlightenment, which had seemed so seductive to historically oppressed groups, into a usable truth at a certain moment in history[7]. By responding to Dalit attacks on Periyar with the truth, Tamils can reunite Tamils once again. With unity Tamil society can work to comprehensively end untouchability in Tamilnad. Alongside Tamils can work to reunite India. In the previous section on India we had stated that the wisest course that Indians can take is to think about the contours of a post-democratic order. Tamils can offer India such an order centered on Periyar's ideal of self-respect. Self-respect can only come to India if Hinduism is de-brahminised. Tamilnadu is the only state in the Union of India that has the political will to de-brahminise Hinduism. Tamilnadu is also one of the most developed states in the Union of India. Such development in Tamilnadu is a consequence of the dynamism and creativity that gets unleashed by their more pure Dravidian culture. Therefore the people of India can embrace a parentalistic order in which Tamil societies will have core responsibility within the Union of India. Historically speaking there are two Tamil societies known to us. One is Tamilnad which is in India and the other is Eelam which is in Sri Lanka. However Eelam Tamils must on their own accord choose to come inside India. Other competent states that can fulfill the non-Brahmin vision in the Union of India can along with Tamils constitute a fraternity that would help shepherd the Indian nation. Needless to say the three southern states would be part of this fraternity along with Tamils. In addition the Sinhala nation, Pakistan and Bangladesh would also be welcome to join India. If they willfully join then the Sinhala nation, greater Punjab and greater Bengal can also be part of the national fraternity of responsible states. No state in India must be forcibly kept within the Union against its will. The parentalistic order can be created by evolutionary means. Today the democratic government in India is formed by the party that has the majority of the members in the People's assembly or Lok Sabha. The parentalistic government can be formed from the States assembly or Rajya Sabha in which only competent states that can implement the non-Brahmin vision would be members. Alternately Indians may respond favorably to parentalism when they come face to face with the inevitable. In the last few decades large cities like Mumbai (formerly Bombay) and Bengaluru (formerly Bangalore) have a huge influx of migrant workers from other states including Tamilnadu. As a consequence in these cities the language of the immigrant has become the language of the street. This is understandably resented by the native population in these cities. As a gesture of goodwill, Tamils through the offices of the government of Tamilnadu can offer to help these cities. Either Tamilnadu can advocate that these Tamil immigrants learn the local language and assimilate or alternatively in some phased manner find new employment opportunities for these migrant workers in Tamilnadu itself so that these migrants can return home. Tamil self-respecters have always held that the Ramayanam was an insult to Dravidians. Ramayanam is read reverentially by Hindus and its protagonist Ram is worshipped as God by millions of people all over India. Both as gesture of good will and out of sensitivity to religious feelings of worshipping Hindus, Tamils can use secular criteria to pursue the ideal of self-respect instead of attacking the Ramayanam and the Hindu God Ram. If Eelam Tamils on their own accord come inside India, then, one secular way that could help remove some of the insult experienced by Tamils due to the Ramayanam would be by taking the capital of India in lands historically occupied by Eelam Tamils - either Trincomalee or Jaffna may be good candidates. If the ideal of self-respect is used to transform the socio-political order in India then it is only reasonable that the transformation is extended to the symbolic. Some of the symbols of Indian nationalism are vestiges of the Indian independence era. As an example, the saffron and green of the Indian national flag were directly taken from the flag of the Indian National Congress, the political party which led India to independence. If India is to make the journey from independence to interdependence then it is only appropriate that the color of the political movement that facilitates this transformation finds its place in the Indian tricolor. The successors of the Self-Respect movement had all along identified with the colors red and black. However, unlike the DMK flag, the red should be on top and the black should be at the bottom to signify that the light had triumphed over darkness. In attempting to incorporate the ideal of self-respect into the national flag, Tamils should not disrespect or insult the existing Indian flag. A parentalistic order, so created, would be historically just. De-Brahminisation of Hinduism would provide Dalits, Backward castes and Dravidian self-respecters with answers in their search for meaning. Likewise it could prospectively help reassure Muslims and Sikhs and bring them back once again into the mainstream of national life. The Hindi heartland in Northern India and forward caste Hindus in Northern India can rest in the satisfaction that the Union of India would be saved for posterity. Many of the states in peninsular India that lie outside the Hindi heartland will find that in this order their relative competence has received pan-civilizational recognition. One should not dismiss such recognition as lacking in purpose or merit as such recognition is bound to have enormous significance in eastern cultures where group identity is greatly prized. Nor should anybody worry about the order prospectively becoming a hierarchical order in which people with authority and recognition think they are superior to others because the narrative or story of their coming together will cherish Periyar's ideal self-respect and therefore emphatically and continuously deny that there is any notion of superior or inferior among the people. Tamils need not stop with unifying India alone under a parentalistic order. They can pursue the ideal of self-respect even further and help unify the world. As a consequence Tamils can earn the respect of the world. Tamils are a language centered people. It is true that just as there are no two suns over the Chinese sky and there are no two emperors for the Chinese people so also there are no two pre-eminent languages for the Indian people. But no language group can claim a space for its language outside its native lands as a prerogative. Only the respect that Tamils earn through their deeds can translate into growth for their language.

Islam. As long as Islam uses violence for the destruction of evil, it is to be welcome. But if Islam uses violence to impose its way of life on others then that would be wrong. Islam can take the help of other nations in its development efforts. If a religious movement towards the creation of Israel takes root in the Middle East making a persuasive case for Israel on religious grounds then the Arabs may very well welcome such an Israel. A religious movement by definition would be ethical. Also a religious movement would be morally resourceful in ways that would be unfathomable to us. Therefore such a movement would disassociate with Jewish notions of being a "Chosen People". The international community can then advise Muslim societies to take such an Israel as the core state of the monotheistic world.

Israel. Modern Israel, strictly speaking, is not making an ideological claim on modernity. But Israel is so central to the politics of Islam and the politics of the West that it has profound repercussions. So we include it here. Jews have been waiting for their Messiah[8]. They have held that a religious movement will take the Jewish diaspora back to Israel. However the movement to create modern Israel has not been a religious movement but a secular movement called Zionism. Modern Israel in reality is not a Jewish state; rather it is the nation state of the Jewish people. Herein lies the difficulty. A modern nation state by definition is created in a place where people currently live. If a people have to migrate elsewhere and form a nation based on historical claims then that nation would not be a modern nation state. Such a nation may be a civilizational nation. Such a civilizational nation would be ethical in the way in which it is created and be a great nation. Since it would be ethical it would succeed in getting the consent of the Arabs. But one has to be patient. It is not evident that politicians will succeed in creating a civilizational nation. Modern Israel has the backing of America and the Arabs have a legitimate grievance and an overwhelming demographic advantage. The current struggle is bound to be bloody until a religious movement brings peace between the contending parties. The best secular human effort can only reduce the violence and will not succeed in delivering an enduring peace. On the other hand if a religious movement succeeds in obtaining Arab consent in re-creating a new Israel then such an Israel can use its natural advantages in the sphere of development and help Islamic nations. A religious movement by definition would be ethical and therefore would have disassociated with Jewish notions of being a "Chosen People". When this happens the international community can advise Islamic nations to accept the so created Jewish state of Israel as the core state of their civilization. Such an Israel can have a fraternal relationship with Turkey and Iran and a parental relationship with other Islamic nations in the Middle East, North Africa and Central Asia and help all these countries in their developmental efforts.

Asia Pacific Nations. Here we include Japan, all countries besides Vietnam in South East Asia (in this we include both mainland South East Asian countries like Laos, Myanmar, Thailand and Cambodia and maritime South East Asian countries like the Philippines, Indonesia, Malaysia, Brunei and Singapore), Australia, New Zealand and the Islands of Polynesia, Melanesia and Micronesia. Not only has this Asia Pacific region been relatively more developed than most other parts of the world but it has achieved this development with considerable civilizational diversity. Diverse nations in this region have succeeded in working together co-operatively for their mutual benefit. In addition, this region has come up with an alternate approach to working together dubbed *the Asian Way*, which values pragmatism and results rather than insisting on prerogatives. Not only do nations in this region belong to varied civilizational traditions but they are mostly free of the historical baggage that characterizes these civilizations in their traditional lands. Islam in South East Asia is relatively mild. Hindus and Buddhists living in South East Asia do not practice untouchability. Singapore does not regard non-Singaporeans as barbarians. While Japan certainly has issues with the Dowa, which we could regard as a historical baggage, the percentage of the Dowa is not demographically large and for a country with an ancient history as Japan the segregation of the Dowa was official only during the Tokugawa (Edo) period 1603-1867[9]. Distinct peoples in this region also exhibit considerable diversity in their ability to independently come to terms with the requirements of modernity. Japan, Australia, New Zealand and Singapore are the most developed nations in this region. Malaysia, Indonesia, Philippines and Thailand are somewhere in the middle and most other South East Asian nations and Polynesian nations can benefit from substantial help. Given the inclination of these nations towards pragmatic and result oriented solutions, we can expect this region to spontaneously gravitate towards a parentalistic order. If it does then Japan could be the core state having a fraternal relationship with Australia, New Zealand and Singapore and a parental relationship with the other countries in this region. Through much of its history, Japan was, for all practical purposes, only aware of two nations – China and Korea. Japan, occasionally, not unlike other nations, may have nursed a sense of superiority. However such a sense of superiority is not a central theme in Japanese history. Unless one is pedantic there is no loss of self-respect in nations from this region taking help from Japan and other developed nations in the region.

Third World. The word *third world* is a hangover from the cold war years. Today the word third world ought to refer to any nation that has difficulty in its development efforts. The first thing that the third world can do is to acknowledge that it has difficulty in its development efforts. In this book we have primarily cited cultural reasons for the difficulty experienced by third world nations. Therefore the third world need not persist with blaming others. To be sure there has and continues to be exploitation. But even if all the exploitation ended instantaneously, the woes of the third world would not be significantly reduced. The third world can begin an honest conversation about the need for help. The third world need not be hesitant in taking help from developed nations provided this help is offered without condescension. If the nobility of intent of the developed nation becomes apparent then the third world nation may even consider handing over complete authority of the state to the developed nation provided the developed nation does not consume any more than what it needs and is not making an attempt to absorb the third world nation into a narrative that inferiorizes the third world nation.

PEACE

Great opportunity exists for peace in the world. In this book we have spelt out a way by which peace on earth can be realized. Poverty can be completely eradicated. All peoples of the world can have the same facilities that exist today in advanced countries for education, health care and transportation. All this can be achieved by preserving the self-respect and dignity of all peoples. True and honest co-operation between nations can take place. The world can be politically united under one government. In such a world there would be no war. America, of all nations, is in the best position to bring such lasting peace to the world. President Barrack Obama spoke about – "the fierce urgency of now" - during his first Presidential election bid. America needs to act with the fierce urgency of now to create such a world. If America succeeds in creating such a world then it could be assisted by a fraternity of states in Japan, China, Tamil centered India, prophetic Israel as different from the Zionist state and either one or two nations from both Eastern and Western Europe in serving humanity.

In creating this world order America must be sensitive to the aspirations of other nations, especially in Asia. In the present world order, America is the most powerful nation, English, which is America's national language, is the lingua franca of the world and the headquarters of the United Nations is located in America. While America ought to retain responsibility for the world with itself, it would be well advised to take the language of the core state of one civilization as the lingua franca and a city from another core state as the headquarters of the new United Nations.

Appendix

Appendix 1

List of Countries of Central and Eastern Europe and Countries of the Former Soviet Union arranged in Order of Geographical Proximity to the West along with Development and Freedom Indicators

Country Name	HDI Rank for 2013	HDI Rank for 2011	Freedom House Rating for Political Rights in 2014	Freedom House Ratings for Civil Liberties in 2014
Germany	5	9	1	1
Austria	18	19	1	1
Czech Republic	28	27	1	1
Slovenia	21	21	1	1
Croatia	47	46	1	2
Poland	39	39	1	1
Bosnia and Herzegovina	81	74	3	3
Hungary	37	38	1	2
Slovakia	35	35	1	1
Montenegro	52	54	3	2
Albania	70	70	3	3
Serbia	64	59	2	2
Macedonia	78	78	3	3

Country Name	HDI Rank for 2013	HDI Rank for 2011	Freedom House Rating for Political Rights in 2014	Freedom House Ratings for Civil Liberties in 2014
Romania	56	50	2	2
Russia	55	66	6	5
Bulgaria	57	55	2	2
Ukraine	78	76	4	3
Lithuania	41	40	1	1
Latvia	44	43	2	2
Estonia	33	34	1	1
Belarus	50	65	7	6
Moldova	113	111	3	3
Georgia	72	75	3	3
Armenia	87	86	5	4
Azerbaijan	82	91	6	6
Kazakhstan	69	68	6	5
Turkmenistan	102	102	7	7
Uzbekistan	114	115	7	7
Tajikistan	125	127	6	6
Kyrgyzstan	125	126	5	5

Observations on Reading the Table in Appendix 1

- You generally see **a trend** in the table in Appendix 1 and that is, the closer to the West a country is the more developed and the freer it is.
- Germany which is closest to the West is most free and most developed.
- Uzbekistan, Tajikistan and Kyrgyzstan are farthest from the West but have among them the least development and the least freedom.
- This trend has **notable exceptions**.
- The countries that came out of the former Yugoslavia were affected by the Yugoslavian war and had to rebuild. The only country in substantial measure to have escaped the ill effects of the war was Slovenia.
- The Baltic Sea states Lithuania, Latvia and Estonia along with Poland have historically been more associated with the West than their geographical position suggests.
- Belarus and Moldova can be viewed as transition nations. Belarus's freedom is all but the worst whereas Moldova's development indicators are much lower than what its geographical proximity to the West might suggest.
- Russia's territory is expansive. Its developmental indicators showing a proximity to the West and its Freedom indicators showing its vast reach into the East.

Appendix 2 - Latin American Countries Ethnic Composition Based on Latinobarometro Informe 2011 and Correlated with Freedom and Development Indicators, in decreasing order of white population.

Country Name	Year of Independence	Ethnic Composition in Perentages							HDI Rank for 2011	HDI Rank for 2013	Freedom House Rating for Political Rights in 2014	Freedom House Rating for Civil Liberties in 2014
		Mestizo	White	Native American	Biracial	Black	Others	Asian				
Uruguay	1825	7	74	1	4	3	3	0	48	51	1	1
Argentina	1816	26	61	1	1	1	3	0	45	45	2	2
Chile	1810	25	59	8	1	0	2	0	44	40	1	1
Brazil	1822	17	49	1	13	17	1	0	84	85	2	2
Costa Rica	1821	31	40	4	17	3	1	1	69	62	1	1
Venezuela	1811	33	32	4	21	8	0	0	73	71	5	5
Paraguay	1811	55	29	3	1	1	2	0	107	111	3	3
Guatemala	1821	15	29	45	1	1	1	0	131	133	3	4
Colombia	1810	47	26	5	5	6	2	0	87	91	3	4

Appendix 2 - Latin American Countries Ethnic Composition Based on Latinobarometro Informe 2011 Correlated with Freedom and Development Indicators in Decreasing Order of White Population

Country Name	Year of Independence	Ethnic Composition							HDI Rank for 2011	HDI Rank for 2013	Freedom House Rating for Political Rights in 2014	Freedom House Rating for Civil Liberties in 2014
		Mestizo	White	Native American	Biracial	Black	Others	Asian				
Panama	1821	53	16	7	5	10	1	1	58	59	2	2
Dominican Republic	1844	29	11	4	24	26	0	3	98	96	2	3
El Salvador	1821	68	10	5	4	4	0	2	105	107	2	3
Honduras	1821	62	9	13	5	2	1	1	121	120	4	4
Peru	1821	76	6	7	1	1	1	1	80	77	2	3
Nicaragua	1821	67	6	8	2	3	0	1	129	129	4	3
Mexico	1810	52	6	19	2	0	3	1	57	61	3	3
Ecuador	1822	81	4	7	3	3	0	1	83	89	3	3
Bolivia	1825	57	4	27	1	1	1	0	108	108	3	3

Appendix 3 - Latin American Countries Ethnic Composition Based on Latinobarometro Informe 2007-11 averages Correlated with Freedom and Development Indicators (countries ordered as in Appendix 2)

Country Name	Year of Independence	Ethnic Composition							HDI Rank for 2011	HDI Rank for 2013	Freedom House Rating for Political Rights in 2014	Freedom House Rating for Civil Liberties in 2014
		Mestizo	White	Native American	Biracial	Black	Other	Asian				
Uruguay	1825	6	78	1	3	2	3	0	48	51	1	1
Argentina	1816	20	68	1	1	1	3	0	45	45	2	2
Chile	1810	25	60	7	1	0	1	1	44	40	1	1
Brazil	1822	28	35	2	15	15	2	0	84	85	2	2
Costa Rica	1821	28	46	3	14	2	1	1	69	62	1	1
Venezuela	1811	35	30	4	17	7	0	1	73	71	5	5
Paraguay	1811	36	35	2	1	1	4	0	107	111	3	3
Guatemala	1821	29	17	44	2	1	2	1	131	133	3	4
Colombia	1810	43	29	5	5	7	1	0	87	91	3	4

Appendix 3 - Latin American Countries Ethnic Composition Based on Latinobarometro Informe 2007-11 averages Correlated with Freedom and Development Indicators.(order as in Appendix 2)

Country Name	Year of Independence	Ethnic Composition							HDI Rank for 2011	HDI Rank for 2013	Freedom House Rating for Political Rights in 2014	Freedom House Rating for Civil Liberties in 2014
		Mestizo	White	Native American	Biracial	Black	Other	Asian				
Panama	1821	55	17	5	5	11	1	2	58	59	2	2
Dominican Republic	1844	28	12	5	25	27	0	2	98	96	2	3
El Salvador	1821	64	10	5	3	2	2	1	105	107	2	3
Honduras	1821	56	14	12	3	3	1	2	121	120	4	4
Peru	1821	72	7	8	2	2	1	0	80	77	2	3
Nicaragua	1821	66	8	7	3	4	1	1	129	129	4	3
Mexico	1810	49	30	8	1	4	2	3	57	61	3	3
Ecuador	1822	78	6	7	3	3	0	0	83	89	3	3
Bolivia	1825	60	4	27	1	0	1	0	108	108	3	3

Appendix 4 - Latin American Countries Ethnic Composition Based on Dr. Francisco Lizcano Fernández's work in 2005 Correlated with Freedom and Development Indicators (countries ordered as in Appendix 2)

Country Name	Ethnic Composition									HDI Rank for 2011	HDI Rank for 2013	Freedom House Rating for Political Rights in 2014	Freedom House Rating for Civil Liberties in 2014
	Mestizo	White	Native American	Biracial	Black	Other	Asian	Creoles & Garifunas					
Uruguay	8	88	0	4	0	-	0	0	48	51	1	1
Argentina	11	85	1	0	0	-	3	0	45	45	2	2
Chile	26	69	5	0	0	-	0	0	44	40	1	1
Brazil	0	54	0	39	6	-	1	0	84	85	2	2
Costa Rica	15	82	0	1	0	-	0	2	69	62	1	1
Venezuela	38	17	3	38	3	-	2	0	73	71	5	5
Paraguay	75	20	2	4	0	-	1	0	107	111	3	3
Guatemala	42	4	53	0	0	-	1	0	131	133	3	4
Colombia	53	20	2	21	4	-	0	0	87	91	3	4

Appendix 4 - Latin American Countries Ethnic Composition Based on Dr. Francisco Lizcano Fernández's work in 2005 Correlated with Freedom and Development Indicators. (countries ordered as in Appendix 2)

Country Name	Ethnic Composition									HDI Rank for 2011	HDI Rank for 2013	Freedom House Rating for Political Rights in 2014	Freedom House Rating for Civil Liberties in 2014
	Mestizo	White	Native American	Biracial	Black	Other	Asian	Creoles & Garifunas					
Panama	32	10	8	27	5	-	4	14	58	59	2	2
Dominican Republic	0	15	0	75	8	-	0	2	98	96	2	3
El Salvador	91	1	8	0	0	-	0	0	105	107	2	3
Honduras	86	1	8	2	0	-	1	3	121	120	4	4
Peru	32	12	46	10	0	-	1	0	80	77	2	3
Nicaragua	78	14	7	0	0	-	0	1	129	129	4	3
Mexico	70	15	14	1	0	-	1	0	57	61	3	3
Ecuador	41	10	39	5	5	-	0	0	83	89	3	3
Bolivia	28	15	55	2	0	-	0	0	108	108	3	3

Appendix 5 - Latin American Countries Ethnic Composition Based on CIA World Factbook Correlated with Freedom and Development Indicators (arranged by decreasing order of White Population)

Country Name	Ethnic Composition								HDI Rank for 2011	HDI Rank for 2013	Freedom House Rating for Political Rights in 2014	Freedom House Rating for Civil Liberties in 2014
	Mestizo	White	Native American	Biracial	Black	White & Mestizo	Mixed	Other				
Uruguay	8	88			4				48	51	1	1
Argentina		97						3	45	45	2	2
Chile			5			95			44	40	1	1
Brazil		54	1	39	6			2	84	85	2	2
Costa Rica			2		3	94		2	69	62	1	1
Venezuela	67	21			10			5	73	71	5	5
Paraguay	95					59			107	111	3	3
Guatemala			41	14					131	133	3	4
Columbia	58	20	1		4		3		87	91	3	4

Appendix 5 – Latin American Countries Ethnic Composition Based on CIA World Factbook Correlated with Freedom and Development Indicators. (arranged by decreasing order of White Population)

Country Name	Ethnic Composition								HDI Rank for 2011	HDI Rank for 2013	Freedom House Rating for Political Rights in 2014	Freedom House Rating for Civil Liberties in 2014
	Mestizo	White	Native American	Biracial	Black	White & Mestizo	Mixed	Other				
Panama	70	10	6				14		58	59	2	2
Dominican Republic		16			11		73		98	96	2	3
El Salvador	90	9	1						105	107	2	3
Honduras	90	1	7		2				121	120	4	4
Peru	37	15	45					3	80	77	2	3
Nicaragua	69	17	5		9				129	129	4	3
Mexico	60	9	30					1	57	61	3	3
Ecuador	65		25		3			7	83	89	3	3
Bolivia	30	15	55						108	108	3	3

Reading Appendix 2, 3, 4 and 5

1. In Appendix 2 and Appendix 3 the total percentage of all the ethnic communities in a nation does not add up to 100. These tables are based on self-identification surveys in which respondents could choose Don't know/No Response. We have not included this column into the table because of space constraints.
2. In Appendix 4 and Appendix 5, the data had decimal places in them. We have rounded these decimals to the nearest whole number percentages.
3. We have used the term biracial to mean Afro-biracial born in Latin America between one parent who is predominantly European and one parent who is pre-dominantly African.
4. The 18 Latin American countries we have included are a subset of countries that are found in all the different sources. The most conspicuous exception in this list is Cuba. Cuba has been included by Dr.Lizano (Appendix 4) and in the CIA World Factbook (Appendix 5) but omitted by Latinobarometro Informe.
5. According to Dr. Francisco Lizcano Fernández's work in 2005, Cuba's population is 37% White, 51% Afro-biracial, 11% Black and 1% Asian.
6. According to the CIA World Factbook, Cuba's population is 65 % White, 10% Black and 25% Mixed.
7. Cuba's HDI rank for 2011 is 51. Cuba's HDI rank for 2013 is 59. The Freedom House Rating for Political Rights in Cuba in 2014 is 7 and the Freedom House Rating for Civil Liberties in Cuba in 2014 is 6.

Notes

Notes

Preface
1. Gayatri Spivak in the preface to her translation of Jacques Derrida's *Of Grammatology* cites the very existence of a preface to suggest the inherent incompleteness of any book. I am dismayed by the currency this line of reasoning receives in the academy and among the intelligentsia. As for me, a preface is best defined by the book *Words into Type* where it contrasts the preface with an Introduction – '*A preface or foreword deals with the genesis, purpose, limitations, and scope of the book and may include acknowledgments of indebtedness*'. One may write a new book on high school mathematics so as to present the same material in a different light. In this case the author would put the motivation for the new presentation in the preface. The preface would not have anything about mathematics proper and would not add anything to the mathematical content of the book. Nor would the absence of such a preface take away anything from the completeness of the mathematical content of the book.

Chapter 1: An Ethical Interrogation into the Pre-Modern World
1. We use the term transcendental to mean historically transcendental. This should not be confused with metaphysical transcendence which could refer to a better place that we have not experienced like heaven or a better state we have not experienced like the Buddhist nirvana.

Since modernity is historically transcendent we could experience the greater possibilities here in this world.
2. Jacques Barzun has written a book titled *From Dawn to Decadence: 1500 to the Present: 500 Years of Western Cultural Life*. As the title suggests extraordinary changes began taking place in Western civilization in the year 1500 and has continued ever since. Paul Kennedy explicitly states this process began in the year 1500 in his book *The Rise and Fall of Great Powers*. In the *Cornel West Reader*, Cornel West refers to the period 1492-1945 as the age of Europe.
3. See *The Oxford History of Western Philosophy* edited by Antony Kenny page 210 in the section under Marx in Chapter 4 titled "Continental Philosophy: Fichte to Sartre" for Marx's six stages of historical development. This chapter is written by Roger Scruton.
4. See the section The Rise of Mao Zedong on pages 301-305 under Chapter 15 titled The Second Coming of the Communist Party in John King Fairbank's *China: A New History* where one can see Mao Zedong substituted the peasantry for the urban proletariat and made a break with Marxist-Leninist analysis of history advocated by the Comintern.
5. See Lev Grossman's Time magazine article titled "2045: The Year Man Becomes Immortal" in Time dated Thursday, Feb. 10, 2011 in the Science section for a technological vision in which humans and machines would merge with one another into a singularity radically increasing human life expectancy. This has led to the speculation that death could be transcended and human immortality could be realized. Such a realization we believe will constitute a transcendental moment in world history. The theorist popularly associated with Singularity is Ray Kurzweil.

6. **Aristocracy.** See page 144 of T.G.Parkin's *Demography and Roman Society* (1992) for Life expectancy in the Roman Empire.
7. **Aristocracy.** In Public Agenda, Andrew.L.Yarrow had written an article titled "History of U.S.Children's Policy, 1900-PRESENT" where he stated that in the year 1900 in the United States about 1 in 4 children under the age of 5 had died. (Public Agenda is a non-partisan, non-profit think tank in the United States).
8. **Aristocracy.** See the section Formation of Gentry Society on pages 101-107 under Chapter 4 titled China's Greatest Age : Northern and Southern Song in John King Fairbank's *China: A New History* for a discussion on China's gentry class and its relationship to the working class.
9. **Aristocracy.** See the Chapter titled "The Elites" in Bernard Lewis's *The Middle East: A Brief History of the Last 2,000 years*. In Islamic terminology the aristocrats were referred to as Khassa (meaning special) and the working classes as Amma (meaning general). In fairness, the Doctors of Law constantly strove in Islam to dissuade differences from arising within the Muslim community.
10. **Aristocracy.** For early Indian history, I have taken the view that Indus valley civilization was a Dravidian civilization and that **most** of the indigenous people of India who lived in India before the early Aryans arrived were Dravidians. Please see the views expressed by researcher Iravatham Mahadevan in *Towards a scientific study of the Indus Script* in The Hindu Magazine dated Sunday, Feb 04, 2007. In addition, also see Asko Parpola's *Deciphering the Indus Script*. Both these researchers subscribe to the Dravidian origins hypothesis. In addition, Karen Armstrong says that the majority of the people who lived east of the Ganges were indigenous people in her

book *The Great Transformation: The Beginning of our religious Traditions.* See pages 232-238 in Chapter 6 titled Empathy in the Great Transformations which depicts life in India between 530B.C.E and 450B.C.E. I am further persuaded in this view by the presence of a Dravidian substratum in North Indian Indo-European languages. Modern scholars, of late, tend to think that in early India there were three or four language speakers. Several language speakers may co-habit a place and some may even speak more than one language but that does not constitute a homogenized population. Their ethnicity is inseparable from their native language. In the case of early India, the ethnic difference is conspicuously self-evident in the Vedic social organization. Varnashrama Dharma is the name for the Vedic social order. It was a term that was coined in early India. 'Varna' means color. The Vedic social order was made up of four Varnas or four colors, meaning skin color. If the principals who created the Vedic social order in early India thought it appropriate to refer to their order on the basis of racial categories, then why must we exhibit reservation in calling it 'racism', especially when the subsequent history of that caste order in India has been horrendous? Besides among the non-Aryan ethnic groups that lived in early India, the Dravidians were demographically numerous and culturally more advanced. By virtue of ethnicity, language and civilization it is the Dravidian who has hierarchically been inferiorized with respect to the Aryan. The tribals, on the other hand, have continued to live at the periphery of mainstream society, mostly independently, until modernity intruded into their lives. Objectivity should not be used to blur the centrality of Dravidian humiliation in the writing of the early history of India.

11. **Aristocracy.** See pages 83-84 under Chapter 4 titled Modernization and Social Equality in Bernard Lewis's *What Went Wrong? : Western Impact and Middle Eastern Response* where Lewis says that as late as the early 19th century it was more likely for a man of humble origins to attain to wealth, power and dignity in the Islamic World than in Christian Europe.
12. **Aristocracy.** Niccolo Machiavelli in *The Prince* makes the case that it is better a ruler derives his support from the people rather than from the nobles in the Ninth Chapter titled "Concerning a Civil Principality" in page 73. Likewise Aristotle extols the aristocracy in his famed treatise *Politics*. Aristotle gives us three ideal forms of government namely Monarchy, Aristocracy and Constitutional Government in this order. Their corresponding corrupt forms are Tyranny, Oligarchy and Democracy. Since in the Aristotelian view Aristocracy is regarded as an ideal form of government next only to Monarchy we say that Aristotle extolled the Aristocracy.
13. **Aristocracy.** The decadence in Florentine Italy during the Renaissance becomes evident through the life and work of Girolamo Savonarola, who lived then and avidly campaigned to rid the city of vice.
14. **Economy.** Norman Roth, who edited the *Medieval Jewish Civilization: An Encyclopedia* (Please use the internet link below in the Bibliography to go to Norman Roth's article on Jewish Money Lending. This article appears in the MyJewishLearning website), says that The Church prohibition against usury was at its height from the end of the 12th century and all through the 13th century. However he goes on to say that it was ineffectual as many church leaders including the Pope himself flouted it. There also were Italian gentile moneylenders in France and Germany. While Norman Roth may be right and all these may

certainly be true it does not explain specifically why Jews took to moneylending in large numbers. The stigma against Jews who were viewed as Jesus killers apparently segregated them socially and the prohibition of the Church while certainly not comprehensive must have had some effect on the faithful.
15. **Economy.** For deriding mercantilism in China see John King Fairbank's *China : A New History*. In this, Fairbank shows how in each major dynasty mercantilism was derided. In page 55 he shows how it was derided by the Qin, in page 59 how it was derided by the Han, in page 96 how it was derided by the Neo-Confucians, in page 108 mercantilism is least esteemed of the four occupations of China, in page 135 he shows the Ming detestation of mercantilism. Only in the late imperial period would the merchants may have moved around with some ease and as reference for it see page 180 in the Fairbank book. We see profound expressions of charity in the Sangam poems, in the Thirukural, in Avaiyar's Nall Vazhi and in the life of the Saivaite saint Pattinathar in the Tamil tradition. Charity is one of the five pillars of Islam and it is obligatory on the part of Muslims. Charity is referred to as Zakat and is next only in importance to submission to God in the Islamic faith. For social welfare carried out by the Methodists in the 18th century in England see chapter 5 under The British Enlightenment titled Methodism: "A Social Religion" and for moral sentimentality see chapter 6 tilted "The Age of Benevolence" in Gertrude Himmelfarb's *The Roads to Modernity: The British, French, and American Enlightenments*.
16. **Ethnicity.** The ideological basis of the English Enlightenment in the 18th century was moral sentimentality and as reference for it see Chapter 6 tilted "The Age of Benevolence" in Gertrude Himmelfarb's *The Roads to*

Modernity: The British, French, and American Enlightenments. Moral sentimentality meant practicing arbitrary acts of kindness and generosity in response to the pain and suffering that one sees around oneself. The anti-slavery movement took root in the moral universe of moral sentimentality. The anti-slavery movement began with the Quakers in the 18th century and later was more widely advocated. For references to the anti-slavery movement see pages 210-214 in the Chapter titled Race and Slavery in Thomas Sowell's book titled Race and Culture: A World View.
17. **Religion.** In Chapter 4 of this book titled Civilizational Narratives we try to show how each one of our major cultural traditions were ethical in their inception when discussing their respective ideals. Three out of our four major cultural traditions are religious traditions.
18. **Religion.** All the great religious teachers we have highlighted may not have explicitly spelled out love as their primary message but love is evidently implied in the totality of their message.
19. **Religion.** In Chapter 4 of this book titled Civilizational Narratives we try to show how each one of our major cultural traditions failed to live up to their ethical ideals when discussing the respective realities of their existence as is manifest in their respective histories.
20. **Religion.** Please see Premarital sexual intercourse among adolescents in Malaysia: a cross-sectional Malaysian school survey conducted by L.K.Lee, P.C.Y.Chen, K.K.Lee and J.Kaur. Pre-marital sex especially among teenage girls is a good indicator of the sexual permissiveness in a society. This survey finds around 2% of teen age girls in Malaysia had pre-marital sex. In Asia the range is between 2-11% whereas it is much higher in Britain, America, Sub-Saharan Africa and Brazil. Also see

a journal article in Journal of Sex Research v35, n4 dated Nov, 1998. by Eric.D.Widmer, Judith Treas and Robert Newcomb titled *Attitudes Toward Nomarital Sex in 24 Countries* where you see huge discrepancies between the two Asian countries Japan and the Philippines that were part of the survey and the rest – made of Western and East European nations including Russia - when asked whether sex before marriage was not wrong at all. The least number of people from the two Asian countries said that it was not wrong at all.

21. **Outcastes.** We have used the first part of George Hart's book *The Poems of Ancient Tamil, Their Milieu and Their Sanskrit Counterparts to* help us understand the origin of untouchability in India.

22. **Outcastes.** We see two perspectives emerging on the condition of the Osu. One is an expression of outrage on the condition of the Osu based on their place in traditional society and the other insisting that their condition greatly worsened after colonialism.

23. **Outcastes.** Modern scholars have studied the ancient Tamil Sangam poems and have tried to reconstruct life in that period. They argue that Untouchables then were regarded as being lowly. However we must understand that the Sangam poems in Tamil are an anthology. An anthology is a collection of literary works. An anthology is neither a canon nor does it necessarily constitute a national or religious narrative. Ancient Tamils discovered the medium of writing and composed poems. The Sangam anthologies have poems in them that are lofty. The renowned poem in Purananuru (poem number 192) beginning with the words Yadhum oorae Yavarum Kalir (யாதும் ஊரே ; யாவரும் கேளிர்) says that we need not look up at people above us and even more importantly must not be condescending to those below us. So in

ancient Tamilnad while people may very well have looked down on their fellow human beings, there were also enlightened individuals who cherished the brotherhood of men. However, neither of these dispositions of the people had an ideological basis. They merely reflected the attitudes of individuals.
24. **Vegetarians.** Yogendra Yadav and Sanjay Kumar in a front page article titled "The food habits of a nation" in the Indian newspaper called The Hindu dated Monday, Aug 14, 2006 report on a *Hindu-CNN-IBN State of the Nation Survey* which says that about 31% of India's present population is vegetarian and another 9% consumes eggs but is vegetarian otherwise.

Chapter 2: Western Modernity
1. Samuel Huntington makes a reference using citations from other scholarly sources in Chapter 3 – A Universal Civilization? Modernization and Westernization under the heading The West and Modernization on page 68 of his book *The Clash of Civilizations and the Remaking of World Order* where he says the scientific, technological and industrial developments which began in the 18th century in Europe and led to a highly developed complex form of life is comparable to in the scale of its advancement to the establishment of river valley civilization (civilization in the singular) which began on the banks of the rivers Tigris, Euphrates, Nile and Indus around 5000 B.C.
2. In Ancient Rome you had the rule of the law. According to Aristotle it is the Constitution that defined the State and Democracy was practiced in ancient Greece. (See Aristotle's Politics). The ancient Chinese had instituted the bureaucracy during the Han dynasty (See Fairbank's

China: *A New History*). Plato's Republic was a communist state and of course the institution of family has existed since time immemorial.
3. In the History of Western philosophy disparate thinkers like Kant and Hegel are typically grouped together under German idealism to contrast it from empirical approaches that were largely associated with the British. Barzun uses the term idea-ism to signify that the idea presupposed the comprehension of reality. See pages 507-509, ironically in a Chapter titled *Cross Section: The view from Paris 1830 in* Jacques Barzun's Dawn to Decadence for a discussion on German Idea(l)ism. In a technical sense this sort of classification may be right but the nature of reality that is comprehended is vastly different. Kant is using categories to further understand empirical observation whereas Hegel views the Spirit unfolding all through history. Given that many of the prominent thinkers of German origin use history as source material to make important socio-political and historical observations it would not be particularly inaccurate in associating German thinkers with ideas using history as source material.
4. Kant is the closest among major Western Philosophers in seeking resolution between love and reason but does so in verbiage that is far less accessible than 'Love thy neighbor as thy self'.
5. In modern India, ideologically based political movements, which did not have the enthusiastic support of communities that were relatively better placed in the caste order, effortlessly compromise their ideals on taking political power. One just has to witness the sharp distinction between the Dalit leader Mayawati's BSP and the Marxists in relation to the BJP, the radical right wing Hindu party. Mayawati entered into an alliance with the BJP whereas the Marxists have steadfastly been opposed

to the BJP. The Marxists draw their constituents from both forward caste intellectuals and trade union workers. The presence of the forward caste gives them the cultural and historical resources to draw upon in upholding their ideals. So also it is with the Dravidian movement. As long as non-brahmin groups that were relatively better off in the caste order enthusiastically participated in public affairs the Dravidian movement did not compromise on its ideals.

6. See the Prologue of Gertrude Hilmmelfarb's *The Roads to Modernity: The British, French, and American Enlightenments*. On page 5 she says that reason was the most prominent of the many values espoused during the Enlightenment.

7. See the Prologue of Gertrude Himmelfarb's *The Roads to Modernity: The British, French, and American Enlightenments*. On page 5 she says that virtue was noticeably absent during the discourse on the Enlightenment. In this book I have used the terms like morality, ethics, virtue and righteousness interchangeably.

8. Gertrude Himmelfarb in her book *The Roads to Modernity: The British, French, American Enlightenments* attempts to bring to the forefront, the missing ethical dimension of the Enlightenment, but succeeds only in demonstrating that this missing ethical dimension was the moral sentimentality of the English Enlightenment. See Chapter 6 tilted "The Age of Benevolence" in this book.

9. Socrates shows Tracymachus that it is advantageous to be good in Book 1 of Plato's *Republic*.

10. See the section titled *Enlightenment and Revolution* in the Chapter titled *The French Enlightenment: The Ideology of Reason* from Gertrude Himmelfarb's book *The Roads to Modernity: The British, French, American Enlightenments*. (pages 181 -187).

11. For Burke's political philosophy see pages 334-337 in The Oxford History of Western Philosophy.
12. Gandhi's quote "100,000 Englishmen simply cannot control 350 million Indians, if those Indians refuse to co-operate" is most easily accessible in Richard Attenborough's 1982 Oscar winning film Gandhi. This quote by Gandhi is part of Gandhi's response in the film when he was asked by a Brigadier whether he expected the British to simply walk away from their empire.
13. See pages 20, 21 and 77 in Francis Fukuyama's *The End of History and the Last Man* in which he attributes the end of apartheid in South Africa to its inherent unsustainability.
14. For Anglo-Russian rivalry in the 19th century see Henry Kissinger's Diplomacy pages 89, 98, 100, 142, 151, 171 and 188.
15. See section 7 with sub-heading titled 'Hegel' and section 8 with sub-heading titled 'Hegel and Marx' under PART III with heading "Towards a threshold of scientific history" from pages 113 to 126 in R.G.Collingwood's book *The Idea of History*.
16. The idea that God was the czar's junior partner is taken from Samuel Huntington's book *The Clash of Civilizations and the Remaking of World Order*. In page 70 of this book in Chapter 3 titled A Universal Civilization? Modernization and Westernization under the heading The West and Modernization, Huntington observes that in lands in which the civilizational affiliation was "Orthodoxy", "God" was "the Caesar's" (Czar in Russia) "junior partner".

Chapter 3: Post-Modernity

1. Commentators say that post-modernity is a condition. We are concerned here in this chapter primarily about the truthfulness and relevance of post-modern ideas. I chose the term post-modernity ahead of the term post-modernism or postmodern philosophies to denote post-modern ideas. Modernism is an art movement and so using postmodernism would denote an artistic successor to modernism. Until recently, I have rarely come across the term postmodern philosophies used to denote postmodern ideas. Therefore I have settled for the term post-modernity itself to describe ideas associated with the post-modern condition.
2. Post-modernity encompasses a wide array of views. To go into the different strands of ideas that can be broadly classified under post-modernity is beyond the scope of this book. In this chapter we have generally engaged with a broad set of core ideas that are generally referred to as being post-modern. For a seminal work on the post-modern condition and some of the ideas associated with it see Jean-François Lyotard's book *The Postmodern Condition : A Report on knowledge*. Along with it also see Jacques Derrida's of *Grammatology*. For those looking for brief simple introduction to Post-modern ideas see Christopher Butler's *Postmodernism : A Very Short Introduction*.
3. The seminal book on deconstruction is Jacques Derrida's of *Grammatology*.
4. The primary evidence we can ascribe for eastern thought is Lao Tzu's *Tao Te Ching*.
5. The former chief minister of the state of Tamilnadu in India and the renowned Dravidian leader C.N.Annadurai regards the most venerated Indian epic, the Ramayanam, as an allegory representing the Aryan conquest of the

Dravidian South. Annadurai argues that in the Ramayanam, the Southern Dravidian King Ravanan who was based in Lanka was depicted as a demon. Annadurai was engaged in a couple of debates with Tamil scholars on the worthiness of the Ramayana. Later on, the substance of at least one of these debates was published in a Tamil book titled (Tī paravaṭṭum). For those who cannot read Tamil they could look at pages 63-71 in R.Kannan's *Anna- The Life and times of C N Annadurai* where the context and substance of these debates are summarized in English. Also see page 97 in Section XIII titled Mahabharata under Chapter Four: The Discovery of India in Jawaharlal Nehru's book *The Discovery of India*, where Nehru says that the Ramayana was a story of expansion to the South of India.

Chapter 4: Civilizational Narratives
1. Though Gandhi lived in the 20th century, during his lifetime much of India lived in pre-modern conditions. So we regard Gandhi's attempt to interpret Hinduism in the light of the truth both as modern and a pre-modern phenomenon.
2. For much of the ancient history in this chapter and elsewhere in this book I have found Karen Armstrong's book *The Great Transformation* invaluable. Her work is scholarly and yet reasonable people cannot accuse her of partiality as she is a well-meaning scholar who is not known to have a political agenda or an ideological bent. For Islamic history I have found the many works of Bernard Lewis cited in the bibliography valuable. In addition I have also used *A History of Islamic Societies* by Ira Lapidus. For Chinese history I have found John Fairbank's book on China that has been cited in the bibliography very useful. For the main themes in the

history of Christendom that I have presented in this chapter I have essentially accepted the widely prevalent narrative of modern scholarship. Indian history is certainly a passionately contested area. However here the basis of disagreement is indisputably political and ideological. For ancient Indian history, I subscribe to the Dravidian origins and Aryan migration theory (see Notes for Chapter 1 – entry 10). Now to be sure modern scholarship does not regard this theory as conclusive but the most plausible among the rest and to that extent I am objectively correct. Readers of this book will find out on completion that the theory of truth that we have spelt out in this book does not privilege objective knowledge but non-pedantically encompasses it. For those who read the contents of this book with an open mind, we believe, the Dravidian origins theory will conform to the notion of truth we have spelt out in this book.

3. The historical origins of renunciation and by extension the origins of other Indian metaphysical ideas are shrouded in mystery. See Karen Armstrong's The Great Transformation pages 120 and 121 where she says that renunciation and by extension Indian spirituality could have been indigenous to the native inhabitants of India or a natural development of Vedic religion or an entirely new ideology. I find that it is a natural development of Vedic religion problematic because the reference to this ideology in the earliest Vedic text, the Rig Veda, is very sketchy. We cannot say with certainty that this ideology is indigenous in origin as neither the Atharvana Veda nor early Tamil sources from the Sangam poems are centered on this ideology. The argument that it was a new ideology is inherently very speculative. The historical origins of Indian spirituality seem to be rooted in fringe groups who could have been either indigenous Dravidians or non-

Vedic Aryans. In this book we have taken the view that pre-Aryan Indian civilization was Dravidian and we have given our reasons for it in the Notes for Chapter 1, titled *An Ethical enquiry into the pre-modern world*. Since the pre-Aryan Indian civilization was Dravidian we in this book have taken the view that the spirituality also originated in a Dravidian fringe group. The Vedic world recognized this spiritual wisdom through the Upanishads. The word Upanishad means to sit near. Sitting near whom? From our perspective these were indigenous Dravidian Siddhas or perfect masters. So the Vedic Aryans sat near these Dravidian Siddhas and listened to their discourses and absorbed the teachings of these Dravidian Siddhas into the Upanishads. So we attribute the historical origins of the spiritual heritage of India to Dravidians and the subsequent assimilation and propagation of the theistic version of this spirituality to mostly the Vedic Aryans.

4. The Gods that were prominent in the Rig Veda like Indra and Varuna had lost out to indigenous Gods. See page 360 in Karen Armstrong's Great Transformation where she says that Rudra who was a minor God in the Vedic religion was merged with the indigenous Shiva. Indeed none of the major Gods that Hindus today worship can be traced back to the Rig Veda indicating that these Gods were absorbed into the brahminical religion from pre-Aryan sources. The magical incantations from indigenous sources were absorbed into the Atharvana Veda.

5. See K.Veeramani's *Collected Works of Periyar E.V.R.* pages 218-219.

6. The former chief minister of the state of Tamilnadu in India and the renowned Dravidian leader C.N.Annadurai regards the most venerated Indian epic, the Ramayanam, as an allegory representing the Aryan conquest of the Dravidian South. Annadurai argues that in the

Ramayanam, the Southern Dravidian King Ravanan who was based in Lanka was depicted as a demon. Annadurai was engaged in debates with Tamil scholars on the worthiness of the Ramayanam. Later on, the substance of these debates was published in a Tamil book titled Tī paravaṭṭum. For those who cannot read Tamil they could look at pages 63-71 in R.Kannan's *Anna- The Life and times of C N Annadurai* where the context and substance of these debates are summarized in English.
7. For Christian Ideals we have taken some of the most profound pronouncements on love that are found in the Gospels and have tried to imagine a world order that would have emerged in the pre-modern world if these ideals had been embraced.
8. See the section titled Usury in Christianity under Wayne A.M Visser and Alastair McIntosh's article *A Short Review of the Historical Critique of Usury*. In addition also use the internet link below in the Bibliography to go to Norman Roth's article on Jewish Money Lending. This article appears in the MyJewishLearning.com website.
9. For Islamic truth we have presented some of the most well-known ideals and have stated that these ideals were pertinent to the circumstances of the pre-modern world. We have also tried to place in historical context the institution of slavery in Islam and we have also grappled with the provision for violence in Islam. Please see the Holy Quran and the many books on Islam and Islamic societies cited in the bibliography.
10. On page 6 in the first Chapter titled 'Slavery' in Bernard Lewis's book titled *Race and Slavery in the Middle East: An Historical Enquiry* the author states that the slave had a certain status in Islam and was not mere chattel.
11. On page 6 in the first Chapter titled 'Slavery' in Bernard Lewis's book titled *Race and Slavery in the Middle East:*

An Historical Enquiry the author states that manumission was encouraged in Islam and one's sins would be expiated as a result of it.
12. See page 59 in Chapter 4 titled 'The Caliphate' in Ira.M.Lapidus's book *A History of Islamic Societies* for the death of Hussein and its significance for Shite Islam. Also see C.M.Naim's *MUHARRAM : The Spirit Of Karbala* published in OutlookIndia, web edition, dated Feb 6, 2007 where C.M.Naim makes the case that each year on the day of Muharram it is Islam that comes alive. In other words long ago on this day in Muharram needless violence had stained Islam and Muslims were yearning ever since for the pristine Islam that characterized its origin.
13. See pages 54-58 in Chapter 4 titled 'The Caliphate' in Ira.M.Lapidus's book *A History of Islamic Societies* for the history of the first four caliphs. In page 54 of this book, these four caliphs are described as having been rightly guided.
14. See page 43 in the Chapter 3 titled 'The Arab Conquests' and pages 242-244 under the sub title "Conversion to Islam" in the 2nd part of Ira.M.Lapidus's book *A History of Islamic Societies* where the author says that the majority of peoples converted to Islam voluntarily.
15. See page 6 in the first Chapter titled 'Slavery' in Bernard Lewis's book titled *Race and Slavery in the Middle East: An Historical Enquiry,* where the author states that the slave had a certain status in Islam and was not mere chattel. In addition this book also compares slavery under Islam with slavery elsewhere at other times.
16. For the political and social organization of Chinese life in the feudal age period see pages 25-36 in the first chapter titled The Axial Peoples (c. 1600 to 900 B.C.E.) from Karen Armstrong's *The Great Transformation: The Beginning of our Religious Traditions.*

17. For a history of China see John King Fairbank's *China: A New History*.
18. For a discussion on Confucius and his ideas see pages 200–211 in the sixth Chapter titled Empathy (c. 530 to 450 B.C.E) from Karen Armstrong's *The Great Transformation: The Beginning of our Religious Traditions*.
19. See Li Tianchen's To *learn from the past is to serve the present: a Confucian lesson*.
20. For the restraint shown by the warrior and the gentleman (referred to as Junzi in China) see pages 148-152 from Chapter 4 titled Knowledge (c. 700 to 600 B.C.E.) in Karen Armstrong's *The Great Transformation: The Beginning of our Religious Traditions*.
21. For nepotism in China's examination system see the section titled Education and the Examination System on pages 93-95 in Chapter 4 titled 'China's Greatest Age: Northern and Southern Song' in Part One titled 'Rise and Decline of the Imperial Autocracy' in John Fairbank's book *China: A New History*.
22. From Francis Fukuyama's lecture at SAIS at John Hopkins University on Wednesday, September 16, 2009 entitled, "Getting to Denmark: Where the State, Rule of Law and Accountable Government Come From". Fukuyama followed this up with his book *The Origins of Political Order: From Prehuman Times to the French Revolution*.

Chapter 5: Gandhi, India and the Quest for an Ethical Response to Modernity

1. See the essay 'Gandhi's Ambedkar' in Ramachandra Guha's book *An Anthropologist Among the Marxists: And Other Essays* where Guha says that Gandhi is the mother of all debates about India's future.

2. See Indian Critiques of Gandhi which is part of the SUNY Series in Religious Studies Edited by Harold Coward for the differences Indian leaders had with Gandhi. In addition, see the essay Gandhi's Ambedkar in Ramachandra Guha's book *An Anthropologist Among the Marxists: And Other Essays* for the conversations between Ambedkar and Gandhi, where Guha lays out the differences.
3. See the book *Mind of Mahathma Gandhi* edited by R. K. Prabhu & U. R. Rao under the section 'Gospel of Truth'. Further look for the topic "Absolute Truth". Here Gandhi says we humans do not know the absolute truth and all that we know is relative truth. Also see Nirmal Kumar Bose's book titled *Selections From Gandhi* in a section titled 'God' under the heading 'The Character of Truth' where Gandhi says truth (meaning relative truth) is self-evident and would become clear if we remove the cobwebs of ignorance surrounding it.
4. Socrates shows Tracymachus that it is advantageous to be good in Book 1 of Plato's *Republic*.
5. For a reference for Amos see pages 87-89 from Chapter 3 titled Kenosis (c. 800 to 700 B.C.E.) in Karen Armstrong's *The Great Transformation: The Beginning of our Religious Traditions*. Yahweh, the God of Israel, informs through his Prophet Amos that the ancient Israelites will be punished because of the injustices that existed in ancient Israel at the time. A people will lose their favored status with their God as a punishment for their inequities. Mere observation of rituals and ceremonies alone is not enough. It must be accompanied by justice and integrity.
6. See page 34 from Chapter 1 titled The Axial Peoples (c. 1600 to 900 B.C.E.) in Karen Armstrong's *The Great*

Transformation: The Beginning of our Religious Traditions.

7. In *Hind Swaraj* in the section 'Why was India lost?' Gandhi says that British colonial rule in India was created and sustained by Indians.
8. The Round Table Conference was based on the British view that interests of different communities in India needed to be safeguarded and the implication clearly being that from the British standpoint Gandhi did not represent all of India.
9. As quoted from OECD report Monitoring the World Economy authored by Angus Maddison published in 1995 in Gurucharan Das's essay *India : How a rich nation became poor and will be rich again* which says that the Indian economy grew at 0.8 % between 1900-50. We have approximated 0.8% to 1%. Gurucharan Das's essay can be found in the book titled *Developing Cultures : Case Studies* edited by Lawrence.E.Harrison and Peter Berger.
10. As quoted from OECD report Monitoring the World Economy authored by Angus Maddison published in 1995 in Gurucharan Das's essay *India : How a rich nation became poor and will be rich again* which says that the Indian economy grew at 3.5 % between 1950 to 1980. Gurucharan Das's essay can be found in the book titled *Developing Cultures : Case Studies* edited by Lawrence.E.Harrison and Peter Berger.
11. See page 183 Table A4 'Emerging and Developing Economies: Real GDP' in *World Economic Outlook* published by the International Monetary Fund (IMF) for India's growth rate after liberalization beginning in the early 1990s.

12. See page 183 Table A4 'Emerging and Developing Economies: Real GDP' in *World Economic Outlook* published by the International Monetary Fund (IMF) for India's accelerated growth rate after 2002.
13. See the essay 'Gandhi's Ambedkar' in Ramachandra Guha's book *An Anthropologist Among the Marxists: And Other Essays* where he says that that Gandhi was a rural romantic.
14. Gandhi's views on modernity were not strictly constant but his book Hind Swaraj gives a good account of how he generally looked upon modernity.
15. See Gandhi's Speech before the Inter-Asian Relations Conference on 2nd April, 1947. Also see Chapter Forty Five titled 'Asia's Message to the West' in Louis Fischer's book *The Life of Mahatma Gandhi*.
16. See Ian.A.Talbot's *Jinnah and the Making of Pakistan* in History Today where he says that Jinnah was not a devout Muslim and that he ate pork and drank alcohol. See Ashis Nandy's article titled *Unclaimed Baggage* in 'the little magazine' where Nandy states that many of the founder leaders of the Hindutuva political formation were non-believers.
17. See A.Prasad's *Sarvodaya Movement: Developing a Macro Perspective From Grassroots Collective Actions* presented at The 12th Biennial Conference of the International Association for the Study of Commons held at Cheltenham, Gloucestershire, U.K. on July 14-18, 2008 for an account of the Sarvodaya movement in India.
18. See Census of India 2001.
19. See A.T.Ariyaratne's *Basava Sree Award Acceptance Speech*. This speech was made at a Ceremony held at Sri Muruga Math, Chitradurga – Karnataka, India on Monday the 15th August 2011. In this speech Mr.Ariyaratne says

that Sarvodaya serves 15000 villages in Sri Lanka. This is a large number of villages in a small country like Sri Lanka.
20. Many of Periyar's speeches and writings have not been translated from Tamil to English. However there exists a mathematical treatise which applies mathematical methods to Periyar's views on untouchability. This has been published as a book in English. This book is written by W. B. Vasantha Kandasamy and Florentin Smarandache and is titled *Fuzzy and Neutrosophic Analysis of Periyar's Views on Untouchability*. Much of the latter sections of this book contain Periyar's views on untouchability. This may give the reader a peek into the mind of Periyar. In addition it may be useful to see *Collected Works of Periyar E.V.R* by K.Veeramani for Periyar's views on different topics. This Collected Works is not a collected works in a literal and comprehensive sense but a selection of many of Periyar's views and opinions. This is in English and would give the reader a broad exposure to the mind of Periyar.
21. Periyar was practical and utility oriented and this is what we mean here by utilitarian. In the last few years, especially after the widespread use of the worldwide web we see greater interest in usability engineering. Much of Periyar's practical suggestions would have fallen into the usability domain.
22. Periyar rejects the Socialist parties because these parties were led by ethnic Brahmins who were at the apex of the Hindu caste order.
23. Please see RaviKumar's "Re-Reading Periyar", Raj Sekhar Basu's "Dalit Politics in Tamilnadu" in the Seminar magazine and M. Venkatesan's book E V Ramasamy Naickarin Marupakkam (The other side of E V Ramasamy

Naickar) (This book is written in Tamil and not available in English) for Dalit critiques of Periyar.

Chapter 6: Expositions of the Truth

1. For Existence in eastern thought see Lao Tzu's Tao Te Ching. Tao Te Ching gives its exposition on Existence in a few lines. I have allowed theistic Indian metaphysical depiction of existence to seamlessly flow into these Taoist expositions to give me greater elucidations on existence. In Indian theism, Existence is represented as a female God and is referred to in Tamil as Adi Para Sakthi.
2. I came to the conclusion that love infused into existence is the truth after reflecting on the abode of my Guru Shirdi Sai Baba. Sai Baba lived in a mosque in Shirdi. Sai Baba has said that the presiding deity in the Mosque is Dwaraka Mai, (See Sai Satcharita which is the inspired biography of Sai Baba) which means Divine Mother in English. Divine Mother in Indian theistic tradition encompasses the different facets of existence like ego, time, nature, matter and energy. Sai devotees believe that Sai Baba embodies the Hindu Gods Sivan, Raman, Krishnan and Maruthi. Sivan in Indian theism is none other than Love. Sai Baba has also said that he never speaks untruth in his Mosque. Since Sai Baba is love, the mosque is existence and since he says that he never speaks untruth in that mosque, we conclude that love infused into existence is the truth. Needless to say the source of such a conclusion is my own personnel faith. I do not present this as evidence but to elucidate how I arrived at this conclusion. Now the reader can use their intuition or rational judgment and arrive at the same conclusion that I have arrived at as a consequence of my faith.

3. See Nirmal Kumar Bose's book *Selections from Gandhi* under the topic *God* in the section titled *Character of the Truth*.
4. This pan civilizational metaphysical perspective on the truth is my own perspective on the truth. It is very difficult, almost impossible, for me to enlist all the sources which shaped this perspective of mine. Despite being raised in a religious Tamil Hindu family, to this day I have hardly read any of the great works of the Hindu canon in translation (I could have only read these works in translation as I do not know Sanskrit !!!), including the well-known Bhagavat Gita. I am a Shirdi Sai devotee and that certainly must have contributed to my perspective. I have had several discussions with Swami Sivanandha who resides in Southern Tamilnadu in India. Swami Sivanandha was a disciple of the Hindu Goddess Mahalakshmi and told me that he was spiritually influenced by Siddhars in Tamilnadu. So that must have influenced my metaphysical views as well. In addition I have been influenced by Lao Tzu's Tao Te Ching, the writings of Meher Baba and the writings and speeches of Sathya Sai Baba - especially those pertaining to his expositions on love. In addition, over the years I have, informally, more than familiarized myself with the central themes of the great religions of the world.
5. See Lao Tzu's *Tao Te Ching*. Here I am substituting nothingness for Tao.
6. Nothingness becoming aware of its potentialities is an idea borrowed and adapted from the writings of Meher Baba. Meher Baba himself did not use the word nothingness. He calls it unconscious God. See Meher Baba's *God Speaks*.
7. The one entity pervading all of existence is the central metaphysical message in almost all the theistic religions of India. Sikhism, certain strands of Sufism and mainstream

Hinduism along with the many perfect masters from India are all metaphysically centered on this message.
8. See Lao Tzu's *Tao Te Ching*.
9. Both 'Righteousness is truth applied' and 'Evil is truth misplaced' are again attributed to Gandhi.
10. It is not possible to make ethical judgments on existence. There is nothing morally superior in summer over winter or the vice versa. So also there is nothing morally superior in morning over evening or the vice versa. This is plain common sense and should be apparent to anybody. However for academic interest among the books we have cited in the Reference List one could look at Indian Critiques of Gandhi edited by Harold Coward for Aurobindo's critique of Gandhi where such ideas on existence are explicitly stated.
11. An entire body of Buddhist literature deals with the past lives of Buddha in the Jatakas.
12. The results of the Archaeological excavations are directly taken from Karen Armstrong's *The Great Transformation*. See pages 39-40 in The Great Transformation. The texts quoted are the author's words in the book. The opinion of scholars that is stated in this context is also taken from this book. The fact that ancient Jews were not writing objective history is also taken directly from these pages in Karen Armstrong's *The Great Transformation*.
13. Montaigne in his essay titled *Of Experience* says that a certain man in ancient Greece could feel an egg in his farm and was by experience able to identify the hen that had laid it. See *Great Books of the Western World Vol 25*.
14. Barzun says that by the time of the reformation, Catholics in Europe had taken to worshiping saints and this had become a sort of polytheism. Different saints were worshipped for different purposes. For Travelers Saint Christopher, for sailors Saint Elmo, for old maids Saint

Catherine, for sick children Saint Germain, for lost keys Saint Sythe, for getting rid of detested husbands Saint Wilgefortis and for those in hopeless trouble Saint Jude were worshipped. See Jacques Barzun's *Dawn To Decadence* in Part 1 under the chapter The New Life on page 22.
15. Most of those who lived west of Iran and Arabia were formerly Christian before their conversion to Islam. See the page 4 of Introduction in Bernard Lewis's *What went wrong?*
16. See Richard M.Eaton's *The Rise of Islam and the Bengal Frontier,1204-1760* for a recent scholarly account on how Islam came to Bangladesh.
17. See Freedom in the World 2012 report published by Freedom House for the combined scores of different countries.
18. This is based on my experience as a Software Engineer and Software Consultant in American companies for over 20 years. Other immigrant engineers, especially those from India, concurred with me in private.

Chapter 7: Ethical Resolutions in the Light of the Truth

1. The conception of the modern nation state began in the early 19th century and it acquired greater force during the 19th century. Romanticism is the movement that brought the nation state to the forefront. Its ideological origins are to be found in the German philosopher Johann Gottlieb Fichte's notion of the Volk. See Lewis Mumford's *The Natural History of Urbanization* in *Man's Role in Changing the Face of the Earth* edited by W.L.Thomas Jr. where Mumford says that modern urbanization began as the third stage of urbanization in the 19th century in the section titled *Modern Forces of Expansion*. See Jacques

Barzun's *From Dawn To Decadence* pages 539-544 for discussion on the effect of railways in Europe. Barzun says this began in 1830 and found widespread use rapidly. Though the Industrial Revolution took place in the 18th century in England its effect in creating modern life greatly increased with above mentioned changes in other areas in the 19th century.
2. See the Brooking's Institution's research paper by Lex Rieffel titled *Reconsidering the Peace Corps*.
3. See Francis Fukuyama's *End of History and the Last Man*.
4. See Freedom Status, 1972–2011 Table in Freedom House's Freedom in the World 2012 report where the number of free countries peaks in 2006 and 2007 but it has been consistently at the highest levels since 1998.
5. The five countries ruled by communist parties today are China, Vietnam, Laos, Cuba and North Korea.
6. See Leszek Kolakowski's essay *Modernity on Endless Trial* in his book *Modernity on Endless Trial*.
7. See Table 1 titled *Human Development Index* and its components on pages 127-130 under Statistical Tables of the *Human Development Report 2011*. Though the latest *Human Development Report 2014* and the *Human Development Report 2013* are now out we have only referenced the *Human Development Report 2011*. We believe the conclusions we have drawn from the 2011 Report for this book would not have been fundamentally different if we had referenced the later Reports. Besides the 2011 Report allows us to engage with a Caribbean country as a very highly developed country.
8. Look under Economy for the countries of Qatar, UAE and Brunei in *The World Factbook 2009* published by the Central Intelligence Agency.

9. Look under Economy for the country of Bahrain in *The World Factbook 2009* published by the Central Intelligence Agency.
10. See the table TOURIST (STOP-OVER) ARRIVALS AND CRUISE PASSENGER VISITS IN 2011 Table in *Latest Tourism Statistics 2011* published by the Caribbean Tourism Organization. Barbados is one of the 9 destinations in this table with over half a million tourist arrivals in the year 2011.
11. See IMF Working Paper WP/07/87 by Ahmed Zoromé titled *Concept of Offshore Financial Centers: In Search of an Operational Definition* where in page 7 an Offshore Financial Center (OFC) is defined as a country or jurisdiction that provides financial services to nonresidents on a scale that is incommensurate with the size and the financing of its domestic economy.
12. Look for GDP - composition by sector: under Economy for the country of Singapore in *The World Factbook 2009* published by the Central Intelligence Agency. You will see that industry accounts for roughly 26% of GDP.
13. From *World Federation of Exchanges – Statistics/Monthly* published by World Federation of Exchanges and archived from the original on 21 August 2010.
14. See *The Panama Canal: A plan to unlock prosperity* in The Economist dated 3rd December 2009. This article says that the Colón Free Zone, in the Atlantic end of the Panama Canal, is the second largest re-exporter after Hong Kong.
15. See Chapter 1 titled Introduction in Edward. E.Telles's *Race in Another America: The Significance of Skin Color in Brazil*. When the Chapter from this book is seen in conjunction with Appendix 2, 3, 4,

and 5, the account we have provided for race in Latin America will be affirmed.
16. In Chapter 1 titled Introduction in Edward. E.Telles's *Race in Another America: The Significance of Skin Color in Brazil*, the author says that White Brazilians would point to the presence of blacks and afrobiracials in their family albums.
17. Since this happens to be a politically controversial issue we referred to three sources to ensure the correctness of our perspective. These are Francisco Lizcano Fernandez's Culturales del Continente Americano al Comienzo del Siglo XXI, Informe Latinobarómetro and *The World Factbook* published by the CIA. The Informe Latinobarómetro asks respondents to self-identify their race in its survey. Francisco Lizcano Fernandez's work is a scholarly work. Despite the variation in these approaches their results confirm our basic thesis. There are not significant variations in the demographic constitution of different countries in Latin America in these three sources. Where there is a difference, the difference is either a consequence of different methods of classification or it only confirms our thesis more emphatically. See Appendix 2, Appendix 3, Appendix 4 and Appendix 5. The Latinobarometro web site is http://www.latinobarometro.org/lat.jsp and the link http://en.wikipedia.org/wiki/Ethnic_groups_in_Latin_ America provides averages for the Latinobarometro surveys for the years 2007-2011, a tabulation of the CIA World Factbook data and Dr.Lizano 's results. The Latinobarometro 2011 survey has a table titled Tabla N°16: Raza a la que pertenece por país 2011 on page 58 which gives the survey results for the year 2011. We have not used genetic data because the notion of race and

ethnicity in Latin America is fluid and can at best be described as cultural. Therefore we believe methods of identification and perception would be a more accurate indicator of ethnicity than biological certitude.
18. Gujarat has a higher per capita GDP than Tamilnadu but its HDI score is lower than Tamilnadu. Kerala has a higher HDI score than Tamilnadu but Kerala's income is not so much a consequence of development from within but from remittances sent by Keralites living in Gulf countries. Maharashtra has a higher HDI score than Tamilnadu but that is because the city of Mumbai (formerly Bombay) is included in calculating Maharashtra's score. The cultural ethos of Mumbai (formerly Bombay) is pan-Indian unlike Tamilnadu's largest city Chennai. So the score for Mumbai (formerly Bombay) justly should not be included along with Maharashtra if we are comparing cultural fit for modernity. However Punjab and Himachal Pradesh have marginally higher HDI numbers than Tamilnadu. They are just developed as Tamilnadu and can be regarded as front runners in overall development. See Table 2.3 titled Human Development Index of States in India on page 23 of the Meghalaya Human Development Report 2008. Unfortunately we just have to do with the 2008 report because there is time lag in getting HDI Scores for sub-nationalites.
19. Please see an insightful internet article titled LEADING TRIBES OF PUNJAB AND THEIR ORIGINS available at http://www.paklinks.com/gs/culture-literature-and-linguistics/73172-leading-tribes-of-punjab.html.
20. See Thomas Sowell's *Race And Culture: A World View* where he discusses cultural disposition of certain ethnic groups to succeed in business. He counts Gujaratis among these groups and discusses their success in foreign lands. See pages 2 and 194.

21. **Ethnicity.** See the article *The slaughter of sacred cows : Some cherished policies are being re-examined* in the The Economist dated Apr 3rd 2003.
22. **State.** See Eric Hobsbawm's *Nations and Nationalism Since 1780: Programme, Myth, Reality.*
23. **State.** See Benedict Anderson's *Imagined Communities: Reflections on the Origin and Spread of Nationalism.*
24. **Outcastes.** In Jeffrey Toobin's *The Nine: Inside the Secret World of the Supreme Court* on page 210 four liberal judges in the U.S. Supreme Court believe that affirmative action is justified on the grounds that it would redress prior discrimination or foster the goal of diversity. Prior discrimination would be wrong only if a structural alternative could have been possible in a previous age. Secondly for prior discrimination, affirmative action would be justifiable only for a certain amount of time. Whereas if the goal was to promote diversity then in multicultural, multiethnic societies, talented members of groups which had been historically disadvantaged would have more enduring opportunities for fulfillment and self-expression. Nor should anybody worry that affirmative action would displace merit as a criterion for opportunities. Affirmative Action can co-exist with merit. I came to this view independently before I read this book.
25. **Entertainment.** Here we regard Mahatma Gandhi and Mother Teresa as extraordinary examples of selfless service but are not resorting to mindless reverence. Being aware of our own failings and limitations, recognizing the extraordinary selflessness of both these individuals and with great humility on our part, we make some observations on these two extraordinary people. When in Delhi, Gandhi stayed at the Harijan colony but towards the end of his life stayed at Birla's House. Birla was then the richest man in India. Birla wasn't practicing the trusteeship

that Gandhi advocated, whereby one would keep all the wealth that was over and above one's needs in trust and spend it on public welfare. When such was the case Gandhi should not have stayed in Birla's house. Gandhi could very well have rented a room in a decent hotel. Likewise Christian missionaries in India do resort to aggressive proselytization. In the last generation, Mother Teresa along with the likes of Nelson Mandela and Elie Wiesel has been regarded as a person with moral authority in the world. Yet Mother Teresa never publically took a stance against such proselytization. If the motivation for proselytization is theological, then I believe it is absolutely unnecessary. Each person has to be guided by her or his own inner light.

26. See The Economist article titled *Africa rising : The hopeful continent* dated Dec 3rd 2011.
27. See the Mckinsey Quarterly report titled *What's driving Africa's growth* dated June 2010 by Acha Leke, Susan Lund, Charles Roxburgh, and Arend van Wamelen.
28. See The Economist article titled *Sad South Africa : Cry, the beloved country* dated Oct 20th 2012.
29. See the Mckinsey Quarterly report titled *What's driving Africa's growth* dated June 2010 by Acha Leke, Susan Lund, Charles Roxburgh, and Arend van Wamelen.
30. See Brooke Donald article titled *At Stanford, Bill Gates says foreign aid is threatened, but big ideas can turn the tide* published by Stanford News Service, Stanford University. This report was emailed to all who had signed up for Stanford News via the Stanford Report on April 5, 2012.
31. See *Case1 : Eradicating Smallpox* of the Millions Saved Initiative from the Center for Global Development.
32. See pages xxvi and xxvii in the Introduction titled Why Culture Matters edited by Lawrence E Harrison from the

book titled *Culture Matters: How Values Shape Human Progress* by Lawrence E. Harrison and Samuel P. Huntington where he says life is better than death, health is better than sickness, liberty is better than slavery, prosperity is better than poverty, education is better than ignorance and justice is better than injustice. I have obviously, if somewhat subconsciously, borrowed this idiom: *is better than* – and have used it in a similar context to reflect my preferences.

33. At the bottom of page 2 in the SUMMARY section of Oxfam International Briefing Paper 178 dated Jan 20th, 2014 and titled *WORKING FOR THE FEW: Political capture and economic inequality* it says that 85 of the richest people in the world are as wealthy as the bottom half of the world population, which is roughly 3.5 billion people.

34. See in page 8 of The *State of Food Insecurity in the World 2013: The multiple dimensions of food security*, which is prepared jointly by the Food and Agricultural Organization (FAO) of the United Nations, the International Fund for Agricultural Development (IFAD) and the World Food Program (WFP) and published by the FAO.

35. See pages 52 and 55 of the United Nations' *The Millennium Development Goals Report 2012*.

36. See *the UNESCO Institute for Statistics (UIS) FACT SHEET No.26* dated September 2013.

37. Please see TABLE S.12. TEN COUNTRIES OR AREAS WITH THE HIGHEST AND THE TEN COUNTRIES OR AREAS WITH THE LOWEST LIFE EXPECTANCY AT BIRTH, for the period 2005-2010 and TABLE S.13. LIFE EXPECTANCY AT BIRTH, BOTH SEXES COMBINED, BY

COUNTRY FOR SELECTED PERIODS, for the period 2005-2010 in the *United Nations, Department of Economic and Social Affairs, Population Division's World Population Prospects : The 2012 Revision, Key Findings and Advanced Tables. Working Paper No. ESA/P/WP.227.*
38. Please see TABLE S.14. INFANT MORTALITY RATE BY COUNTRY FOR SELECTED PERIODS for the period 2005-2010 in the *United Nations, Department of Economic and Social Affairs, Population Division's World Population Prospects : The 2012 Revision, Key Findings and Advanced Tables. Working Paper No. ESA/P/WP.227.*
39. See the last section in Chapter 5 of this book titled *The Alternate Gandhi*.

Chapter 8: An outline for a discourse on Civilizations
1. See Samuel P. Huntington's book *The Clash of Civilizations and the Remaking of World Order*. The definition that is quoted here is taken from Chapter 2 titled Civilizations in History and Today under the section The Nature of Civilizations on page 43 of this book.
2. In his book *The Clash of Civilizations and the Remaking of World Order* Samuel P. Huntington identifies 7 or 8 distinct civilizations. Huntington's choice of civilizations can be found in Chapter 2 titled Civilizations in History and Today under the section The Nature of Civilizations on pages 45-47 of this book.
3. See Henry Kissinger's *On China*.
4. See Arnold J. Toynbee's A Study of History, Vol. 1 of the abridged edition where he says all civilizations went through roughly similar phases of civilizational evolution.

5. See Henry Kissinger's White House Years for complete details of Nixon's China trip. Kissinger reproduces Nixon's speech from Los Angeles announcing the Nixon trip in pages 759-760. Nixon's trip to China was simultaneously announced by both Chou En Lai and Nixon in their respective countries at the same time. In this announcement the Chinese premier Chou-En-Lai on knowing of President Nixon's expressed desire to visit China extended an invitation to him on behalf of the Chinese government.
6. See Herbert.S.Klein's *The Changing American Family* in Hoover Digest 2004 No.3 published by the Hoover Institution at Stanford University. In this article Klein clearly states that during the 1970s the disintegration of the family was perceived as a matter of public concern.

Chapter 9: India: A World within the World

1. Cadets for the officer cadre of the Indian Armed forces are initially trained for a period of 3 years in India's National Defense Academy. The National Defense Academy is India's equivalent of West Point. On entering the academy they are attached to a squadron. The names of these squadrons are Alpha, Bravo, Charlie, Delta, Echo, Foxtrot, Golf, Hunter, India, Juliet, Kilo, Lima, Mike, November, Oscar, Panther, Quebec and Romeo. All of which, including the term India, are English or European names and in a way illustrates the continuing British influence in the Indian armed forces.
2. This quote by Winston Churchill is taken from Shashi Tharoor's book *India from Midnight to the Millennium*. This quote appears at the beginning of the first chapter.

3. See the Minutes on Education by T. B. Macaulay, dated the 2nd February 1835 in *Selections from Educational Records, Part I (1781-1839)* edited by H.Sharp.
4. The Achaemenid Persian Empire or first Persian Empire ruled between 550B.C.E. and 330B.C.E. Historians may slightly vary on the exact date when the Roman Republic transitioned into the Roman Empire but we would not be way off the mark if we take the year 27B.C.E. as the year when the republic became an empire. In 27 B.C.E. the Roman Senate gave Octavian the title of Augustus and made him Princeps or Emperor. The Chinese Empire was unified in the year 221B.C.E.
5. See Peter F Drucker's 1997 Foreign Affairs article titled *The Global Economy and the Nation-State* where he says that India was rarely united except under a foreign conqueror. We agree that mostly it was the foreigner who united India however such unity was only a rarity in antiquity. From the late medieval period onwards the notion of unity has been gaining far more steam.
6. In antiquity Alexander also reached India as an invader. After Alexander the Greeks co-opted non-Greeks via culture and language. The Greek language emerged as the lingua franca of the Mediterranean world. However there is no evidence that the Greek cultural reach encompassed India in a substantial way.

Chapter 10: The Chinese Mind

1. See pages 140-141 in Chapter 6 titled Is the world made up of Nouns or Verbs from Richard E. Nisbett's *The Geography of Thought : How Asians and Westerners Think Differently... and Why?*
2. See page 167 in Chapter 6 titled First Steps toward China in Part 1 titled 1969: The Start of the Journey from Henry

Kissinger's *White House Years* where Kissinger says Huang Hua was lone Chinese ambassador serving abroad in 1969, being stationed in Cairo, Egypt.
3. Please see BBC NEWS internet article titled *How China is ruled*.
4. See John King Fairbank's book *China: A New History* where he has a section titled Co-relative Cosmology. He discusses co-relative cosmology when he discusses the Han dynasty in China.
5. See page 151 in Chapter 4 tilted Knowledge (c.700 to 600 BCE) from Karen Armstrong's *The Great Transformation: The Beginning of Our Religious Traditions* for the inculcation of self-discipline in China from the earliest times.
6. See transcript of Henry Kissinger's remarks at the 14th Annual John.M.Ashbrook Memorial Dinner at Ashland University on September 11, 1997. The transcript is available at http://ashbrook.org/events/kissinger-transcript/.
7. Please see internet article available at http://factsanddetails.com/china/cat2/sub1/item31.html
8. China has two indigenous schools of thought namely Confucianism and Taoism. Confucianism advocates self-cultivation of the individual but it does not contain any axiomatic inviolable first principles nor does it have a set of laws which must be adhered to at all times. Taoism advocates inaction. Therefore neither of these indigenous Chinese systems can be called ideologies. China certainly had co-relative cosmology which evolved indigenously. But then co-relative cosmology was more a method to uncover reality than an ideology. Co-relative cosmology was to China what reason has been to the modern West and faith has been to Islam.

9. For Nixon's trip to China see Henry Kissinger's *White House Years*. Kissinger has four chapters in this book in which he gives a firsthand account on the China trip. These chapters are titled *First Steps towards China, An Invitation to Peking, The Journey to Peking and Nixon's trip to China*.
10. Kissinger reproduces Nixon's speech from Los Angeles announcing the Nixon trip in pages 759-760 of Kissinger's book *White House Years*. Nixon's trip to China was simultaneously announced by both Chou En Lai and Nixon in their respective countries at the same time. In this announcement, the Chinese premier Chou-En-Lai on knowing of President Nixon's expressed desire to visit China extended an invitation to him on behalf of the Chinese government.
11. See page 781 in Chapter 19 titled The Journey to Peking under the subsection Polo II in the book *White House Years* by Henry Kissinger.
12. See Margaret MacMillan's *Nixon and Mao: The Week That Changed the World*.

Chapter 11: The Ethical and Historical Dimensions of Islam's Interaction with Modernity

1. See Bernard Lewis's *What Went Wrong? : Western Impact and Middle Eastern Response*.
2. See part V titled The Challenge of Modernity in Bernard Lewis's book *The Middle East: A Brief History of the Last 2,000 years* where he says that in the 20th century many European political concepts were tried in the Middle East. This part of the book can be read for facts relating to Islam's interaction with modernity.
3. See *The Roots of Muslim Rage* by Bernard Lewis in The Atlantic Magazine dated September, 1990.

4. See Bernard Lewis's article titled *Freedom and Justice in Islam* in The Imprimis magazine dated September 2006 - Volume 35, Number 9, in which he says that Islam neither had a caste system like India or an aristocracy like Europe.
5. In Bernard Lewis's book titled *Istanbul and the Civilization of the Ottoman Empire* in Chapter V titled The City on page 127 Lewis says that Islam was essentially an urban civilization.
6. The difference in the meat content of a Muslim diet and a non-Muslim diet becomes evident when one visits an Indian Restaurant and a Pakistani Restaurant. The cuisine from Northern India and Pakistan is essentially the same. However for the same dish one is bound to get more meat in a Pakistani Restaurant than in an Indian Restaurant.
7. See web article titled "Controversy. Naachne Gaane Waali Aurat" in OutlookIndia.com in which the Indian activist and film star Shabana Azmi says that the Quran does not insist on the veil. The article also has snippets of reactions to her views from other Muslims. Moderates are supportive of her but the religious establishment voices its opposition to her views. This is generally indicative of the disposition of moderate Muslims and Muslim intellectuals, who favor women's rights and the religious establishment which insists on the veil.
8. The per capita consumption of Amphetamines, Cocaine, Ecstasy drugs and even Cannabis is mostly predominant in relatively more progressive countries of the new world and Europe whereas in Asia and Africa it is relatively less. Only Opium consumption is relatively large in Asia and Africa. See the maps in ANNEX 1 on pages i (133), ii (134) and iii(135) in the UNODC's World Drug Report 2013. See the OECD Family Database 2012 using the Structure of Families indicators to get data on single parent homes and dissolution of the family in OECD countries.

9. See SJR — SCImago Journal & Country Rank. Middle East scholar Bernard Lewis says that the non-fossil exports of Middle East countries is not much. (See Bibliography for works by Bernard Lewis. In particular see part V titled The Challenge of Modernity in Bernard Lewis's book *The Middle East: A Brief History of the Last 2,000 years*). Outside the Middle East, Malaysia and Indonesia are two Islamic countries which have diversified economies with considerable industrial outputs but then the Chinese community plays a disproportionately large role in the economy and commerce of these countries.
10. See Gandhi's article titled "THE JEWS" in the Harijan dated November 26, 1938.
11. See Karen Armstrong's *Islam : A Short History* page 11.
12. See pages 16-18 in Karen Armstrong's *Islam : A Short History*.

Chapter 12: Secular Historical Reflections on the Second Coming

1. The idea that God was the czar's junior partner is taken from Samuel Huntington's *Clash of Civilizations and the Remaking of World Order*. In page 70 of this book in Chapter 3 titled A Universal Civilization? Modernization and Westernization under the heading The West and Modernization, Huntington observes that in lands in which the civilizational affiliation was "Orthodoxy", "God" was "the Caesar's" (Czar in Russia) "junior partner".
2. See pages 20, 21 and 77 in Francis Fukuyama's *The End of History and the Last Man* in which he attributes the end of apartheid in South Africa to its inherent unsustainability.
3. In his book *The Clash of Civilizations and the Remaking of World Order* Samuel P. Huntington shows that though

Buddhism went to China from India, it did not affect China's civilizational distinctness. Please see pages 47-48 from Chapter 2 titled Civilizations in History and Today under the section The Nature of Civilizations in this book.

4. We had stated in Chapter 10 of this book titled The Chinese Mind that in response to Winston Churchill's comment, that China was a civilization that was looking for a nation, the Chinese retorted that America was a nation that was looking for a civilization. Our observation in this book that the West needs a civilization born anew merely reiterates such observations that others have made about Western civilization.

Chapter 13: The Way Forward

1. The oft quoted words of the American Declaration of Independence reads: "We hold these truths to be self-evident, that all men are created equal, that they are endowed by their Creator with certain unalienable Rights that among these are Life, Liberty and the pursuit of Happiness".
2. See page 133 in the book *The Wisdom of Confucius* edited by Epiphanius Wilson. This quote can be found in the book under the section The Sayings of Mencius in Book V Part 1 titled Wan Chang.
3. I have deliberately preferred the phrase *the truth* is *upholding Gandhi* over the phrase *the truth is vindicating Gandhi*, despite the fact that the word *vindicating* would have literally conveyed the meaning. This is because truth is inherently purely good and even when it seems vindictive the object of such vindication is transformation of individuals and societies.
4. Most of the great religious and cultural traditions in the world begin with the narrative of a great flood from which

they were rescued. The Vedic tradition in India held that a fish rescued the Vedas from this great flood. The fish which rescued the Vedas was according to the Vedic tradition the first Avatar of the Hindu God Vishnu. Tamil Saivam, which is a Hindu religious order, holds that the fish rescued not just the Vedas but also the Tholkappiyam which is essentially a work on Tamil Grammar from the Second Tamil Sangam. In Thirumular's Thirumantiram, at the time of his marriage in Mount Kailash in the Himalayas, the highest God of the Hindu pantheon, Sivan on seeing that all the people have come to the north to see the marriage asks the great sage Agastya to go south so that the world does not lose its balance. Asking Agastya to go south is presented as evidence for the fact that Sivan is a just God. In addition, we are told that Sivan gives Agastya the opportunity to see Sivan's marriage while Agastya meditates, even though he is far away in the south. We are also told that Sivan confers this favor on Agastya because the quality of Agastya's meditation is superior to that performed by all other sages. In the fish creation myth and in the justice of the highest Hindu God Sivan being manifest in his asking the great sage Agastya to go south to ensure the balance of the world, Tamil Saivam establishes the southern Tamil tradition as being morally equivalent to the northern Vedic tradition.
5. The earliest book of the Aryans is the Rig Veda. The major Gods of the Rig Veda like Indra, Varuna and Agni are not worshipped as Gods by the vast majority of Hindus today.
6. Puja is of Dravidian Origin. See George Hart's *The Poems of Ancient Tamil, Their Milieu and Their Sanskrit Counterparts.*
7. Only the historical legacy of Periyar was realized at a certain moment in time. The ethical legacy of Periyar is

for the ages. Periyar's ideal of self-respect ought to be regarded as the highest ethical ideal in the coming future.
8. The British-Pakistani writer and film maker Tariq Ali spoke at the Rothko Chapel in Houston Nov 13, 2009 on the topic "The Uses and the Abuses of History". In this speech he cites a Jewish Israeli writer Shlomo Sand's book on Jewish history. Shlomo Sand apparently showed in his book that the majority of today's Jews were not descendants of the ancient Israelites and their ancestors had never lived in ancient Israel. According to Shlomo Sand, the descendants of most of the people who lived in ancient Israel later converted to Islam. This is the general stance we have taken in this book. In this book we tend to refer to the Israelites of antiquity as ancient Israelites and to modern Jews simply as Jews. However we hold that the pain, suffering and struggles of the Jews throughout their history is real and simply the fact that they have carried their yearning for Israel in their bosom is sufficient reason to deserve it, regardless of the objective historical evidence. But we also hold that such an Israel can be formed only through a religious movement and not through Zionism.
9. See the entry for Burakumin in Encyclopedia Britannica. The Dowa in Japan were once referred to as Burakumin in Japan. Now the term Burakumin is regarded as a derogatory term and the term Dowa is preferred.

References

Reference List

- Anderson, Benedict.2006.Imagined Communities: Reflections on the Origin and Spread of Nationalism. [Paperback]. London : Verso (Verso is an imprint of the New Left Books).
- Annadurai, C.N. and Rā Pi Cētup Piḷḷai. 1950. ஸ்ரீ பரவட்டும் (Tī paravaṭṭum). Pondicherry : Ñāyiṟu Nāṟ Patippakam.
- Aristotle (Author), Jowett, Benjamin (Translator) and Lerner, Max (Introduction).1943. The Politics of Aristotle. New York : The Modern Library.
- Ariyaratne A.T. *"Basava Sree Award Acceptance Speech"*. At the Ceremony held at Sri Muruga Math, Chitradurga – Karnataka . India On Monday the 15th August 2011
- Armstrong, Karen.2006. The Great Transformation: The Beginning of Our Religious Traditions. New York : Alfred.A.Knopf , a division of Random House.
- Armstrong, Karen.2000. Islam : A Short History. New York : The Modern Library
- Baba, Meher.1997.God Speaks : Dodd Mead
- Barzun, Jacques.2000. From Dawn to Decadence: 1500 to the Present: 500 Years of Western Cultural Life. New York : HarperCollins.
- Basham, A.L.1954. The Wonder That Was India : A survey of the culture of the Indian sub-continent

before the coming of the Muslims. New York: Grove Press.
- Basu, Raj Sekhar. "Dalit Politics in Tamilnadu". Seminar. February 2006, New Delhi.
- Bose, Nirmal Kumar.1960. Selections From Gandhi (Encyclopedia of Gandhi's Thoughts). Ahmedabad, India : Navajivan
- Butler, Christopher.2002. Postmodernism : A Very Short Introduction. [Paperback]. New York : Oxford University Press.
- Collingwood, R.G.1956. The Idea of History. [Paperback]. New York : Oxford University Press
- Coward, Harold (Editor).2003. Indian Critiques of Gandhi (Suny Series in Religious Studies). [Paperback]. Albany, New York : State University of New York Press
- Derrida, Jacques and Translated by Spivak, Gayatri Chkravorty.1976. of Grammatology. [Paperback]. Baltimore and London : The John Hopkins University Press.
- Donald, Brooke. "At Stanford, Bill Gates says foreign aid is threatened, but big ideas can turn the tide". Stanford Report, April 5, 2012 published by Stanford News Service, Stanford University.
- Drucker, Peter F. "The Global Economy and the Nation-State", *Foreign Affairs,* Vol. 76, no. 5, 1997.
- Eaton, Richard M.1993. The Rise of Islam and the Bengal Frontier, 1204-1760. Berkeley: University of California Press.

- Ehrman, Bart D.2007. The New Testament : A Historical Introduction to the Early Christian Writings, 4th ed. New York: Oxford University Press.
- Fairbank, John King. 1992. China : A New History. Cambridge, Massachusetts: Belknap Press of Harvard University Press.
- Fernández, Francisco Lizcano. May-August 2005. Culturales del Continente Americano al Comienzo del Siglo XXI.
- Fischer, Louis.1983. The Life of Mahatma Gandhi. [Paperback]. New York : Harper & Row, Publishers Inc
- Fukuyama, Francis.2011.The Origins of Political Order: From Prehuman Times to the French Revolution.[Paperback].New York : Farrar, Straus and Giroux
- Fukuyama, Francis.1992. The End of History and the Last Man. New York: The Free Press, Macmillan.
- Gandhi, Mohandas Karamchand (Mahatma) and Translated by Desai, Mahadev H.1957.Gandhi, An Autobiography: The Story of My Experiments with Truth [Paperback]. Boston : Beacon Press
- Gandhi, M.K.1938. Hind Swaraj or Indian Home Rule. Ahmedabad, India : Navajivan Publishing House
- Gandhi, M.K. Speech before Inter-Asian Relations Conference. 2nd April, 1947. Published in Harijan on 20th April, 1947.
- Gandhi, M.K. "THE JEWS". Harijan, November 26, 1938.
- Gay, Robert.M. and Skillin, Marjorie.E. 1974. Words into Type. [Paperback] .Prentice Hall.

- Grossman, Lev. "2045: The Year Man Becomes Immortal". Time .Thursday, Feb. 10, 2011in the Science section.
- Guha, Ramachandra.2001. An Anthropologist Among the Marxists: And Other Essays. Delhi : Permanent Black
- Haleem (Translator), M. A. S. Abdel.2008. The Qur'an (Oxford World's Classics). [Paperback]. New York : Oxford University Press
- Harrison, Lawrence E. and Huntington, Samuel.P.2000. Culture Matters: How Values Shape Human Progress. [Paperback]. New York : Basic Books
- Harrison, Lawrence E. (Editor) and Berger, Peter (Editor). 2005. Developing Cultures : Case Studies. New York : Routledge
- Hart, George.L.1975. The Poems of Ancient Tamil, Their Milieu and Their Sanskrit Counterparts. Berkeley: University of California Press.
- Hart, George.L. (Translator) and Heifetz, Hank (Translator).2002. The Four Hundred Songs of War and Wisdom: An Anthology of Poems from Classical Tamil: The Purananuru. New York : Translations From the Asian Classics-Columbia University Press.
- Himmelfarb, Gertrude.2004. The Roads to Modernity: The British, French, and American Enlightenments. New York : Alfred.A.Knopf
- Hobsbawm, Eric J.1992. Nations and Nationalism Since 1780: Programme, Myth, Reality. 2nd ed. Cambridge University Press.
- Hourani, Albert. 2002. A History of the Arab Peoples. Faber & Faber

- Huntington, Samuel P.1997.The Clash of Civilizations and the Remaking of World Order. New York : Simon and Schuster.
- Hutchins, Robert Maynard (Editor).1952. Great Books of the Western World. Chicago : Encyclopedia Britannica.
- Johnson, Paul.1998. History of the American People. New York : HarperCollins.
- Kandasamy, W. B. Vasantha and Smarandache, Florentin.2005. Fuzzy and Neutrosophic Analysis of Periyar's Views on Untouchability.[Paperback] : Hexis
- Kannan.R.2010. Anna- The Life and times of C N Annadurai. New Delhi : Penguin India Group (Viking)
- Kennedy, Paul M.1987.The Rise and Fall of the Great Powers. New York : Random House.
- Kenny, Antony (Editor).1994. The Oxford History of Western Philosophy. Oxford and New York : Oxford University Press
- Kissinger, Henry.A.2011. On China. New York : Penguin Group.
- Kissinger, Henry.A.1995. Diplomacy. New York : Simon and Schuster.
- Kissinger, Henry.A.1979. White House Years. Boston : Little, Brown and Company
- Kissinger, Henry.A.1969. American Foreign Policy : Three Essays. New York : W.W.Norton and Company.
- Klein, Herbert. S. "The Changing American Family". Hoover Digest 2004 No.3 on Population, Hoover Institution, Stanford University.

- Kolakowski, Leszek(Author), Czerniawski, Stefan (Translator), Freis, Wolfgang (Translator), Kolakowska,Agnieszka(Translator). 1991. Modernity on Endless Trial. Chicago : University Of Chicago Press
- Lapidus, Ira M. 2002. A History of Islamic Societies. Cambridge: Cambridge University Press.
- Lee LK, Chen P C Y, Lee K K, Kaur J: Premarital sexual intercourse among adolescents in Malaysia: a cross-sectional Malaysian school survey. *Singapore Med J* 2006, 47(6):476-481.
- Leke, Acha, Lund, Susan, Roxburgh, Charles and Wamelen, Arend van. "What's driving Africa's growth". Mckinsey Quarterly (published by the Mckinsey Global Institute). JUNE 2010.
- Lewis, Bernard.1997. The Middle East: A Brief History of the Last 2,000 years. Simon and Schuster.
- Lewis, Bernard. "Freedom and Justice in Islam". Imprimis. September 2006. Volume 35, Number 9.
- Lewis, Bernard.2004. From Babel to Dragomans: Interpreting the Middle East. New York : Oxford University Press.
- Lewis, Bernard.2002. What Went Wrong? : Western Impact and Middle Eastern Response. New York: Oxford University Press.
- Lewis, Bernard.1990. Race and Slavery in the Middle East: An Historical Enquiry. New York : Oxford University Press
- Lewis, Bernard. "The Roots of Muslim Rage". The Atlantic Magazine, September, 1990.

- Lewis, Bernard.1963. Istanbul and the Civilization of the Ottoman Empire. Norman : University of Oklahoma Press.
- Lyotard, Jean-François (Author), Bennington, Geoff (Translator) and Massumi, Brian (Translator).1984. The Postmodern Condition : A Report on knowledge. Minneapolis: University of Minnesota, Press.
- Machiavelli, Niccolo.1993. The Prince. Hertfordshire : Wadsworth Editions Ltd
- MacMillan, Margaret.2007. Nixon and Mao: The Week That Changed the World. New York : Random House.
- Maddison, Angus.1995.Monitoring the World Economy, 1820-1992. [Paperback]. Paris : Organisation for Economic Co-operation and Development (OECD)
- Martin, Dale.B.2012. New Testament History and Literature. New Haven : Yale University Press.
- Moore, John Hartwell (Editor-in-Chief).2008. Encyclopedia of Race and Racism. Detroit : Thomson Gale.
- More, Thomas(Author), Logan, George M. (Editor) and Adams, Robert M. (Editor).2002. More : Utopia. (Cambridge Texts in the History of Political Thought) [Paperback]. Cambridge, U.K. : Cambridge University Press.
- Mumford, Lewis. "The Natural History of Urbanization," in Man's Role in Changing the Face of the Earth. Thomas Jr, W.L. (Editor). Chicago: University of Chicago Press, 1956.

- Naim, C.M. "MUHARRAM : The Spirit Of Karbala". OutlookIndia, web edition, dated Feb 6, 2007.
- Nandy, Ashis. "Unclaimed baggage". the little magazine, Vol III : issue 2.
- Nehru, Jawaharlal.1946.The Discovery of India. New York : The John Day Company
- Nisbett, Richard.2003.The Geography of Thought : How Asians and Westerners Think Differently... and Why?. New York: Free Press.
- Parkin, T.G.1992. Demography and Roman Society. The Johns Hopkins University Press
- Parpola, Asko.2009. Deciphering the Indus Script. [Paperback]. Cambridge University Press.
- Plato (Author), John M. Cooper (Editor) and D. S. Hutchinson (Editor).1997. Plato: Complete Works. Indianapolis and Cambridge: Hackett Publishing Company.
- Prabhu R. K.(Compiler).1960. India Of My Dreams. Ahmedabad, India : Navajivan
- Prabhu R. K. and Rao, U. R. (Compilers and Editors).1960. Mind of Mahatma Gandhi (Encyclopedia of Gandhi's Thoughts). Ahmedabad, India : Navajivan
- Prasad.A. "Sarvodaya Movement: Developing a Macro Perspective From Grassroots Collective Actions". The 12th Biennial Conference of the International Association for the Study of Commons : IASC Conference 2008, Cheltenham, Gloucestershire, U.K. on July 14-18 available at : http://iasc2008.glos.ac.uk/conference%20papers/papers/P/Prasad_210801.pdf. Retrieved on Oct 26th, 2013.

- RaviKumar. "Re-Reading Periyar". Seminar. February 2006, New Delhi.
- Rieffel, Lex. "Reconsidering the Peace Corps". Brookings Policy Brief Series Number # 126, The Brookings Institution, December, 2003.
- Roth, Norman.2003.Medieval Jewish Civilization: An Encyclopedia. New York : Routledge-Taylor and Francis Group.
- Sand, Shlomo and Lotan, Yael (Translator).2010. The Invention of the Jewish People. [Paperback]. New York : Verso-New Left Books
- Sharp, H (Editor).1920. Selections from Educational Records, Part I (1781-1839). Calcutta: Superintendent, Government Printing. Reprint. Delhi: National Archives of India, 1965.
- Sowell, Thomas .1994. Race And Culture: A World View. [Paperback]. New York : Basic Books
- Talbot, Ian.A. "Jinnah and the Making of Pakistan". History Today. Volume: 34 Issue: 2 1984
- Telles, Edward E.2006. Race in Another America: The Significance of Skin Color in Brazil. [Paperback]. Princeton, New Jersey : Princeton University Press.
- Tharoor, Shashi.1997. India from Midnight to the Millennium. New York : Arcade Publications.
- Tianchen, Li.1998. "To learn from the past is to serve the present: a Confucian lesson," Culture Mandala: The Bulletin of the Centre for East-West Cultural and Economic Studies: Vol. 3: Iss. 1, Article 6. Available at: http://epublications.bond.edu.au/cm/vol3/iss1/6 and Retrieved on Oct 20th, 2013.

- Toobin, Jeffrey.2007. The Nine: Inside the Secret World of the Supreme Court. New York : Doubleday.
- Toynbee, Arnold J.1987. A Study of History, Vol. 1: Abridgement of Volumes I-VI by D.C.Somervell.[Paperback]. Oxford : Oxford University Press.
- Tzu, Lao and Translated into German by Wilhelm, Richard and Translated into English by Oswald, H.G.1995.Tao Te Ching: The Book of Meaning and Life. New York : Penguin Books
- Veeramani, K.2005. Collected Works of Periyar E.V.R.. The Periyar Self-Respect Propaganda Institution: Chennai.
- Venkatesan, M. E V Ramasamy Naickarin Marupakkam (The other side of E V Ramasamy Naickar) (This book is written in Tamil and not available in English).
- Visser, Wayne A.M. and McIntosh, Alastair. "A Short Review of the Historical Critique of Usury". Accounting, Business & Financial History, 8:2, Routledge, London, July 1998, pp. 175-189.
- West, Cornel. 2000. The Cornel West Reader. [Paperback]. New York: Basic Civitas Books.
- Widmer, Eric D, Treas, Judith and Newcomb, Robert. Attitudes Toward Nomarital Sex in 24 Countries. Journal of Sex Research v35, n4 (Nov, 1998):349
- Wilson, Epiphanius (Editor).1995. The Wisdom of Confucius. New York : Wings Books.
- Yadav, Yogendra and Kumar , Sanjay. "The food habits of a nation". The Hindu. Monday, Aug 14, 2006 in the front page.
- Yarrow, Andrew.L. History of U.S.Children's Policy, 1900-PRESENT. Public Agenda, April, 2009.

- Zoromé, Ahmed. "Concept of Offshore Financial Centers: In Search of an Operational Definition". IMF Working Paper WP/07/87, International Monetary Fund, April, 2007.
- *Gandhi.* Dir. Richard Attenborough. Perf. Ben Kingsley, Rohini Hattangadi, Roshan Seth, Saeed Jaffrey, Virendra Razdan, Candice Bergen and Edward Fox. Columbia. 1982. Film.
- World Economic Outlook. Washington.D.C. : International Monetary Fund, Publication Services. September, 2011
- Freedom in the World 2012 : Freedom House. (Available at: http://www.freedomhouse.org/sites/default/files/inline_images/FIW%202012%20Booklet--Final.pdf). Retrieved on Sept 20, 2013.
- Freedom in the World 2014 : Freedom House. (Available at: http://www.freedomhouse.org/sites/default/files/Freedom%20in%20the%20World%202014%20Booklet.pdf). Retrieved on May 17, 2014.
- Human Development Report 2011 : United Nations Development Programme(UNDP). (Available at: http://hdr.undp.org/en/media/HDR_2011_EN_Complete.pdf). Published by Palgrave Macmillan, New York. Retrieved on Sept 20, 2013.
- Human Development Report 2013: United Nations Development Programme(UNDP).

- World Drug Report 2013 : United Nations Office on Drugs and Crime (UNODC). (United Nations publication, Sales No. E.13.XI.6)
- The World Factbook 2009. Washington, DC: Central Intelligence Agency, 2009.
- Latest Tourism Statistics 2011: Caribbean Tourism Organization
- World Federation of Exchanges – Statistics/Monthly : World Federation of Exchanges. Archived from the original on 21 August 2010.
- Meghalaya Human Development Report 2008 published by the Government of Meghalaya, Shillong, India. Available at http://megplanning.gov.in/MHDR/Human_De.pdf. Retrieved on Sep 29, 2013.
- Informe Latinobarómetro, Latinobarómetro. 2011.
- "WORKING FOR THE FEW: Political capture and economic inequality". Briefing Paper 178, Oxford: Oxfam GB for Oxfam International, Jan 20th, 2014.
- FAO, IFAD and WFP. 2013. The State of Food Insecurity in the World 2013. The multiple dimensions of food security. Rome, FAO.
- The Millennium Development Goals Report 2012. New York : United Nations, 2012.
- "ADULT AND YOUTH LITERACY". UNESCO Institute for Statistics (UIS) FACT SHEET September 2013, No.26
- United Nations, Department of Economic and Social Affairs, Population Division(2013). World Population Prospects : The 2012 Revision, Key Findings and Advanced Tables. Working Paper No. ESA/P/WP.227.

- Encyclopædia Britannica. Encyclopædia Britannica Online. Encyclopædia Britannica Inc., 2013. Web. Available at: http://www.britannica.com/EBchecked/topic/84894/burakumin Retrieved on 23 Sept, 23, 2013
- Please see the internet article titled LEADING TRIBES OF PUNJAB AND THEIR ORIGINS which is available at http://www.paklinks.com/gs/culture-literature-and-linguistics/73172-leading-tribes-of-punjab.html. Retrieved on Sept 20, 2013.
- Please see BBC NEWS internet article titled *How China is ruled* which is available at : http://news.bbc.co.uk/2/shared/spl/hi/in_depth/china_politics/government/html/4.stm. Retrieved on Sept 21, 2013.
- Please see internet article on Jewish Moneylending available at : http://www.myjewishlearning.com/history/Ancient_and_Medieval_History/632-1650/Christendom/Commerce/Moneylending.shtml. Retrieved on Oct 24, 2013.
- "Controversy. Naachne Gaane Waali Aurat". OutlookIndia – web edition. 29 October 2006. See internet article at http://www.outlookindia.com/article.aspx?232969. Retrieved on Sept 21, 2013.
- "The Panama Canal: A plan to unlock prosperity". The Economist. 3 December 2009.

- "The slaughter of sacred cows : Some cherished policies are being re-examined". The Economist. Apr 3rd 2003.
- "Africa rising : The hopeful continent". The Economist. Dec 3rd 2011
- "Sad South Africa : Cry, the beloved country". The Economist. Oct 20th 2012.
- "Towards a scientific study of the Indus Script". The Hindu Magazine, Sunday, Feb 04, 2007.
- "Case1 : Eradicating Smallpox" of the Millions Saved Initiative by the Center for Global Development.
- OECD (2012), OECD Family Database, OECD, Paris (http://www.oecd.org/social/family/database). Retrieved on Sept 21, 2013.
- SCImago. (2007). SJR — SCImago Journal & Country Rank. Retrieved July 15, 2013, from http://www.scimagojr.com
- Please see internet article available at http://factsanddetails.com/china/cat2/sub1/item31.html Retrieved on Feb 12, 2014.
- "Burakumin". Encyclopædia Britannica. Encyclopædia Britannica Online. Encyclopædia Britannica Inc., 2013. Web. Available at: http://www.britannica.com/EBchecked/topic/84894/burakumin
Retrieved on 23 Sept, 23, 2013
- http://www.latinobarometro.org/lat.jsp
Retrieved on June 8, 2014
- http://en.wikipedia.org/wiki/Ethnic_groups_in_Latin_America
Retrieved on June 8, 2014.

- http://ashbrook.org/events/kissinger-transcript/ Retrieved on November 8, 2015

Index

A

AIADMK 237
Aboriginal 114
Academy 10, 37, 241
Adam 110
Africa (also see Sub-Saharan Africa and South Africa) 18, 19, 79, 94, 122, 125, 138, 150-153, 169, 180, 213, 219, 248
African 123, 151, 167, 169, 186, 198
African Americans 38, 79, 158, 186
Africans 12, 202
Age of Discovery 102, 106
Agricultural laborer 144
Ahimsa 63, 85
Ali 53
Allah 13, 39, 52, 85, 95
Ambedkar 61, 71, 72, 74
America (also see United States) 8, 13, 33, 34, 43, 47, 53, 65, 67, 98, 107, 126, 135, 138, 140, 148, 160, 177, 180, 186, 187, 193, 196-200, 215, 226, 227-231, 233, 247, 250.
American 5, 8, 13, 34, 126, 149, 175, 177, 187, 196, 198, 199, 215, 227-230
American Exceptionalism 200
American Revolution 29
Americans 200, 227-229
Amos 63, 101, 231
Anderson, Benedict 137
Anglo-American 211
Anglo-Russian rivalry 34
Anti-colonialism 31
Apartheid 32, 152, 153, 214
Arab 119, 136, 138, 178, 202, 211, 247
Arab-Israeli 135, 210
Arabia 39, 94, 201
Arabic 138
Arabs 136, 138, 186, 211, 246 247
Arranged marriage (and marriages that are arranged) 146, 207
Archaeological 92
Argentina 119, 121-123
Aristotle 10, 15, 231
Aristotelian 15, 51, 126
Aristocracy 8-10, 15, 28, 29, 38, 48, 125-127
Aryan 20, 47, 124, 159, 172, 220, 239, 240

Aryans 12, 21, 41, 47, 78, 124, 125, 158, 159, 178
Asia (also see South East Asia) 15, 44, 61, 68, 69, 94, 124, 150, 151, 163, 248
Asia Pacific 226, 248
Asian 230
Asian Way 248
Astrology 84, 99, 100
Athenian 10
Atom Bombs 68, 69, 99
Atomic Tests 69
Aung San Suu Kyi 63
Aurangzeb 105
Australia 248, 249
Automation 143
Avatar 6
Avatars 5, 6

B
BSP (Abbreviation for Bahujan Samaj Party) 242
BJP 234, 235, 242
BIMARU 111, 151, 185
Back-to-Africa movement 79
Backward Caste 172, 175
Backward Castes 22, 66, 68, 73, 76, 158, 172, 234, 245
Bahrain 119, 120

Bangalore 184, 244
Bangladesh 71, 75, 95, 96, 97, 186, 233, 234, 243
Barbados 119, 120, 122
Barzun, Jacques 3
Beijing 199
Bengal 185, 243
Bengaluru 132, 244
Berlin wall 113, 188
Bestiality 217
Bikini 146
Binary (as in binary opposition and the like) 37, 40
Bodhisattva 45
Bodhisattvas 89
Bombay (also see Mumbai) 125, 244
Book of Changes 190
Bose, Subash Chandra 69, 70, 234
Brahmin 21, 47, 48
Brahminical 20, 104, 180, 181, 183, 239
Brahmins 11, 18, 19, 20, 21, 47, 57, 78, 80, 81, 126, 178, 236, 240, 241
Brazil 185
British 13, 61, 64, 65, 66, 70, 78, 80, 126, 177, 178, 179, 181, 189, 230, 234

British Raj 65, 177
Brunei 119, 248
Buddha 13, 45, 68, 81, 87, 179
Buddhas 5, 6
Buddhism 48, 56, 72, 74, 81, 82, 104, 148, 168, 181, 183, 194, 220, 241
Buddhist 181, 191
Buddhists 102, 104, 248
Bumiputra 131, 132, 134
Bureaucracy 27, 41, 65
Bureaucratic 57, 127
Burke, Edmund 31
Byzantine 203
Byzantium 213

C
Caliph 53
Caliphs 53
Caliphate 53, 103
Canaan 92
Canada 123, 133, 138
Capital punishment 141
Capitalism 3, 51, 61, 68, 76, 77, 110, 115, 118, 119, 127, 128, 129, 180, 188, 221, 227
Caribbean 119, 120, 122
Caste 9, 11, 12, 13, 14, 29, 47, 48, 57, 62, 66, 71, 72, 73, 74, 76, 78, 81, 82, 102, 103, 104, 105, 124, 125, 126, 135, 136, 159, 170, 174, 172, 178, 179, 183, 204, 237, 241, 242, 245
Castes 22, 29, 66, 73, 104, 105, 136, 159, 177
Catholics 14
Catholicism 168, 169
Chaos 41, 85
Chastity 18, 79, 86
Chile 119, 121, 122, 123
China 4, 9, 11, 15, 18, 34, 35, 36, 45, 54, 55, 56, 57, 68, 100, 103, 104, 107, 111, 121, 122, 126, 138, 148, 151, 152, 155, 168, 170, 171, 173, 175, 179, 180, 184, 187, 188, 189, 190-200, 203, 204, 206, 219-221, 226, 227, 231-234, 249, 250
Chinese 14, 33, 54, 55, 56, 63, 103, 104, 131, 132, 134, 148, 168, 173, 175, 186, 187-200, 201, 202, 207, 220, 246
Christendom 9, 11, 18, 44, 51, 94, 167, 168, 169, 174, 203, 209, 213, 219, 220
Christian 9, 14, 28, 41, 49, 50, 57, 67, 79, 85, 94, 95, 100, 173, 174, 203, 212, 213, 217, 219, 231

Christian Coalition 65, 186
Christianity 13, 14, 37, 38, 50, 62, 94, 95, 102, 113, 168, 169, 173, 203, 209, 210, 213, 219, 221
Christians 11, 67, 94, 95, 113, 209
Church 28, 38, 50, 51, 67, 94, 95, 113, 169, 213
Churches 209
Churchill, Winston 178, 193,
Circumcision 50, 90
Civil Rights 13, 72, 73, 74, 115, 160, 229
Civilization 3, 9, 12, 16, 17, 20, 21, 27, 31, 33, 34, 38, 41, 42, 48, 57, 61, 66-68, 100-102, 104, 111, 114, 119, 121, 128, 135, 137, 138, 150, 151, 152, 163, 164, 167, 171, 172, 174-180, 181, 183, 184, 190-193, 196, 201, 202-204, 208, 209, 213, 215, 217-221, 226, 231, 236, 247
Civilizational narrative 175
Civilizational narratives 44, 45, 57, 84, 85, 147
Civilizations 4, 7, 8, 23, 27, 49, 98, 104, 112, 117, 138, 146, 165, 167, 170, 172, 179, 180, 183, 186, 199, 201, 203-206, 218-220, 226, 248
Co-relative Cosmology 190
Cold War 34, 42, 110, 118, 132, 175, 180, 202, 249
Colonialism 61, 64, 80, 111, 126, 149, 150, 151, 169, 178
Communism 3, 4, 11, 12, 27, 35, 36, 61, 80, 180
Communist 3, 18, 35, 80, 115, 119, 121, 180, 185, 187, 188, 196, 197, 198
Communists 35, 76, 187, 196, 237
Confucian 3, 11, 44, 56, 57, 85, 96, 111, 120, 121, 152, 167, 168, 192, 219, 230, 231
Confucianism 14, 54, 56, 148, 193
Confucius 13, 14, 54, 192, 232
Conservative 148, 185
Conservatives 66, 98, 116, 148
Constantinople 169, 213
Cosmopolitanism 138, 139
Costa Rica 122, 123
Croatia 119
Crucifix 50
Cuba 122, 123, 185

Cuban Missile Crisis 196
Cultural Anthropology 57
Cultural Capital 42, 122
Cultural Revolution 197
Czar 36, 213
Czech Republic 119

D
DMK 80, 237, 242, 245
Dalai Lama 63
Dalit 61, 65, 71, 73, 74, 81, 82, 172, 241-243
Dalits 18, 68, 71, 72, 73, 74, 76, 82, 172, 186, 241, 242, 245
Dark ages 101, 102, 104, 203, 233
De-brahminisation (also de-brahminise and de-brahminised) 241, 243, 245
Debt 216, 217, 227, 231
Decolonization 32, 150, 171, 176
Deconstruction 37, 115
Deconstructionist 81, 241
Deconstructionists 37
Deng (also Deng Xiaoping) 121, 178, 190, 191, 193
Democracy 16, 27, 29, 33, 34, 96, 97 110, 112, 113, 115, 118, 170, 176, 177, 180, 184, 189, 193, 215, 220, 221, 235
Democratic (also Democratically) 29, 33, 76, 81, 85, 96, 113, 135, 142, 148, 149, 178, 188, 234, 235, 244
Dowa 18, 19, 206, 248
Dravidian 19, 20, 47, 74, 81, 124, 172, 220, 236, 237, 239, 240, 241, 242, 243, 245
Dravidians 20, 41, 61, 78, 124, 158, 159, 172, 236, 240, 241, 242, 244

E
East Asian 3, 9, 57, 96, 111, 119, 120, 167, 168, 186, 192, 219, 230, 231, 248, 249
Eastern Orthodox Church 213
Eelam 243, 244
Egypt 92, 138, 152, 153, 190
Egyptian 92, 202
Empiricism 27, 99
Empirical 27, 40, 89, 92, 93, 98, 99
Enlightenment (also includes the English Enlightenment and the European Enlightenment) 12,

13, 27-33, 36, 38, 42, 44, 51, 61, 73, 78, 81, 102, 106, 201, 221, 236, 243
Entertainment 16, 106, 144, 145, 147, 154, 207, 222
Environmental degradation 164
Equality 9, 15, 29, 30, 40, 48, 51, 62, 131, 149, 160, 189, 190, 204, 205, 209
Estonia 119
Ethics 7, 10, 14, 15, 17, 23, 29, 34, 38, 55, 61, 62, 63, 66, 85, 86, 91, 96, 101, 117, 144, 154, 181, 189, 193, 194, 198, 212, 227
Ethiopian 198, 199
Eve 110
Evolutionary 244
Evolutionary Biology 57
Evolutionary Psychology 58
Evolutionary Trajectory 88, 110,
Evil 233, 246

F
Falsehood 243
Feudalism 3, 48
Fossil fuel 210
Fraternity 30, 31, 74, 164, 243, 250

Freedom 15, 28, 32, 52, 67, 85, 96, 110, 114-117, 131, 140-142, 149, 171, 172, 176, 193, 208, 213-218, 220, 228, 234
Freedoms 28, 67
Freedom House 96
French 12, 137
French Revolution 30, 31, 42
Frescoes 113, 209
Fukuyama, Francis 110, 118, 127, 188

G
GDP 120, 121, 227
Gandhi 32, 45, 61-64, 66-72, 74-80, 83, 85, 101, 130, 138, 145, 160, 174, 181, 182, 210, 233-239
Ganges 90
Gay 115
Gays 146
Gay marriage 146, 171, 215, 217
Gene pool 101
Genetic 101
Genghis Khan 191
Gentiles 113, 173
Gentry 11, 57
Gentry-Scholar (also Scholar-Gentry) 9, 126

German 34, 109, 179
Germans 12, 159
Germany 27, 34, 70, 98, 101, 102, 104, 117, 137, 158, 159
Globalization 68, 77, 138, 147, 152
Golden temple 174
Great War of 1857 150
Greco-Roman 9, 173, 174, 219
Greek 91, 102, 168
Greeks 50, 62
Greenpeace 64
Greece 10, 15, 62, 101, 179
Gujarat 125, 185
Gujarati 125
Gurus 89

H
HDI (also Human Development Index) 120, 121, 123-125, 151
Habitat 143
Han Dynasty 190
Haryana 124
Herder 34
Hegel 34, 35, 160
Hellenism 102
Hesiod 231
Himachal Pradesh 124
Hindi 41, 76, 151, 177, 245

Hindu 6, 9, 11-13, 18, 20, 21, 29, 41, 45-49, 57, 61, 65-67, 71, 72, 75, 76, 78, 82, 91, 102, 103, 105, 113, 124, 125, 126, 147, 159, 167, 172, 174, 175, 178-183, 186, 191, 220, 235, 236, 238-242, 244
Hindu Nation 75
Hindu Nationalism 71, 75, 147, 174
Hindu Nationalist 172, 174, 175
Hindu Nationalists 61, 186
Hinduism 13, 21, 48, 61, 67, 68, 91, 102, 175, 182, 203, 235, 238-240, 243, 245
Hindus 14, 72-76, 95, 96, 102, 104, 105, 113, 175, 182, 244, 245, 248
Hindustani 201
Hindutuva 75, 76, 174, 234
Hitler 12, 70, 97, 102, 158, 159
Hobsbawm, Eric 137
Hong Kong 119-121, 151, 155
Human Development Index (also see HDI) 119, 122, 123
Hungary 119

Huntington, Samuel 167, 219, 220

I
Icons 113, 209
Idealism 84, 85, 180, 193, 200, 239, 242
Ideology 12, 13, 28, 35, 75, 76, 84, 96, 98, 147, 148, 187, 188, 192, 203, 204, 226, 234, 235, 242
Ideological (also ideologically) 12, 13, 38, 40, 45, 61, 75, 83, 85, 113, 114, 180, 187, 194, 197, 206, 225, 226, 235, 239, 242, 246
Idolaters 52
India 3, 11, 14, 18-23, 29, 41, 45, 47, 48, 49, 57, 61, 62, 64-66, 68-78, 80-82, 85, 96, 97, 98, 100, 102-104, 107, 110, 111, 124-126, 132, 133, 136, 148, 150-152, 158, 159, 170, 172, 174, 175, 177-187, 191, 194, 199, 203, 204, 206, 219-221, 226, 233-236, 241-246, 250
India-Pakistan war 97
Indian 9, 13, 14, 19, 20, 22, 29, 44-47, 49, 51, 61, 62, 64-66, 69-77, 95, 102, 105, 124, 125, 132, 136, 138, 148, 150, 167, 174, 177-184, 186, 220, 233-235, 237-239, 243, 245, 246
Indians 22, 32, 41, 62, 64-66, 69, 76, 78, 80, 174, 177-179, 181, 184, 187, 201, 202, 203, 207, 234, 235, 243, 244
Indonesia 248
Industrial Revolution 27, 102, 106, 137
Infant mortality 8, 17, 32, 155, 164
Inner Asian tribes 56, 170, 189
Intellectuals 97, 194, 197, 201, 204, 242
Intelligentsia 50, 80
Iran 9, 103, 138, 175, 185, 186, 220, 247
Iranian Revolution 33, 175, 202
Iraq 138
Italy 10, 137
Islam 3, 9, 11-13, 42, 44, 48, 51-54, 61, 67, 74, 81, 82, 85, 94-96, 102, 103, 105, 113, 136, 160, 167, 169, 171, 173, 175, 182, 186, 193, 201-210, 219, 220, 221, 226, 227, 231, 246, 247, 248

Islamic 15, 18, 36, 51-53, 57, 75, 85, 94, 95, 105, 107, 119, 138, 167, 173, 175, 178, 186, 201-206, 208-210, 219, 220, 247, 248
Israel 17, 79, 92, 98, 119, 121, 180, 193, 210, 211, 226, 246, 247, 250
Israelites 104, 233
Ivy League 126

J
Jaffna 244
Jainism 48, 183, 241
Jains 102
Japan 9, 18, 19, 29, 68, 100, 111, 119-121, 126, 138, 155, 168, 206, 219, 221, 248-250
Japanese 34, 68, 126, 167, 192, 202, 206, 207, 249
Jerusalem 88, 90, 210
Jesus 13, 14, 35, 41, 49, 50, 51, 68, 85, 94, 104, 212, 233, 236
Jews 11, 12, 41, 49, 79, 92, 97, 100-102, 113, 121, 136, 158, 159, 180, 210, 211, 247
Jinnah, Muhammad Ali 61, 75, 202, 233, 236
Joseph 92, 94
Judaism 13, 51, 94, 219

Junzi 55

K
Kamaraj 237
Karma 88
Kennedy, Paul 3
Kerala 124, 185
King, Martin Luther 63
Kissinger, Henry 196-199
Korea 111, 119-121, 151, 168, 249
Korean 196
Kublai Khan 191
Kurzweil, Ray 5

L
Lapidus, Ira 53
Latin 169
Latin America 119, 121-124, 152, 180, 185, 219
Latin American 123, 167, 185
Latvia 119
Lenin 29, 107
Lewis, Bernard 53, 203
Lesbian 115, 215
Lesbians 146
Li 192
Liberal 14, 31-33, 37, 73, 98, 113, 146, 148, 149, 156, 171,

173-175, 185, 193, 205-208, 215, 219, 241
Liberals 31, 148, 189, 193
Liberalization 64, 65
Libertarian 35, 130
Libertarians 215
Liberty 30, 85, 86, 135, 160, 176, 209
Liberty, Equality and Fraternity 30
Lincoln, Abraham 215
Lithuania 119
Lok Sabha 244

M
MNC (Multinational Corporations) 156-158
Machiavelli 10
Maharashtra 125, 185
Major Cultural Traditions 9, 18, 44, 45, 53, 54, 57, 58, 167, 168, 170, 172, 176, 188, 203, 213, 225
Malay 132, 134
Malays 131, 134
Malaysia 131-134, 248
Manchus 189
Mandate of Heaven 189
Manumission 52
Mao Zedong (also Mao) 4, 126, 190, 197-199

Marijuana 215
Marx 34, 35
Marxism 34-37, 194
Marxism-Leninism 107
Marxist 3, 11, 28, 85, 127, 140, 142
Marxists 3, 61, 242
Mary 94
Mayawati 242
Mecca 39, 210
Medieval 42, 95, 112, 191, 221
Medina 210
Meditation 46, 69, 88
Melanesia 248
Mencius 232
Mercantilism 11, 68
Messiah 247
Messiahs 5, 6
Mestizo 123
Mestizos 122
Methodists 11
Mexico 122, 123
Micronesia 248
Mill, John Stuart 78
Ming 104
Modernity 3, 4, 6, 7, 12, 32-34, 37, 38, 42, 43, 45, 61, 62, 66, 67, 68, 72, 98, 106-108, 111-114, 117-119, 123-127, 131, 133-137, 143, 147, 149,

151, 153, 163, 164, 168-172, 174-176, 181, 188, 191, 195, 201, 203, 204, 206, 210, 215, 218, 225, 226, 232, 246, 248
Mohammed, the Prophet 13, 14, 53, 68, 85, 210
Mongol 103, 201
Mongols 103, 189
Monotheism 94-96, 98, 112, 113, 203, 209
Moral Sentimentality 11, 13, 30
Morality 29, 30, 61, 67
More, Thomas 35, 231
Morocco 152, 153
Moses 13, 68, 98
Muharram 53
Multiculturalism 13, 160, 217, 218, 229
Mumbai 125, 132, 244
Muni 45
Mythological 86, 89, 91
Mythology 41, 46, 47, 91, 238

N
NAACP (National Association for the Advancement of Colored People) 65
NAFTA (North American Free Trade Agreement) 123
Nandi Kadal 237, 238
Napoleonic 42
Nasser, Gamal Abdel 138, 202
Nation State 106, 131, 137-139, 202, 210, 211, 247
Nationalism 36, 71, 75, 130, 132, 133, 142, 147, 174, 202, 245
Nationalisms 211
Native American 123, 169
Native Americans 122
Nayanmars 240
Nazi 70, 98, 101, 102, 104, 117, 158, 159
Nehru, Jawaharlal 61, 180, 182
Neo-Confucian 85
Neo-Liberal 194
Neo-Marxism 36
New Zealand 248, 249
Nietzsche 34, 117, 216
Nirvana 87, 88
Nixon, Richard 121, 175, 180, 187, 195-199, 203
Non-Brahmin 80, 241, 243, 244
Non-Brahmins 74, 240, 241

O

Obama, Barrack 229, 231, 240, 250
Offshore Financial Center (OFC) 120
Organizing principle 81, 109, 159, 160, 161
Osu 18, 19
Ottoman Empire 201, 202, 206
Outcaste (also outcastes) 18, 19, 21, 23, 108, 142

P

PRC (People's Republic of China) 121, 175, 195
Pagutharivu (பகுத்தறிவு) 78, 81
Paine, Thomas 31
Pakistan (also see India-Pakistan war) 61, 65, 71, 75, 95, 172, 186, 202, 233, 234, 236, 243
Pakistani 71, 75, 233
Pakistanis 69, 196
Palestine 211
Panama 123
Paramount leader 190
Parentalism 149, 160, 163, 225, 226, 232
Paul 50, 219
Pauline 94, 173, 219
Peace Corps 107
Periyar, E.V.Ramasamy 61, 74, 78-82, 85, 98, 160, 161, 163, 225, 226, 230, 232, 236, 237, 239, 241- 243, 246
Persian 126, 178, 220
Plato 35, 63, 231
Philippines 248
Poland 119
Poles 12
Polo 2 197
Polynesia 169, 248
Polynesian 249
Poonool (the Tamil name for the Hindu sacred thread) 241
Portugal 150
Post-colonial 66, 131
Post-modernity 37-40, 42-44
Prabhakaran, Vellupillai 234, 238, 239
Pre-Islamic 9
Pre-modern 3, 4, 6-18, 21-23, 27-29, 34, 35, 44, 46, 48, 50, 52, 54-58, 61, 66, 73, 90, 103, 105, 106, 108, 118, 121, 126, 137, 139, 143, 151, 154, 163, 170, 193-195, 203, 204, 230, 242
Pre-Pauline 85
Primatology 57

Proletariat 127, 197
Prophet 5, 13, 14, 53, 68, 85, 210
Prophetic 99, 100, 136, 203, 231, 250
Prophets 5, 6, 68, 83, 92, 93, 98
Proselytizing 50, 94, 182, 208, 221
Prostitution 18, 52, 139-141, 204
Protestant Reformation 169
Protestants 14
Punjab 124, 185, 186, 243

Q
Qatar 119
Queen Catherine 201
Quran (also Koran) 204, 209
Qutub 45

R
RSS 174
Racism 18, 21, 48, 111, 228
Rajya Sabha 244
Ram 244
Ramayanam 244
Realpolitik 84, 180, 187, 188
Realism 84, 200
Red Guards 197
Red sea 92

Reformation (also see Protestant Reformation) 51, 102, 106
Renaissance 10, 100, 102, 106, 128
Republican 148
Rig Veda 47
Righteousness 29, 86, 91, 102, 184
Rishi 45
Roma 132, 135
Roman 91
Romania 132, 185
Romans 50, 104, 233
Roman Empire 8, 51, 101, 102, 168, 169
Rome 169
Rule of the law 27, 29, 65, 113, 129, 156
Russia 34, 36, 42, 107, 201, 213
Russian 29, 33, 34
Russians 202

S
Sacred Thread 47, 90, 241
Sages 46, 68, 83, 89
Saivam 240
Sanatani 78
Sanskrit 48, 178, 201, 236, 240

Sarguru 45
Sarvarkar 75
Sathyanarayana 21
Sati 48, 204, 206
Saudi Arabia 120
Science 27, 37, 61, 84, 98-101, 107, 110, 177, 191, 202
Scientific 3, 27, 98, 100, 142, 202, 210
Scientific Revolution 102
Scramble for Africa 150
Second Coming 212, 213, 222
Self-Respect 57, 61, 78-81, 85, 98, 104, 141, 149, 160-163, 220, 225, 226, 230, 232, 236, 237, 239-241, 243-246, 249, 250
Sentimentality (also see moral sentimentality) 30, 51
Sex Worker 140
Sexual Permissiveness 15, 206-208, 222
Siddhar 45
Siddhars 13, 47
Sikh 105, 174
Sikhs 186, 245
Sinic 167
Sino-Soviet 187, 196
Singapore 119, 120, 151, 248, 249
Sinhala 131, 238, 243
Sinhalese 71, 238
Sivan 20, 238
Slovakia 119
Slovenia 119
Smallpox 153
Socialism 3, 16, 61, 130, 193
Socialist 61, 64, 76, 77, 123, 130, 180
Socratic Method 30
Socrates 30, 35, 63, 101, 231
South Africa 32, 152, 153, 214
South East Asia 186, 206, 248
South East Asian 186, 248, 249
South Korea 111, 119-121, 151, 168
Soviet bloc 119, 121
Soviet Union 35, 154, 169, 180, 187, 188, 196, 202
Spain 150
Spengler 34
Sri Lanka 71, 77, 131, 237, 243
Sri Lankan 131, 234, 237, 238
Sub-Saharan 111, 125, 128, 152-155, 185
Sudra 47

Sufi 203
Suyamariyadai (சுயமரியாதை) (also see Self-Respect) 78
Swahili 109
Syria 53

T

Taliban 67, 71, 75, 136, 147
Tamil 11, 20, 78, 81, 109, 181, 184, 185, 220, 237-240, 243, 244, 250
Tamil Tigers 237, 238
Tamilnadu 80, 81, 124, 184, 220, 226, 237, 242, 243, 244
Tamils 71, 76, 131, 185, 226, 234, 236-241, 243-246
Tang 104
Tao Te Ching 55, 191
Taoism 54-56, 148
Taoist 102
Tehran 175
Teresa, Mother 145
Terrorism 75, 107, 108
Thailand 248
Theravada Buddhism 241
Third World 33, 38, 106, 128, 130, 139, 149, 150, 152, 156-158, 160, 162, 217, 226, 229, 230, 249, 250
Thirukural 20

Tracymachus 63
Transgender 146
Transnationalism 138
Tribals 96
Trincomalee 244
Trusteeship 130
Truth 7, 13, 15, 20, 21, 30, 37-39, 44, 45, 49, 51, 54, 55, 59, 61-63, 64, 66-70, 73, 83-91, 93, 96-99, 101-106, 108-110, 114, 115, 117, 118, 141, 142, 147-149, 160, 162, 170, 184, 199, 212, 222, 225, 227, 230, 231-239, 241, 243
Truths 37, 39, 45, 46, 101, 147, 148
Tunisia 152, 153
Turkey 138, 202, 247
Turkish 138
Turks 138, 169, 213
Tzu, Lao 14, 55, 191

U

U.A.E.(also UAE) 119, 120
UN DESA 155
UNESCO 155
United Nations 114, 150, 155, 164, 180, 229, 230, 250
United States 33, 39, 122, 123, 133, 153, 196-198, 202, 215, 217, 218

Untouchability 19-21, 71, 72, 74, 82, 228, 237, 243, 248
Untouchable (see also Dalit) 18-21, 66, 67, 71, 234
Untouchables (see also Dalits) 18-20, 47, 61, 68, 102, 104, 105, 158, 159, 172, 175, 206, 210, 241
Untruth 44, 70, 111, 147
Urbanization 106
Uruguay 122, 123
Usury 11, 51, 52, 204
Uttar Pradesh 65

V
Vaccine 154
Vedas 48
Vegetarian 21, 22, 143
Vegetarians 22
Vegetarianism 21-23, 49
Veil 18, 53, 146, 204
Vietnam 168, 187, 248

W
WFP 155
Weber 34
West, Western (as in Western Nations, Western culture, Western civilization, Western Christendom, Western thought, Westerners, Western Half of the Roman Empire) 3, 27, 30, 31, 33, 34, 38, 41, 42, 51, 67-69, 78, 96, 100-102, 104, 107, 111, 113, 119-121, 123, 128, 129, 132, 135, 137, 146, 148, 151, 152, 167, 168, 169, 171-176, 178, 180, 181, 184, 185, 187-189, 192, 193, 202, 203, 205-209, 213, 215, 217-222, 226, 230, 231, 233, 246, 250
West, Cornel 3
Wollstonecraft, Mary 31
Women 17-19, 23, 31, 33, 48, 52, 53, 56, 108, 136, 139-142, 171, 176, 204, 205, 214, 215, 238
Women's rights 176

Y
Yagna (Yagam in Tamil) 240
Yagnas 240
Yang 148, 191, 207
Yin 148, 191, 207

Z
Zionism 210, 211, 247
Zionist 211, 250
Zionists 211

Zoroaster 68
Zoos 143

www.ingramcontent.com/pod-product-compliance
Lightning Source LLC
Chambersburg PA
CBHW051933290426
44110CB00015B/1967